Born in Lancashire and educated at Oxford, **Anthony Holden** enjoyed an award-winning career in journalism before becoming a full-time writer and broadcaster. Besides his bestselling biographies of Shakespeare and Tchaikovsky, Laurence Olivier and the Prince of Wales, Holden is the author of *The St Albans Poisoner*, which became a critically acclaimed film, and a history of Hollywood's Oscars. More recently he has published biographies of the writer-critic Leigh Hunt and of Lorenzo Da Ponte, Mozart's librettist. *Big Deal*, his account of a year as a professional poker player, is regarded as a contemporary classic.

'Holden is the best possible guide to the new worlds of poker. He has seen it before, and lived it. He writes elegantly . . . I hope that, in ten years or so, when Holden finally achieves his glory, we'll all be reading *Biggest Deal*' *Daily Telegraph*

'Shadowy appearances from various "molls", encounters with the old lions, such as Al Alvarez, and many dramatic narratives of particular hands, ballsy bluffs and spectacular "bad beats". As usual, Holden's prose purrs along like the casino's best limo' *Guardian*

'Holden has an endearing way of turning descriptions of botched or brilliant poker hands into page-turning mini-narratives, discussing his mental demons and romantic travails. You can't help rooting for him' *Scotsman*

'The Bill Bryson of the gambling hall, Holden's deceptively laconic and urbane style is full of unexpected facts, colour and insights' *Glasgow Herald*

'Superb . . . highly entertaining. Let's hope he's still around in seventeen years time to write *Biggest Deal*, when poker has taken over the world' *Daily Mail*

'There are enough hands detailed here to keep poker heads in clover, while those who wouldn't know a royal flush from pocket rockets will still find it thoroughly addictive' *Metro*

'Engagingly confessional . . . Holden will never make a big killing. But he remains undefeated as the champion chronicler of those who do' *Times Literary Supplement*

'It's Holden's effortless prose that makes *Bigger Deal* a triumph. His ebullience is infectious' *Poker Player* Magazine

'This urbane account . . . is a fine and curiously life-affirming read' *FT* Magazine

'A brilliantly observed account of the movers and shakers in both Las Vegas and online' *Daily Mirror*

'Riveting' *Independent on Sunday*

D1418642

BIGGER DEAL

A Year on the New Poker Circuit

Anthony Holden

ABACUS

First published in 2007 by Little, Brown
This paperback edition published in 2008 by Abacus

A CIP catalogue record for this book is
available from the British Library.

ISBN 978-0-349-11903-8

Typeset in Baskerville by M Rules
Printed and bound in Great Britain by
Clays Ltd, St Ives plc

Papers used by Abacus are natural, renewable and recyclable
products made from wood grown in sustainable forests and certified
in accordance with the rules of the Forest Stewardship Council.

Abacus
An imprint of
Little, Brown Book Group
100 Victoria Embankment
London EC4Y 0DY

An Hachette Livre UK Company
www.hachettelivre.co.uk

www.littlebrown.co.uk

For
Ben and Salome
with my love

Contents

Author's Note

I have assumed that most people reading this book will know the basics of poker, particularly No Limit Hold 'em, the game played in the 'Main Event' of the World Series as in most other major tournaments these days – and as seen almost ad nauseam on television. For those who don't, there is a brief explanation of the game at the back of this book (pp. 320–22), plus the ranking of hands and the odds against receiving them, which I recommend you read first. It is followed by a glossary of poker terms, most of which are explained in the text on first usage, then employed in the poker parlance most players use.

Prologue

In 1978, the year I first visited Las Vegas for the World Series of Poker, Bobby 'the Owl' Baldwin beat a record field of forty-two players to the title of world champion and a handsome first prize of $270,000. A decade later, in 1988, the first time I played in the main event myself, there were all of 167 starters and the title was worth $700,000. By 2005, when I take part again at the beginning of this book, the field has risen to nearly six thousand. The first prize is $7.5 million and all nine players who reach the final table become dollar millionaires.

By the book's end and the 2006 World Series there are 8773 starters, myself again included, vying for a first prize of $12 million – the richest, by some distance, in all sport. The 2006 prize pool of more than $150 million made the thirty-seventh World Series of Poker, staged over seven weeks in July and August, the biggest sporting event in the history of the planet. No fewer than 44,500 players took part in at least one of its forty-five events. Thanks to a combination of television and the internet, poker was booming as never before since being introduced to the fledgling United States by French sailors landing in

Louisiana in the 1820s. And now some interested parties really do call poker a sport, rather than the game most of us have long considered it.

Thirty-six years ago, when the wily Benny Binion hosted the first World Series at his downtown Horseshoe Casino, the field of runners numbered a mere six, the prize purse $30,000. Today, in terms of participants and prizes, the WSOP No Limit Hold 'em Championship is the world's largest single competitive event, growing at an annual rate of more than 200 per cent for the three years 2002–05. The prize money – $82,512,162 (almost £50 million) in 2006 for the main event alone – dwarfs that of any other global sporting championship.

The not insignificant difference from all other sports is that this prize purse is paid by the players. The romance of the WSOP's world title event lies in the fact that ambitious amateurs can take on the top professionals on equal terms. All you need to play is the $10,000 entry fee – or, these days, not even that. Thanks to the democracy of cyberspace, at least two-thirds of the giant fields of recent years have won their way there via online tournaments for as little as five dollars. The world championships of 2003 and 2004 were both won by players who had earned their $10,000 seats online for forty dollars or less, which they proceeded to parlay into millions.

At no other sport is the opportunity for amateurs to compete against professionals so readily available – at such small prices and for such potentially huge rewards, even without any corporate sponsorship. The 2005 winner, an Australian chiropractor turned mortgage broker named Joe Hachem, put up his $10,000 entry fee himself. But his $7.5 million prize money for a week's work was many more times that of Tiger Woods for winning the Open golf championship the same weekend or Roger Federer's for conquering Wimbledon earlier that month.

This is a radically different world from the one I chronicled almost two decades ago in 1988 and 1989, when I spent a year attempting to earn my living as a professional poker player. It's a long story; but it all really happened by mistake. As a dedicated recreational player in my Tuesday Night Game in London, I had been travelling to Vegas each summer as a journalist, and an envious railbird, for ten years before I surprised myself by winning a seat in the 1988 main event via a $1000 'satellite' (or heat). When I returned to London with my then girlfriend, the American novelist Cindy Blake, I was so insufferably excited by the experience that she suggested (with some feeling) that I get it all out of my system by hitting the road on the pro poker tour – and writing an account of my adventures.

So I played in tournaments from Malta and Morocco to Louisiana and the Caribbean, with the objective of trying to improve on my performance in the following year's World Series. Cindy came along for much of the ride, as did my poker-playing writer pal Al Alvarez; they became 'the Moll' and 'the Crony' in the story of my adventures that I published in 1990 in a book called *Big Deal*. Having set out with a bankroll of £20,000, I finished the year almost as much in profit – even after deducting absurd expenses, including sixteen transatlantic flights, one on Concorde. Satisfying, yes – but not, alas, enough to sustain the extended Holden tribe. So for the rest of the 1990s it was back to writing – and recreational poker.

In the first few years of the twenty-first century poker began to boom, as television and the internet brought the game out of the shadows of smoke-filled back rooms into the mainstream of what passes for everyday life. If *Big Deal* bore witness to the 'old' poker – the pioneers who built Vegas into the game's world capital, the roller-coaster ride of personal triumph and disaster endured by the handful of 'rounders' then making a living from the game – how about revisiting that world, I thought, to see just how much it has all changed, to examine the pros and cons of the 'new' poker?

Modest bankroll in hand, I took myself off to the 2005 World

Series of Poker in Las Vegas to check out the new poker scene. I managed to qualify for the main event – as you will see in the ensuing pages – and refreshed my appetite for a town I had not visited in almost a decade. While renewing old friendships, and making new ones, I swiftly saw that the poker world I had chronicled in *Big Deal* had changed beyond even the wildest rumours, facts, anecdotes or statistics I had heard. After years of resisting the idea, I felt a sequel coming on. The impulse to write *Bigger Deal* became irresistible.

By the early years of the twenty-first century the marvels of modern science have revolutionised a game that used to be the romantic, often shady preserve of a few, of high drama in low dives. Online poker has also changed the way people play the game, and lowered the average age of its leading exponents. Does this count as an improvement? That was among the questions I was intent on exploring as I set off on a twelve-month journey reliving the one I took nearly twenty years before.

This time, as then, I would play poker in as many different locations as possible, from Vegas to the Caribbean, Connecticut to Monte Carlo, London to Walsall, on board ship and online, in rinky-dink home games and the biggest tournament ever staged. Last time around I was a hopeful unknown; this time, thanks to *Big Deal*, my anonymity would be largely blown – and for some events, to my own surprise, I would even receive sponsorship. Such are the rewards, for a player more experienced than inspired, of writing one of the first of the handful of poker narratives (as opposed to the growing shelf-loads of manuals) – somewhat ahead of its time, perhaps, but never out of print and still selling merrily to each new generation of players.

Big Deal has led to numerous encounters with total strangers who have credited it with inspiring them to take up the game, move to Vegas, even give up their jobs and turn professional – many of them, I admit through gritted teeth, have made out far better than me. Over the years since the book first appeared, the most unlikely people have approached me in bars or restaurants, on trains and planes or merely on the street, and told me, *Yes*, this was what they had always wanted to do: to give up their jobs and turn poker pro.

People tell me that *Big Deal* helped to make poker respectable in Britain, where the game had hitherto been regarded almost exclusively as a seedy offshoot of East End, sub-Kray gangsterdom. The book earned me the world's first regular poker column in a mainstream publication, *Esquire*, and the first-ever poker documentary on, of all places, BBC Television. In vain had I spent years attempting to persuade British TV executives that poker could be big; this was the nearest I got – a clunky pilot for a series that never happened – to what would become a multi-million-dollar TV phenomenon. *Big Deal* was also hawked around Hollywood as a potential vehicle for some of the more rugged stars – with one of whom, James Woods, I enjoyed a genial conversation in the queue for a modest satellite into the 2005 World Series, by which time the movie was actually being scripted.

Nick Leeson, the rogue trader who brought down Barings Bank, read *Big Deal* while serving his time in Changi jail, Singapore; now he is a regular player and poker columnist. My copy of *Death Plus Ten Years* by Roger Cooper, falsely accused of espionage and imprisoned in the Ayatollahs' 1980s Iran, is inscribed: 'To Tony, Remembering *Big Deal*, which meant a lot to me at the time, and in daydreams still does . . .'

One of the most startling surprises came when I received a late-night call in London from Erik Seidel in Las Vegas. Runner-up to Johnny Chan in the 1988 World Series (as immortalised in the film *Rounders*) and still a highly respected professional, Erik was then working with Annie Duke, sister of his friend and fellow poker pro Howard Lederer, on a new (but short-lived) poker magazine called *Poker World*. Seidel had just seen Microsoft's founder Bill Gates, he told me breathlessly, playing poker in the card room of the Mirage Hotel. So he had gone over to him and said, 'Excuse me, Mr Gates, I didn't know you played poker.'

'I don't,' says Gates. 'I play bridge. But I've just read this new book about poker and I thought I'd give it a try.'

'That wouldn't be *Big Deal* by Anthony Holden?' asked Erik.

'Yeah,' said Gates, 'that's it.'

'Well, Tony is a friend of mine,' ventured Erik.

'Sounds like a nice guy,' said Gates.

'If I could get him out here from London, would you play a game of poker with him for *Poker World* ?'

'Sure,' said Gates, which is why Erik was calling me in the middle of the night. Nothing ever came of it, of course; but I have since derived some solace, in moments of darkness, from knowing that the world's richest man seems to think I'm a 'nice guy'.

My other favourite moment came the day I was introduced to one of my movie heroes, Walter Matthau, at a Hollywood awards ceremony while writing a history of the Academy Awards in the early 1990s. Right after *Big Deal*, the book was really an excuse to spend more time in that poker-sodden part of the world, as well as gratifying my three (then) young sons' passion for the movies.

Knowing that Matthau's Friday game in LA and my Tuesday Game in London had a particular player in common, the restaurateur Michael Chow, I mentioned the connection and asked Matthau: 'So who's the sucker in your game?'

'If you can't spot the sucker in your first half-hour at the table,' he replied, 'it's you!' – adding that he had just read this line in a 'great' new book about poker.

'What's it called?' I asked.

Matthau couldn't remember.

'It's not, er, *Big Deal*, by any chance?' I ventured.

'That's it!' he smiled. 'That's the one!'

'Um, well, I wrote it.'

Matthau didn't believe me. How could this Limey in a suit and tie, with a new (and rather brutal) haircut, be the guy who had written *Big Deal*? Mutual friends had to be summoned to assure Matthau that I was indeed Holden. At which point he asked when it was due out in paperback and whether a jacket quote from him might help? Soon, I replied, and, you bet. So Matthau summoned pencil and paper, and sat alone in the corner of the room for quite some time, mostly crossing things out and screwing up sheet after sheet. By the time the luncheon had begun and he was needed at the top table, the best he could come up with was: 'Reading *Big Deal* is better than losing at poker.'

Seeing my face fall, Matthau said, 'You're right, it's not great, is it?' – and asked me to come see him again after the meal. Throughout which he sat furiously scribbling away . . . what turned out to be his postprandial speech, when presenting a lifetime achievement award to his old friend Howard Koch, the Hollywood veteran who had (among many other celluloid achievements) written the immortal *Casablanca*.

When the meal finally ended, I hung around for a while as Matthau was mobbed by admirers and thought, Well, he's been terrific, it was a thrill just to meet him. As I was slinking off, without bothering the great man further, that unmistakable voice yelled after me: 'Hey, Holden, where d'you think you're going? I got something for you.'

Matthau came towards me with his place card, which he handed over, saying 'Will *this* do?' On the back of it he had written: '*Big Deal* is the best book about poker I've ever read.'

I thanked him, of course, profusely, and it duly appeared a few months later on the front jacket of the American paperback.

*

Readers of *Big Deal* will be pleased to know that in the year of the book's publication, after several years of cohabitation, I married the Moll at her family's Cape Cod home, with former world seven-card stud champion and long-time WSOP tournament director Eric Drache sharing the role of best man with my friend and former editor, Harold Evans. They may also share my pain to know that ten years later she decided she had had enough of me. But we are still, after a decent interval, the closest of friends; and Cindy was sitting beside me as my wife when perhaps the seminal encounter took place.

It was Saturday evening in the mid-1990s, a few years after the book was first published, when a young American approached me in the bar of London's Victoria Casino (the 'Vic', to its habitués), introduced himself and asked if I was really the guy who had written *Big Deal*.

Indeed I was, I replied with a modest smile, looking over to the Moll for the mocking smile which usually greeted these occasional little boosts to my ego. I asked him what he did. 'I work for IBM in Mississippi,' came the reply. 'At least I did until I read your book. Then I quit my job and became a professional poker player. Just like you.

'And you see my friend over there, that guy at the craps table – he's a lawyer. Works in the office of the Governor of Mississippi. Or he did until I lent him your book. Then he decided to quit his job too, and now we travel the world together as poker partners.

'We're off to Austria on Monday. I was just wondering if you had any tips about the Hold 'em scene in Vienna?'

I was still a sentence or two behind him. It was not just that I then knew nothing at all about the poker scene in Vienna. Never before, despite the polite remarks about their work to which writers become relatively accustomed, had I met someone who had actually given up his job – and a damn good job at that – because of me.

Over the few years since *Big Deal* was first published, I had grown uneasily aware that I had inadvertently altered a few lives. There were regulars here at the Vic, and elsewhere, who had told me that they'd taken up poker because of me and my book. But they hadn't, so far as I knew, given up their jobs, or left their wives and children, or wound up on skid row, or in jail. Or worse.

'My God,' I finally managed to gasp. 'And how are you doing?'

'Um, I don't want to be rude, but the truth is, we're doing rather better than you. We're in our second years as pros now and we're making a lot more money than we ever did back in Mississippi.'

Both Americans proceeded, as that Saturday evening wore on, to reach the final table of the tournament and then to get into the money. The following day they duly flew off to Vienna. Six months later at the World Series of Poker at Binion's in Las Vegas, I met them again. Both were leading contenders for that year's world title.

On my recent forays to Vegas for this sequel, just as much as in Britain, people still come up to me and tell me they're there because of me. They read *Big Deal* and they took up poker. They took up poker and they started to win. They won so much that now, look, here they are in Vegas. In fact, it would be an honour if I sat down with them for a few hands of . . .

There are limits even to my vanity. I am more than aware that the poker played in those (and these) pages is far from world-standard. Whether or not these guys had even opened *Big Deal* – if they hadn't, it was a stylish scam – I knew they were better players than me.

But are they still? Are all the students with laptops who win online tournaments these days really better than wizened old-timers like me with decades of hard-earned experience at the green baize? Has the game changed for better or worse thanks to the internet and TV revolution? Has poker become a young person's game? These were among the questions I have set out to answer by embarking on another tilt at the world title and the coveted bracelet that goes with it.

This time I wasn't going to give up my job – a nice one, as music critic of the *Observer* – or risk the car, even the house, on the turn of a card. There is, at last, no more alimony. My three sons are long through higher education, out in the world earning their own livings. So my modest ambition for *Bigger Deal* was merely to cover my costs in tournament and cash-game winnings – and, oh yes, of course, to win the world title.

Could I still perform in my late fifties at the same (okay, modest) standard as I had when turning forty? What was it about poker that still got my juices going after all these years? While rediscovering all that, I could also check out how the world of poker has moved on from those heady days of nearly twenty years ago. For one thing is beyond doubt: the first few years of the twenty-first century have seen the world of poker, both amateur and professional, alter beyond all recognition.

In terms of active participants, poker is now without question the most popular game (if not sport) on earth. Eighty million people (1.5 per cent of the global population) are said to play regularly – nearly thirty million of them in the United States, five million in Britain, and almost a third of them women. The game's universal appeal, transcending sport's traditional gender barriers, lies in its uniquely democratic spirit. You can sit down to play anywhere in the world, with a table of millionaires and hoboes, and poker's eternal verities at once render everyone equal.

Poker is played against other people, not a bookmaker or casino, so it can truly be said to be the only form of gambling where, if you know what you're doing, you are wagering favourable odds. Lady Luck may (and will) turn against you from time to time; but an expert, if he or she plays accurately and carefully, will win more often than lose. And the losers will always blame anyone but themselves.

In poker, most significantly, you don't need the best cards to win. Bet the right amount and you can push your opponents out of the pot without even showing your hand. In no other game is licensed larceny such a bonus. Thanks to its unique element of bluff, which sets it apart from all other card games and sports, poker is the only contest at which the worst hand can still win all the money.

Poker is, or should be, the triumph of psychology over chance. Skill, in the long run, will overcome luck – unlike other forms of gambling, from lotteries to the horses, or other casino games such as craps, roulette and blackjack, in all of which the odds are stacked against you. This is why casinos have deep-pile carpets and chandeliers. That's not to say luck doesn't play a role in poker – of course it does – but the best players tend to make their own.

Poker has been said to be '100 per cent skill and 100 per cent luck'. That's one way of putting it. Connoisseurs of the game suggest that at its highest level poker really comes down to 80 per cent skill, 20 per cent luck. In the lower echelons, where I reside, that comes as far down as fifty-fifty. But with guile, perception, courage, patience and grit – between them, a definition of what the top players call 'heart' – anyone can bend the odds in their favour and learn to beat the game, maybe even win a fortune on the turn of a card or click of a mouse.

For nearly two centuries, since those former Napoleonic troops landed in Louisiana with a card game called 'poque', whose final 'e' American Southerners pronounced as a separate syllable, poker was associated primarily with card sharps in saloons, where cheating was rife and disagreements settled by bullets rather than floormen. Aces and eights are still called 'Dead Man's Hand', being the cards 'Wild Bill' Hickok was holding when he was shot in the back of the head in Deadwood, South Dakota, in 1876. For most of the twentieth century, to those without their own home games, poker remained largely the preserve of a select few in the movies, usually Westerns, dubious characters who were probably out to cheat you – or would draw a gun if you won their money.

With the advent of legal gaming in Nevada in the 1930s, the game gradually became more honest. You could still get bilked in a back room in Chicago; but play in casinos, or your own home game, was for the most part straight – and a welcome way of relaxing from your everyday woes. Today, in a regulated casino, it is very unusual to get cheated; online, it's increasingly less likely, with proceedings strictly monitored by the websites.

In the 1980s, as the World Series grew, a tournament circuit developed, breeding a few hundred professionals, mostly in the western United States, who ground out some sort of living from poker. Now, suddenly, there are thousands of pros, maybe tens of thousands lurking in cyberspace – and many more amateurs also seeking and earning handsome money, sometimes fortunes. Over the last few years, thanks to the combination of the internet and television, the poker universe has been expanding at a thousand pots a second.

As I lived and wrote this book, around $100 million was being wagered online every day. Websites like PartyPoker were earning £500 a minute from the many millions of hands they dealt twenty-four seven. The flotation of its parent company, PartyGaming, on the London Stock Exchange in 2005 was the UK's biggest IPO in five years. Valued at more than £5.5 billion, the business leapt straight into the FTSE 100. With internet poker expanding at a rate of 16 per cent a month, the popularity of online gaming, and poker in particular, was credited with a major role in rejuvenating the 'new' economy. These days you can even play poker on your mobile phone.

Since its reincarnation online, television coverage has helped poker to explode. Frenzied competition between websites offers famous players lucrative sponsorship deals – and the pros can't believe their luck. Former world champions from Doyle Brunson to Phil Hellmuth Jr are among the few from the pre-internet era to have turned themselves into high-tech cottage industries with their own websites, churning out 'How to' guides, hosting tournaments online, running pricey Vegas boot camps for students of the game, even lecturing at the venerable Oxford Union.

Where once it was a seedy, disreputable pursuit peopled by shifty characters, poker is now not just respectable but fashionable, even chic, with many showbiz names on both sides of the Atlantic showing off their supposed skills on television, some right alongside you in card rooms. Numerous Hollywood players range from James Woods to Tobey 'Spiderman' Maguire, both of whom played in the 2005 WSOP, as did pro golfer Rocco Mediate. Actress Jennifer Tilly won the women's title, with Mimi Rogers also performing strongly in various events. Ben Affleck has won a major tournament; he and his pal Matt Damon head the growing list of the Hollywood community turning to poker as relaxation, even an alternative lifestyle. Other members of the Hollywood poker set include Leonardo DiCaprio, Jack Black, Heather Graham, David Schwimmer and Martin Sheen. A recent British celebrity tournament at the Palm Beach Casino in London featured Ryder Cup golfer Sam Torrance, footballer Teddy Sheringham, actor Michael Greco and snooker players Jimmy White, Mark Williams and Ken Doherty. Their fellow player Steve Davis did well enough to make it into the money at the main event of the 2006 World Series.

At the movies poker is now sufficiently fashionable for James Bond himself (in the rugged new shape of Daniel Craig) to prefer it to baccarat in his 2006 caper *Casino Royale*. John Dahl's 1998 movie *Rounders* also played a significant role in promoting poker and popularising its best-known variant, No Limit Texas Hold 'em. At the time of writing, there are several more major Hollywood poker movies in production. Tune in to America's Travel Channel, Fox, Bravo or ESPN, even occasionally NBC, or the UK's Challenge TV, Player, the Poker Channel, PokerZone or several other cable and occasionally terrestrial channels any night of the week, and you'll find an array of poker shows, from coverage of the WSOP via the globe-trotting *World Poker Tour* and *European Poker Tour* to homegrown fare like the gangster-esque East End *Poker Den* or celebrity *Late Night Poker*.

After launching on Channel 4 in 1999, *Late Night Poker* astonished its Cardiff-based production company by attracting all of a million viewers in the wee small hours of Saturday nights-to-Sunday mornings. The secret of its success was the glass panel revealing the players' hole cards via below-table cameras, enabling the TV audience to join in the cut and thrust of the game. These were the forerunners of the 'lipstick camera', or 'pocket-cam', since used by the World Poker Tour and all other televised tournaments.

Late Night Poker's third series in 2000 was launched with a 'celebrity' special which has since spawned countless imitators. The seven players who started with £1000 each were the actor and writer Stephen Fry, novelist Martin Amis, playwright and screenwriter Patrick Marber, TV comic Ricky Gervais, journalist and TV presenter Victoria Coren and writers (of books about, among many other things, poker) Al Alvarez and, yes, Anthony Holden.

These last two were the final men standing, with a pair of sixes proving enough for your correspondent to beat his old pal Alvarez, the Crony and dedicatee of *Big Deal*, to the £7000 up for grabs. Like I always say, if you're going to win a tournament, try to do it on television. Al remains a constant presence in this sequel, while my three sons – too young, last time around, to enter a casino – join sundry poker writers in taking on the collective role of travelling cronys. The Moll remains the Moll, still popping up all over the place, leaving only a small 'm' (in print, anyway) for the various other molls who have passed through my life since we went our separate ways.

It was Alvarez who wrote the first really elegant literary treatise on poker and its World Series, a collection of articles for the *New Yorker* magazine which became a book entitled *The Biggest Game in Town*, published in 1983. Seminal poker texts, from Herbert O. Yardley's classic *The Education of a Poker Player* to the book that improved more people's games than any other, two-time world champion Doyle 'Texas Dolly' Brunson's *Super/System*, heralded today's voluminous library of memoirs, biographies of great players and manuals on just about every variation and sub-detail of the game.

Maybe you've read one or more of those books. More likely, you've caught the poker bug from the game's compelling coverage on television. So here comes one of the first poker home truths this book has to offer the tempted: poker is nothing like it looks on television. A one- or two-hour TV edit of a much longer contest is clearly going to zero in on the big hands – the largest pots, the moment the celebrities get knocked out, those hands where the centre of chip gravity shifts decisively. These benchmark hands come up all too rarely in real life.

The final table (nine players) of the 2005 World Series, for instance, wound up running for a record fourteen hours before Joe Hachem finally won through. By the time that hard-fought, gruelling marathon was shown on the box, it had been edited down to two TV hours, or some hundred minutes. Each programme showed maybe a dozen hands of the scores actually dealt as the players circled warily around each other, jockeying for position while fighting to stay alive. This slow, cumulative gathering of knowledge about opponents, far more than those dramatic all-in hands, is the true essence of poker.

Poker is a game of constantly changing moods and rhythms. It can, in other words – often should – be boring. But there are worse ways to be bored and countless things you can do while you are. Poker requires, as much as aggression or a poker face, infinite patience. Where bridge is a card game on which you can bet, poker is a game of wagering played with cards. It is a game less of luck or chance or even cards than of people and, above all, situations, for which you simply have to wait. The right one may take its time coming, but it will. As usual, Shakespeare said it first: 'The readiness is all.'

While you're waiting, there's plenty of fun to be had: joshing with the other players, watching and noting their styles of play, calculating your next move – when to hold 'em, as the Kenny Rogers song runs, when to fold 'em – or simply retreating into your own private, above-it-all shell. Yes, it's true what they say about poker: it takes a moment to learn, and a lifetime to master.

As I was about to find out. All over again.

1

Give My Regards to Broadway

The seventh of July 2005 is a date I will always remember, for all the wrong reasons. In London fifty-two commuters were killed, and more than seven hundred horribly injured, when suicide bombers who turned out to be home-grown targeted the public transport system at the height of a Thursday morning rush hour. Me, I slept through it all, five thousand miles away, for reasons I had hitherto considered important.

The first I knew of the dire events back home was some eight hours after they happened, when I woke up in my distant hotel room to a message from a close friend in London saying, in case I was worried, that she was all right. Why would she not be? CNN promptly gave me the answer.

I was immediately assailed by the same feeling of absentee guilt I had known on 11 September 2001 – when I was living in New York but happened to have chosen that one week all year to visit London. In both cities I worked from home, as I have for all of twenty-five years, so was unlikely to have been a victim of the events of either 9/11 or now 7/7. Yet both had happened in my home towns and on neither occasion had I been there. What were the odds against that?

With another surge of guilt, and a sobering sense of life's priorities, I realised I was in the right place for an answer to that question, too. This was the first day of the world championship of poker, the 'Main Event' of the 2005 World Series of Poker in Las Vegas, in preparation for which I had taken a sleeping pill the night before to ensure a good night's rest as I climbed into bed around 1 a.m., to dream of winning the world title as the tragedy in London began to unfold.

Other Brits in Vegas for the tournament had been up all night, after switching on the news as they returned to their rooms or being woken by family and friends calling to reassure them they were okay. It was the main topic of conversation as noon approached and we met each other shambling along 'Convention Way', the lengthy corridor between the Rio Hotel-Casino and the Amazon Room, heart of the vast conference centre where the World Series was taking place.

The news from London had not yet, to tell the truth, sunk in among the world's leading poker players. These are people so wrapped up in what they do that they would barely notice if the President of the United States sat down at their table. During 'Desert Storm' a top pro named Dewey Tomko enquired of his friend Doyle Brunson, doyen of living poker players, just who in hell was this guy Saddam Hussein? He also once asked Brunson what language they speak in England? Were the Channel Islands anywhere near water? Tomko is a former teacher, for pity's sake. Brunson also recalls a legendary player called Felton 'Corky' McCorquodale, none other than the man who introduced Texas Hold 'em to Las Vegas in 1963, asking him at the height of the Vietnam War where in the heck was this place Vietnam? On his first visit to Austria, 1998 world champion Scotty Nguyen apparently expressed an interest in seeing some kangaroos.

Not until three days later, at the beginning of Sunday's play, would there be a solemn announcement of sympathy for British players in the tournament – more misplaced guilt: whose sympathy did I deserve? – and a moment of silence for the victims. In Vegas the real world takes its time to filter through, if it ever does. Besides, this was the moment for which poker players all over the world wait, and prepare, all year. This was the beginning of a seven-day cycle that would see one of them crowned world champion, with a prize of $7.5 million and sponsorship deals to banish all money worries for life.

So the atmosphere as the tournament approached was sombre less because of world events than the sheer scale of what was going on here. Huge amounts of money were at stake – all nine players to reach the final table would become dollar millionaires – and the winner's life was about to be transformed. For the top pros, already multi-millionaires, some already world champions, pride and honour were as much on the line as the value of their website and sponsorship deals.

For me, a decade since I last played in this event, it was an attempt to see if I could still hold my own – at the very least – in a world which had changed beyond recognition since last I dropped by. For the first time in its thirty-five-year history, the World Series was not being held in the place where it all began, the revered but rundown Binion's Horseshoe Casino in seedy, downtown Glitter Gulch – 'where', as they used to say, 'the *real* gamblers go'. Its paterfamilias, Benny Binion, was long dead; just as well, perhaps, as he'd have muttered a few choice curse words on hearing that his brainchild had been hijacked by his loathed Las Vegas 'Strip', with all its garish razzmatazz. Benny's successor, his son Jack, had moved on, his other son Ted had been murdered and his daughter Becky had been bought out by the world's largest gaming company, Harrah's, which owns the Rio.

Harrah's had wanted only the rights to the legendary names 'Horseshoe' and 'World Series of Poker'; the casino itself was promptly sold off to some dot-com squillionaires, recouping most of the $50 million Harrah's had paid for what were to prove priceless assets. This year's climax was to be held downtown at Binion's, but purely as a nod to poker history, to mark the centenary of Las Vegas. So this would be the last time even one day of the World Series would be played at the Horseshoe – rather like taking tennis away from Wimbledon or cricket from Lord's.

In the few days I had already been at the Rio, to get over the jet lag and play in some satellites for the main event, I had mustered a wry smile as I took the long walk towards the card room past the adjacent conference centre, where a gathering of heavy-duty shrinks was discussing borderline personality disorder. Its delegates, I mused, might be better off mingling with these poker fantasists, all in one way or another crazed by the game which had brought them here.

Was that true of me? I guess so, though right now I had no problem with this particular aspect of my undoubtedly addictive personality. Like many old-school poker players, for instance, I'm still a dedicated smoker, frustrated and enraged by the recent victories of the thought police. Once in a while I can drink too much, too. Over more than thirty years at the baize, however, I have largely managed to keep my bankroll under control, if never making it into the money here at the World Series. Which still doesn't stop me trying.

It all started for me back in 1988, when I had already been coming to the tournament for ten years as a journalist (and amateur, or 'recreational', player), recouping my costs by covering this exotic event for just about every newspaper and magazine in Fleet Street and beyond. Every year for a decade I had watched from the rails as an excited but frustrated wannabe, desperately envious of those who – unlike me – could afford the $10,000 entry fee. Then the tournament director, Eric Drache, came up with the first of the bright ideas that would begin to transform poker into the global phenomenon it is today.

Drache suggested to his boss, Jack Binion, that they try something called 'satellites', or heats, to accommodate lesser players by giving them a route into the action for less than $10k, thus swelling the field (and so the prize money) in the process. Ten players, for instance, could sit down at one table for $1000 each and play until one of them had won the lot, thus earning himself a $10,000 seat for a mere thou.

Even a thou then seemed a lot to me, but I found myself signing up for one of these satellites at the end of a profitable day, primarily to escape a deadly dull dollar-ante game with other journalists. Somehow I managed to win the thing and so got to play in the main event for the first time, against such giants of the 'old' poker as Johnny 'the Man' Moss, Doyle 'Texas Dolly' Brunson, Amarillo 'Slim' Preston, Stu 'the Kid' Ungar, Walter Clyde 'Puggy' Pearson and reigning champion Johnny 'the Orient Express' Chan (who won it again that year, a second successive time – an achievement equalling that of Brunson in 1976–77 and now never likely to be matched). I lasted into the second day and went out in ninetieth place out of 167 starters – not even in the top half but respectable enough for a wide-eyed amateur.

No one back home took much interest until someone pointed out that this was then a higher world ranking than any British tennis player. When people heard that they sat up, impressed. As the only Brit in that year's tournament, I also declared myself the British number one by default. It was just a matter of time, surely, before I received my knighthood for services to sport.

But the World Series is not about rankings, as I have to remind myself to this day; it's about money. Pros with bottomless pits of the stuff say the diamond-studded gold bracelet that comes with the title means more to them than the dough. Yet I have always treasured the on-camera reply of Telly Savalas when I was making a BBC TV documentary about the 1991 World Series and had asked him if the prize money was, er, irrelevant.

'Tony,' replied Kojak with a knowing grin, 'a million dollars is *never* irrelevant.'

I have since played in the event several more times but only when I could earn the entry fee at poker, whether in my regular Tuesday Night Game back home or in satellites for the main event – which soon turned into 'super-satellites', with an entry fee of a mere $200, plus rebuys and a field overflowing the casino, building a prize pool so big that most of the players at the final table got $10,000 seats for the Big One. Three times in ten years, this was the way I qualified for the main event.

Slowly but surely countless satellites began to swell the number of entrants to the tournament and thus the prize money. Soon the Vegas pros hung around the rail purely for the chance to sit down in satellites with suckers like me – then known in poker parlance as 'tourists' or 'patsies', these days as 'fish' or 'donkeys'. Anyone who actually put up ten thousand real dollars of his own money to play in the thing was seen as a self-regarding chump with more money than sense, and so easy meat – or, in my favourite new poker phrase, 'dead money'.

With the arrival of online poker at the turn of the twenty-first century, players could win $10,000 seats for forty dollars or less by working their way past giant fields of players with more hope than expectation. This huge influx was swollen almost beyond control by 'the Moneymaker effect' – a clever marketing play on the surreal surname of the 2003 main event winner, Chris Moneymaker, a Tennessee accountant who carried off the $2.5 million first prize for an outlay of just thirty-nine dollars on PokerStars.com.

It was the first time Moneymaker had played poker live in a real casino, rather than online. 'Hey,' went the global response, 'if that guy can win it, so can I!' That year there were 839 starters; the following year, 2004, there were more than three times as many, 2576, competing for a first prize of $5m. At 5619 in 2005, the number of starters had again more than doubled, with as many as two-thirds of them qualifying via the web.

But qualifying online takes time – lots of it, which those with any other kind of employment or commitments, like me, just can't spare. Dominated, of course, by US time zones, these lengthy events also take place in the UK at ungodly hours – which, again, is not usually a problem unless you've actually got something to get out of bed for the next morning. So these days, for those without the time to qualify online, casino satellites are available before the main event for pretty much any amount you care to risk. Play in a one-table tournament (or 'sit-and-go') for $100 and you can win $1000. Only nine thou more to go.

Quite a few of these events now take place all over the world in the months leading up to the World Series; but in Vegas, California and all over the western United States, they're non-stop. For players who live in that part of the world, or arrive in Vegas well in advance of the World Series, it is one way to try your luck at putting the entry fee together without risking too much money. For late arrivals like myself – those weirdo mavericks to whom poker is not their *entire* life and who prefer live poker to its cyberspace counterpart – the risks are more substantial.

But two nights earlier, twenty-four hours after getting here, I had registered as a World Series player – the 17,716th person to do so this year (out of an eventual total of 32,341) – and promptly managed to win $5000 by outlasting nine other entrants at a $500 one-table satellite, the first I entered. So that was half the $10,000 entry fee won for a mere $500. Maybe I wasn't past it, after all?

This was a major moment (witnessed, I'm pleased to say, by

the poker writer Des Wilson, who gave it a generous mention in his diary for *Poker Europa* magazine). I desperately wanted to play in the world title event, the last of the forty-five different tournaments that constitute the month-long World Series. But I knew I had to win the entry fee rather than bring it with me. The flights and two-week hotel bill were already going to make a serious dent in my slender bankroll. There was no way I could put up the $10,000 out of my own pocket; winning half of it on day one smacked of divine intervention.

Immediately I hurried over to lodge my official entry while there was still a chance. There were rumours that Harrah's would cap the year's entries at six thousand – a total said to be fast approaching. Well, I hadn't come all this way not to play. So I took the risk of registering for the tournament now while there was still space for sure. The other $5000 I could win back later – as indeed I eventually did manage, thanks again to the poker gods, in a streak of good cards over several sessions at the $5–$10 No Limit Hold 'em cash game across the Strip at the Bellagio Hotel and Casino.

My ten thousand dollars – half in tournament chips, half in greenbacks – earned me the coveted card giving me my seat placement for the 2005 world title event. And a ten-dollar food voucher. Harrah's, I mused, last of the big spenders. Only after chucking it away in disgust did I learn that it was worth every cent as a pass for jumping the long line at the Rio's coffee shop.

Nonetheless I permitted myself a pat on the back for again managing to enter the $10,000 event for a great deal less, this time just $500 of my own money and $9500 of other people's. This would be the sixth time I had played – never, but never, having had to put up the entry fee in hard-earned cash. For me this had become a matter of superstitious pride as much as financial necessity.

Or in the immortal words of Paul Newman's 'Fast' Eddie Felson to Tom Cruise's Vincent Lauria in *The Color of Money*,

Martin Scorsese's 1986 sequel to that iconic movie *The Hustler*:
'Money won is twice as sweet as money earned.'

Converted into the world's largest poker hall for six weeks, the
Amazon Room in the Rio's convention centre makes a spectacular yet somehow depressing sight for a veteran like me,
however inspirational it may be to all these youthful online
whizz-kids. With more than two hundred tables, capable of
accommodating two thousand-plus players, it resembles nothing
so much as a giant aircraft hangar reluctantly adapted for the
passing purpose, with none of the necessary – and, at Binion's,
familiar – conveniences.

The old poker took place in a card room especially extended
for the World Series, with free buffets within walking distance
and your bedroom right overhead. Here in the world of the new
poker, there is just one small overpriced snack bar where a
dozen hungry people constitute a long, slow line and your room
seems several miles away. The overhead lighting for TV's benefit is brutal, offering a reason to wear shades beyond the mere
desire for inscrutability. Of the many huckster stalls crowding
the narrow corridor outside the card room, only one is offering
anything worthwhile: Put a Bad Beat on Cancer, where you
can sign up to give 1 per cent of your tournament winnings to
poker pro Phil Gordon's worthy cause. Soon there's a giant
cardboard chip up there reading: 'Anthony Holden – for Cindy
Blake.' The Moll may have left me, but a part of me will always
love her; and she has since been through breast cancer, which
has also robbed her of both her sisters, so this for me is a solemn
commitment.

And a brief interval between moans. On a visit to the men's
room, I discover there are just six stalls to cope with the best part
of two thousand desperate males on a ten-minute 'rest' break.
God knows how the women are coping, though they seem as
unhappy as the guys, not least my friend from London, Victoria

Coren, whose disenchantment with the scale of the new poker reaches lyrical heights:

'It is as if your favourite band has landed a huge recording contract, allowing them to make albums of the best quality with the best resources for many years to come. As a fan you are excited and optimistic, proud to share their music and relieved at their security. But you are not entirely certain, all the time, that you didn't secretly love them a little more on those crackly old recordings knocked up years ago in the lead singer's garage.'

With nearly six thousand starters from forty countries, ranging in age from twenty-one to ninety – but room for only two thousand players at a time – the main event of the 2005 World Series of Poker has been divided into three Day Ones, or 'flights', of which I am drawn to play on the first, Day 1-A. At Table 105, to be precise, Seat Three, in the corner of the room mercifully near the snack bar and the men's room. As I settle in, with luck for the long haul, I look warily around the table but see no one I know or even recognise – another hallmark of the new poker.

People ask if you feel nervous as you sit down for a tournament of this scale, with such potentially giant rewards. Not me, to even my own surprise; maybe I've just been doing it for too long. The buzz you feel at the start of a contest of this scale allows no room for nerves; it is a thrill of an order generated by all too few other activities in life. And right now it's not about the money. It's about the pleasures of play.

I know the drill. You think yourself into the right frame of mind for each stage of the contest, which at first means playing tight, risking chips only on monster hands. This is why, on the first hand of the tournament, I put down J-8 suited in early position, only to see the flop bring J-8-8. Not, psychologically, the best sort of start, but you still know you played your cards right. You have to put it behind you. The only consolation at moments like this is the seasoned advice of Amarillo 'Slim' Preston: 'If you can't fold the winning hand, you can't play poker.'

As I try to cheer myself with this old chestnut, word passes round the room that Hollywood's Oliver Hudson has gone out of the tournament on the first hand – a full house beaten by a better full house. There's an audible sigh of relief from 1999 other players in the hall; we've all achieved our first target – not to be the first out. But the rest of my own first hour brings very few playable hands, with all of which I am desperately tentative.

All ten players at the table, myself included, seem intent on holding on to their blinds, the once-per-round compulsory bets that kick off the action – which is absurd when they are still so low, just $25 and $50 a round out of the $10,000 in front of us. But it's a matter of pride, of self-respect, of table-image, of not letting the others push you around. Even so, at $75 every ten hands, with a week to go before this gets down to the final table, no one is yet taking any unnecessary risks. Few veer more than a thousand above or below their original ten in the first hour of play. At the first break, after a hundred minutes, I am a fraction up on $10,400.

I try to go for a pee but the line stretches to the crack of doom. So I decide to go during the next session, once the blinds have passed me. Back at the table, as I'm thinking about all this, I'm dealt A-10 in late position. I raise $500 and am called by an impertinent A-8, which of course wins when his eight pairs on the river. Just my luck. Suddenly I have slid down to $8500. Then, next hand, I am dealt every poker player's dream and potential nightmare – a pair of aces or 'pocket rockets' – which you can expect only once in every 220 hands, a statistic even I can keep in my head. With the blinds now up to $50–$100, I raise what I consider to be a well-judged $500. The guy on my left reraises me $1000. Everyone round to me folds; I reraise him another $2000. To my utter astonishment, he immediately goes all-in – bets everything he has – to the tune of $8000, only five hundred less than I have myself.

What the heck could he be holding? Luckily, I don't have time to wonder. My automatic poker pilot has kicked in and all my chips have somehow reached the middle of the table. Without even pausing to think, I have called.

There can be no more betting, so I turn over my aces and he turns over a pair of queens. Clearly an internet punter, perhaps playing with human beings for the first time in his life, he doesn't seem too fazed by my mighty hand. Especially when the first card I see coming in the flop is . . . yes, a queen. No whooping or air-punching from him, just a calm, quiet assumption that poker justice is being done, as the dealer rolls Q-K-3 to give him a cruel and unusual 'set' (at odds of 8-1 against). In time-honoured fashion I stand up and start gathering what is left of my worldly goods, ready to leave the room and bore for Britain with my bad beat story.

A banged fist on the baize and the turn comes a jack. There is barely time to work it out before the river brings a ten, one of just four cards in the deck (out of the forty-four available, so a 10-1 shot) that could give me top straight, known in the trade as a 'Broadway'.

Give that blessed street my grateful regards. It takes the guy with trip queens a moment to realise that he's lost. He has never got up from his seat or shown the slightest sign of emotion. Now, with all the indignation of a player who's suffered a really bad beat, he picks up his iPod and makes his way out of the arena, muttering darkly as he goes.

Me, I sit down again somewhat a-tremble, but with a satisfying sense that poker justice has been done. The better starting hand, after all, has won the pot. It's been the first real drama at our table, which has now lost its first player. Some looks, even a few words are exchanged with other players for the first time since we sat down two hours ago. 'That wasn't much fun,' I gasp. There are sympathetic murmurs, amid worried looks at my pile of chips. Doubled up to $17,000 I am now, of course, chip leader, in a position to start bullying the table – raising with lesser hands to force out the smaller stacks – and stealing the blinds when they grow big enough to bother.

With immaculate timing, the deadpan voice behind the public address system now intones, 'For internet players, the RAISE button is to your right.' So inured is the vast hall to tedious administrative announcements that the joke takes a moment to sink in, then laughter slowly spreads around the room as it gets repeated and repeated. By the end of the second session, I am still table boss with $18,550.

It's almost a decade since I've been here in Vegas, after not missing a year between 1978 and 1997. The bigger the World Series grew, the more, for me, it began to lose its charm; and in 1999, when Jack Binion was forced out of the Horseshoe by his sister Becky and her husband, his friends were encouraged not to turn up. Jack had been immensely generous to me for twenty years, comping me throughout each year's WSOP, even once assigning me a Horseshoe limo to do my Christmas shopping. So that year, instead, I went down to his new Horseshoe Casino in Tunica, Mississippi, for the rival Jack Binion World Poker Open, hosted by our mutual friends Jack McLelland and the late Jim Albrecht, both of whom had also been frozen out of the Horseshoe by Becky. Even when I lived in New York for three years, between 1999 and 2002, I never made it back to Vegas. Somehow I wasn't even tempted.

But the place to which I have now returned, wondering how I could have been away for so long, is scarcely recognisable. Take a cab down the Strip's twelve-lane freeway and you see the Eiffel Tower beside St Mark's, Venice, alongside the Empire State Building and the Sphinx. This globalisation on the grand scale has all happened while I've been away.

The Colosseum at Caesar's Palace, symbolising Ancient Rome, has long been a landmark along the Strip. But Paris was still going up and the Bellagio a mere glint in the eye of its creator, Steve Wynn, when last I was here, still marvelling at the scale of his Mirage and Treasure Island complexes. In those days each new hotel built in Vegas had to be the biggest; now it also has to be the best, which means the most luxurious. Having sold his properties to the MGM Grand Group for some four billion dollars in 2000, Wynn has now built another one called simply the Wynn. Not a bad name, once you think about it, for a casino. Next to its sumptuous card room – where Daniel 'Kid Poker' Negreanu is paid $1m a year to take on all comers at any form of the game for a minimum of $500,000 – stands Nevada's only Ferrari franchise, a testosterone-tempting reminder of what you can buy yourself if you get lucky enough at the felt.

In 1978, when I first came here, the population of Las Vegas was 200,000. Now it is two million. There are 150,000 hotel rooms in town; all of 100,000 people a day pass through the airport. Visitors have reached nearly forty million a year. Las Vegas is the fastest-expanding city in the United States – and it shows no sign of stopping. Cranes are everywhere, one building a new suburb of Venice. Soon, perhaps, Mars.

Poker rules have changed too, in ways designed to make the game more respectable, more acceptable to would-be new arrivals. The card rooms are all, for a start, non-smoking. No one sensible is drinking hard liquor at the table during the World Series. The use of mobile phones is banned while you're in a hand; even looking at a text message will kill your cards. Any swear word, especially those beginning with 'f' or 'c', earns a ten-minute time-out penalty. Old-timers like me – and, yes, looking around me, I see that my late-fifties suddenly make me that by contemporary standards – could be forgiven for thinking they'd come to the wrong place, maybe stumbled into a Mormon convention.

Until you sit back down in the tournament arena, where players are still being knocked out at the rate of one a minute. So every ten minutes or so sees a table 'broken up' and its players redistributed to the newly empty seats around the room. Halfway through this third session of Day 1-A it's our turn, and I am moved to Table 120, Seat Three.

A move in mid-tournament is always unsettling: you've taken all that time to assess the other players at your table and adjust your game accordingly, and now you've got to start all over again. Where I had been chip leader, I am now third or fourth. There is a guy here with a *huge* pile, maybe $50,000, which makes my respectable, hard-earned $20,000 suddenly feel rather puny. He's in excellent shape to bully the table – not just raising before the flop, in the hope of stealing the blinds (now $100–$200), but betting 'on the come' or betting big on the turn to steal the pot – and he's doing it with irritating regularity. A hundred more minutes and I'm just about holding my own – but no more – with $18,250.

This third interval is supposedly the dinner break, in which several thousand hungry players and their pals have just forty minutes to find themselves some sustenance. It takes almost that long to fight your way through the crowds to the Rio's coffee shop and other restaurants, let alone order something which may or may not be worth eating. I grab a hot dog from the snack bar and head up to my room to lie down for twenty minutes. After five hours of heavy-duty concentration I'm pretty bushed, and there's as much again ahead of me today if I want to make it to Day Two.

It feels good to get away from the bedlam downstairs; but the adrenalin is pumping and I can't lie still, so I email a progress report my support team back in London – all of whom, I'm well aware, have more important things on their minds today than poker. As I re-emerge from the lift, with five minutes until the tournament resumes and a ten-minute walk to get there, an attractive young woman waves to me from a nearby bank of phones. I head over, wondering if she might be one of the countless nubile teenagers who passed through the house during the dating days of my sons, now all in their twenties. Yes, that must be it. Should I give her a friendly kiss on the cheek?

At the last minute something makes me decide against.

'Hi there,' she says with a friendly smile. 'How are you?'

'Just fine,' I reply, still wondering if I'm supposed to know her.

'What'cha doin'?'

'I'm playing in a poker tournament. In fact, I'm late for—'

'Wouldn'cha rather poke me?'

Still unnerved by this encounter, I get back just in time for my big blind, which remains at $200, but now with compulsory antes for all of $25 a hand. At $550 before it starts, each pot is now much more worth stealing. Somehow I manage to pull this off twice in a row on both my blinds. That's one way to keep going in this thing. On the second, I get nervous about the shell-suited young American on my right. I'm holding K-J and the flop has brought a king with rags. I bet $2500 and he thinks for ever before finally, phew, folding. 'That was a big bet,' he drawls, trying to get a tell out of me – an uneasy scratch of the neck, the twitch of a nervous eyebrow. Luckily, as it happens, my pupils do not begin to dilate. But, I suppose, in the circumstances he was right. I was betting like I didn't want a call. Which I'm not sure I did.

As I'm not wearing shades – which I consider pretentious, if not downright cheating – my lit-for-TV face is presumably as a book wherein an opponent may read many things. There could even be a tell-tale bead of sweat on my brow, but as I myself am not sure what I'm thinking, let him read what he likes. *La lutte continue*.

At the next table is my old pal 'Zapata', now known to be the top professional Surinder 'the Cobra' Sunar, who in 2004 famously won the third World Poker Tour's Grand Prix de Paris by remaining impassive to the uncouth taunts of the Australian pro Antanas Guoga – known to the new world of poker as Tony G, or 'the Australian airbag', so loud and unrelenting is his coarse disrespect of other players at the table. Surinder, by contrast, is a gentleman of the old school – or so I thought until he rattles my ego by telling me I've put on weight since last we met. Well, it's been a few years but there are kinder greetings he could have offered. For all that, I'm sorry to see him knocked out soon afterwards at around the same time as another friend from London, my home-game pal Matthew Norman, one of Britain's most versatile journalists. At least Matthew can get a column out of it, I'm thinking, as the news sweeps the room that Barry Greenstein, a respected pro known as the 'Robin Hood of Poker' because he gives his tournament winnings to charity, has also been eliminated. These little details all give my ego a wholly irrelevant (and thoroughly undeserved) boost.

Also out are pro golfer Rocco Mediate and British snooker champion Stephen Hendry – both further examples of the recent invasion of poker by sports and showbiz stars – plus all the former world poker champs playing today except the holder Greg Raymer and 1996's Huck Seed. Fancied professionals such as Phil Ivey, 'the Tiger Woods of poker', and Howard 'the Professor' Lederer are still going strong. As are numerous Brits, including Neil 'Bad Beat' Channing, Poker Million winner John Duthie and a previously unheard-of woman (though we'd soon be hearing a lot more of her) named Tiffany Williamson.

And me. By session five, with the blinds up to $150–$300 and rolling antes still at $25, my stack stands at $17,800 – okay, but still less than the required average, which is now approaching $20,000 with almost half of today's starters gone. During the last break, I've been trying to disarm the table bully, Mr Big Stack, by engaging him in genial conversation. Maybe that will persuade him to take it easy on me? Some hope, even though he turns out to be a pleasant Irishman called Joe Rafferty. I tell him I visited his home town of Enniskillen many times in the mid-1970s while covering the Irish 'troubles' for the *Sunday Times*. He makes kind remarks about my writings on poker; then we go back to trying to destroy each other.

As we move into the ninth and tenth hours some weary players are turning their chairs around and getting massages in their seat – all part of the service laid on here these days, with ten minutes (or 'A pair') costing $15, quarter of an hour ('Three of a kind') $20, and twenty minutes ('Four of a kind') $25. One middle-aged guy at my table is getting the full four of a kind. With a towel round the neck beneath his grimace-stricken face, he looks pretty stupid, it has to be said, and I notice his hands are shaking as he tries to peek at his hole cards while a petite Vietnamese woman kneads away at his back. Every so often he utters murmurs of delight, or pain, or approval, and tells her how good it feels. Surely I can nail this guy while his mind is so far elsewhere?

For most of the next session, however, I get nothing but dismal cards in the wrong position. Every time I see an ace I squeeze out a lousy low kicker, and am never in the right spot to run a bluff. Even the news of the departure of 2000 champ Chris 'Jesus' Ferguson does little to lift my sinking spirits. By midnight, and the fifth break, I'm down to $13,850 – with just one more session, by the look of things, to survive.

But survival is not enough, as I ponder outside in the corridor as hour-eleven moves into hour-twelve. You've got to avoid being short-stacked at the start of Day Two, I keep telling myself; there's no point in clinging to the wreckage of a pile that's going nowhere. Get aggressive now. Mix up your play more.

So what am I doing out here in the corridor? Halfway through each session, every fifty minutes or so, I allow myself to miss a few hands as I go out for a much-needed cigarette break.

'Are you out?' ask passing pals as I stand pensively in the corridor, puffing on a restorative, duty-free Benson & Hedge. 'No way,' I reply indignantly. 'Just taking a ciggy break.' As I brood on the long odds against my missing pocket rockets or a suited ace for one measly cig, I take absurd consolation in one of the few rewards these days for being a smoker. With people being knocked out of the tournament at the rate of one a minute, every cigarette is worth a rise of ten places in the world rankings.

Yet that's the wrong attitude, I remind myself as I stub my cigarette out and thread my way through the TV cables back to my table. You're hanging in there when you should be trying to build your stack. In the distance I see that the latest departee is another friend from London, who wishes to remain nameless, so upset is he about the way he played the hand. At nearly 2 a.m., after fourteen hours of play, with only another half-hour of the first day to go, it's a brutal time to bite the dust. Perhaps that thought makes me play artificially tight for that last half-hour, against all the advice I have just given myself. By the time a halt is called for the day, I am somehow down to a mere $7625.

It's 2.20 a.m. and the counting, labelling and bagging of the chips takes another half-hour. Suddenly I realise that after fifteen hours at the table I'm completely shattered. Still, I can go to bed happy. I may be short-stacked but at least I've achieved the first of my fundamental objectives. I have lived to fight another day.

2
Aussie, Aussie, Aussie!

Mention the name of Tom Moore to most of the players here at the World Series of Poker and they'll look at you blankly before going back to the matter at hand – their cards, their food, their significant other – without showing too much interest. Moore's name does not exactly ring through the history of poker. But it should. Tom Moore is the reason all six thousand of us, from forty countries, are here.

Back in 1969, Texas-born Moore was the new owner of the Holiday Hotel in Reno, Nevada, where he had an idea that sowed the seeds of this biggest annual gathering of poker players on earth. He sent out invitations to all his Texas poker buddies to come to Reno for a week to take part in what he called 'The Texas Gamblers Reunion'. Suggested to him by a casino floorman, 'Vic' Vickrey, whose name also deserves to be remembered, Moore's poker party was really a ploy to woo some high rollers to his new hotel during the slow season.

The twenty or so who showed up included names that have since become a great deal better known to poker history than either Moore's or Vickrey's: Johnny Moss, Amarillo Slim, Doyle

Brunson, Puggy Pearson, Brian 'Sailor' Roberts, Jack 'Treetops' Straus, Corky McCorquodale, Crandall Addington, Benny Binion and his son Jack. Even the legendary pool player Minnesota Fats came along for the ride – as did the notorious hitman Charles Harrelson, a convicted contract killer.

They had such a wild time at Moore's riverside casino, playing a series of poker games across the different disciplines, as to nickname the event 'The World Series of Poker'. That year the winner was simply the guy who went home with the most money – which just happened to be the Man, Johnny Moss. The following year Moore sold his interest in the Holiday and passed the WSOP baton to his pal Benny Binion, who put his son Jack in charge. They invited the same dozen big-time poker players – plus a few more, including the amateurs 'Doc' Green and Curtis 'Iron Man' Skinner – to come to the Horseshoe in downtown Vegas for a few days in May and play the game in all its many forms.

For Benny, the crowd that flocked to watch, and pour money into his pockets via the slots, and the roulette, blackjack and craps tables, was a reminder of the revenue-generating appeal of Moss's legendary five-month game against Nick 'the Greek' Dandalos at the Horseshoe in 1949. The promotional value of the game to Binion was almost as much as the amount Moss had reputedly won – more than $2 million, around $100 million in today's money – by the time the Greek stood up with his celebrated line: 'Mr Moss, I have to let you go.'

An irresistible footnote to that curiously undocumented episode has it that among the spectators drawn to watch the game was none other than Albert Einstein, whom Benny and the Greek took for a walk down Fremont Street, introducing him as 'Little Al from Princeton – controls a lot of the Jersey action.'

Poker, to Binion, was a loss leader; far more revenue would flow into his pockets from covering the same floor space in slot

machines. At the end of this first formal World Series, there was
a steak dinner in the Horseshoe's Sombrero Room, where various awards were handed out. Straus, for instance, was voted
'Most Congenial Player'. Then Jack Binion asked them all to
vote on whom they considered the best all-round player.
Everyone, of course, voted for themselves. 'I couldn't understand why the fuck anybody would want to vote,' said Amarillo
Slim. 'We played for a lot of money and that was the vote.' So
everyone was asked to vote again, this time for the player they
considered the best – apart from themselves. The answer came
up Johnny Moss, who thus found himself elected the first official
world champion of poker.

The following year, either Slim or Puggy Pearson (depending
on whose version you believe) persuaded the Binions that rather
than voting for the winner they should compete for the title: that
is, play a game of No Limit Hold 'em – $5000 entry, rising
blinds – until one player had won all the chips. Thus was born
the poker tournament, in this case a winner-takes-all freeze-
out. There were six starters and it lasted two days. Again Johnny
Moss emerged the winner and carried off a purse of $30,000.

The next year, 1972, there were two events: a $20,000 five-
card stud tournament (won by Bill Boyd) and the $80,000 world
title event, won by Amarillo Slim. There were eight starters,
paying an entry fee doubled by Benny to $10,000 (Slim's idea,
ironically enough) – where it has remained ever since.
Considerably more garrulous than Moss, Slim milked the
moment by hitting the talk show circuit; an anecdote-packed
appearance on Johnny Carson's *Tonight Show* was such a success
that it led to all of a dozen more, as well as three spots on *60
Minutes* and appearances at the National Press Club in
Washington, DC, even the US Senate. In the process of making
himself the world's most famous poker player, Slim also reawak-
ened America's interest in its national game, then largely
confined to down-home kitchen tables.

The late Puggy Pearson took the title the following year and a prize purse of $130,000, as well as winning two of the other four events (seven-card razz, deuce-to-seven draw, seven-card stud and No Limit Hold 'em). Moss won it a unique third time in 1974 ($160,000), Sailor Roberts in 1975 ($210,000) and Doyle Brunson won back-to-back titles in 1976 ($220,000) and 1977 ($340,000).

A year after Amarillo Slim's 1972 victory had alerted the nation to the World Series of Poker, Benny Binion took part in the oral history project of the University of Nevada, telling interviewer Mary Glass: 'This poker game here gets us a lot of attention. We had seven players last year [in fact it was eight] and this year we had thirteen. I look to have better than twenty players next year. It's even liable to get up to be fifty, might get up to be more than that.' He paused, before musing: 'It will eventually.'

Benny's prophecy was realised faster than even he could have expected. The rapid increase in the prize money reflected that in the number of players, also attracted by the smaller events, which had climbed to all of ten by 1978, when twenty-seven-year-old Bobby 'the Owl' Baldwin emerged from forty-two starters to become the first member of the next poker generation to break the monopoly of the old-timers (and the Texans) on the world title. His $270,000 win saw Baldwin launched on a career as a Las Vegas casino executive, for many years Steve Wynn's right-hand man, now one of the most powerful figures in town as chief executive of the MGM Mirage group, with a *salle privée* named after him in the plush Bellagio card room.

After an aberrant year in 1979 – when the title was won by an amateur, Hal Fowler, who rashly turned pro and was never heard of again – the 1980s saw a procession of professional winners, from Stu 'the Kid' Ungar via Johnny Chan (twice) to twenty-four-year-old Phil 'Poker Brat' Hellmuth (still the youngest winner of the world title), all of whom immediately became big poker names. By 1982, seven years before his death at the age of eighty-six, Benny Binion had lived to see his vision come to pass with fifty-two starters, from whom Jack Straus emerged the winner after being reduced, at one point, to a single chip – giving rise to the poker expression, 'All you need is a chip and a chair'. The following year, 1983, saw Tom McEvoy become the first world champion to have won his way into the event via a satellite.

Gradually the idea was spreading and a tournament circuit began to develop across the western United States, even stretching to Europe. By 1991 the first prize in the World Series main event (won by the Vegas pro Brad Daugherty) had become a guaranteed $1 million. With the exception of Stu Ungar's remarkable comeback in 1997, less than a year before his premature death, the 1990s went on as they began, with a parade of local pros mostly staying famous – with honourable exceptions such as Dan Harrington and Scotty Nguyen (pronounced 'win') – for Andy Warhol's proverbial fifteen minutes.

Only as of 2000 and the arrival of the internet did rising young professionals like Chris Ferguson and Carlos 'the Matador' Mortensen begin to win first prizes in excess of a million dollars, before the centre of gravity switched again, this time from pros to amateurs. During this period the main event of the World Series developed into the flagship for some forty other tournaments lasting all of two months. In 2002, from a field of 631 starters, Robert Varkonyi of Connecticut became the first of a series of unknown internet players to emerge as the winner. In 2004, when Greg Raymer won the $5 million world title from 2576 starters, there were thirty-two other events with a prize pool totalling more than $46 million. This year, 2005, there are forty-five generating $106 million.

Tom Moore can have had no idea what he was starting in Reno back in 1969. Even Benny Binion might blink. I think back to the night in 1988 when I shared dinner in Binion's steakhouse with Benny and his buddy Johnny Moss, celebrating seventy-five years of friendship. Not twenty years on, the poker world has been through a wholly unexpected and unpredictable revolution. What a shame that neither lived to see the game they so loved catch fire on this scale all over the world.

With two more Day Ones to go, I won't be playing in the 2005 tournament again until Sunday. On the evening of the next day, Friday, the first of my two days off as almost four thousand other players fight for survival to Day Two, my youngest son Ben arrives in town with his girlfriend, Salome Leventis. They live in Los Angeles, where Ben works in, guess what, the movies. He's been to Vegas with me before, albeit in his early teens, but this is Salome's first visit.

A petite young woman, as smart as she is pretty, Salome takes to the place with all the enthusiasm of a regular. For some reason this surprises as much as it pleases me. Some people just can't take Vegas; I have seen even poker-playing pals arrive (often at my urging), take one look, shake their heads, turn pale and head out again on the next flight. Maybe Salome's sophistication made me think she might not feel at home here in the babble of this latter-day Babylon; but no, she's posing even now for Ben to take her picture pulling the handle of an enormous one-armed bandit, a smile on her face the size of California.

Over dinner in the Rio's lavish Italian restaurant (well, I am a high roller again, at least for now), I tell them about the media tournament they have just missed, which took place – by long-standing annual tradition – the night before the main event started. In the old days at Binion's a few score of hardened journos took this warm-up as seriously as the world title event itself; to win that wedding-cake of a trophy, inscribed FOR EXCELLENCE AT POKER IN LAS VEGAS, not to mention the $1000 first prize, was the height of everyone's aspirations. One year I was absurdly thrilled just to get the satin World Series jacket that went to every player to reach the final table.

The media tournament was originally designed to help reporters who had never before played poker, let alone Texas Hold 'em, get a grasp of the game before covering the World Series. But some of the entrants, such as the Hold 'em correspondent of *Card Player* magazine, were in truth semi-professionals posing as hacks.

Now, like so much else in the poker firmament, the tournament has been showbizzed up to include celebrities. But James Woods was the only name I could put to a face amid a gallery of minor American TV stars who meant nothing to me. The first prize of $10,000 went to charity, but I can't tell you who won it as I didn't last long. My pair of kings was beaten, as is the way in such tournaments, by the 5-2 of a German journalist who had never played poker before in his life.

That same evening two more poker giants were installed in the Poker Hall of Fame – the ultimate accolade to those who have played for high stakes at the top levels over a period of many years, 'playing consistently well and gaining the respect of their peers'. Hall of Famers range from all-time greats such as Wild Bill Hickok and Nick 'the Greek' Dandalos via Johnny 'the Man' Moss and Stu 'the Kid' Ungar, to competitors in this very tournament, such as two-time winners Doyle Brunson and Johnny Chan. This year's honorees were Jack Binion and Crandall Addington, two long-standing friends who both professed mild surprise at the honour, as neither had played poker for years.

A class act, known for dressing to kill at the poker table as elsewhere, oil-man Addington chose his moment in the poker sun to startle the audience by quoting Henry David Thoreau: 'Most men lead lives of quiet desperation, and go to their graves with a song still in them.' However you choose to read this, it got a nod of approval from the least likely figure up there on the podium with the poker bigwigs: a nun, who was now invited to lead us in prayer to thank the 2005 World Series for donating

$1 million to the Las Vegas chapter of Meals on Wheels. My oh my, just how respectable can poker become?

Back in 1985 I was having dinner with Crandall in London at the home of our mutual friend Al Alvarez when a phone call told me that my mother had died, just a week after my father. I rushed straight home. She had been babysitting my three sons; this was the first evening I had left her alone since bringing her back to London from my father's funeral in Lancashire. Crandall and another Hall of Famer, Jack 'Treetops' Straus, who was also there that night, both wrote me touching letters – a rare gesture from any poker player, then as now.

At the awards Crandall and I were just recalling that traumatic evening when Jack Binion loped over to say 'Hi!' I told Jack I had dined the previous evening at the Horseshoe, in the famous steak bar atop the building, which boasts one of the best views of Vegas by night. 'How was it, Tony?' he asked as if, for once, he actually wanted to hear the answer.

'The food was as good as ever, Jack,' I replied. 'But the place was half-empty. And during the World Series!'

Binion's face fell so low that I had to remind him: 'Hey, Jack, you don't own the joint any more. It's not your problem.' So deep does the Binion legend run in Jack's blood that he seemed none too consoled.

The day after dinner at the Rio, my last day off before resuming play in the world championship, Ben and I go heads-up in the card room of the Mandalay Bay, where he and Salome are staying. Suffice it to say that on one flop he pulls quad sixes and does me out of three hundred dollars.

When I go to check on progress back at the Rio, the route to the Amazon Room has been changed. The entrance to the corridor is blocked off and access to the tournament area can be gained only via a trade fair calling itself the Gaming Lifestyle Expo. There are 150 stands offering everything from expensive poker lessons with the masters to books, cards, videos, poker jewellery, fridge stickers and other knick-knacks. Great though it is to pick up armfuls of poker freebies of one sort and another, the whole jamboree strikes me as acutely depressing: visual confirmation that the maverick, bohemian, once back-room game I have loved for so long has now turned into just another branch, logos and all, of corporate American capitalism.

Which puts me in mind of that classic line of Walter Matthau's: 'Poker exemplifies all the worst aspects of capitalism that have made our country so great.'

By Sunday, Day Two of the tournament – or, to be precise, Day 2-A, the first of two Day Twos – the conference on personality disorder has given way to a children's dancing contest. There are little girls in tutus practising their routines along the corridor otherwise peopled by characters their mothers really wouldn't want them to meet.

The first session begins with that moment of silence for the London bomb victims – interrupted only by the deranged yelling of a loud, greasy-haired exhibitionist in an England football shirt, desperate for TV time, who (when he duly gets it) is rightly called 'unspeakable' by ESPN's amiable commentator Norman Chad. In conversation later even Chad admits that TV has a lot to answer for in the etiquette stakes. All these players who leap around with whoops of joy when they win a hand, or get under their opponents' skin with snide remarks and insults, all this is the fault of television, where novices see such conduct from pros who should know better and come to think it's the norm. Back at Binion's, as 1983 world champ Tom McEvoy reminds me, such conduct – disrespecting the game and its other players – would have been 'sorted out later, in the parking lot'.

I am drawn, to my dismay, at Table 85, Seat One. I dislike Seats One or Nine because they are poker's equivalent of 'restricted view' – next to the dealer, around whom you have to crane for a sight of the players at the other end. Also, I like to see the dealer's name-tag so I can address him or her by name in a friendly sort of way. Which may bring me luck. Okay, that's close to being an irrational superstition – and, yes, you could say that all superstitions are close to being irrational; but for super-stitious people like me (entirely the fault of my late mother), some are, some aren't. People hereabouts keep telling me, 'It's unlucky to be superstitious.' Be that as it may, these two seats beside the dealer are far from ideal. Especially if you like, as I do, to keep an inconspicuous eye on your opponents' demeanour, if not every nuance of their body language – i.e., looking for a 'tell', which is at least as important as the cards you are dealt.

I am consoled by a swelling support team rooting for me from the rails: Ben and Salome, Matthew Norman and other friends from London, poker writers Michael Craig, Des Wilson and Richard Sparks, and online entrepreneur Joe Saumarez Smith. The blinds are $300–$600, with $75 rolling antes. After twenty minutes or so I receive A-Q in late position, facing a raise of $1500 from another iPod kid in Seat Three. What the heck, if I'm going to go out, let's do so in style; I reraise him all-in to the tune of $7500. He calls and reveals a pair of nines. The flop brings a king and rags, and I begin to wish I'd been leading a better life lately. Then the turn brings . . . a queen! And the river is . . . another queen! Maybe I have been living right, after all; the cards just took their time to go through the files. As Shakespeare almost said: 'As flies to wanton boys are we to the poker gods; they use us for their sport.'

When the tannoy announces that 2003 world champion Chris Moneymaker has been eliminated, I again reflect how absurd it is to be so chuffed to have outlasted such big names. But these are the straws at which we amateurs clutch. Then, seven minutes before the first break, I'm dealt A-Q again – and all-in I go. This time, though, no callers. So I make it to the first interval back just about where I began three days before, with a little over $10,000. There are 160 tables left, with nine at each table, which by my reckoning equals 1440, so we've lost three-quarters of the field. Or to put it another way, I've lasted longer than 4200-plus players – but am still way below the average chip count. The point of this thing is to *win* it, or at least to get into the money (top 10 per cent), not just hang in there as long as the poker Furies deign to permit.

During the second session I go all in twice more, with K-Q suited and J-10 suited, but no one calls. Am I getting respect or what? No, I'm just lucky that no one has cards good enough to call these less than premium hands.

Then I am moved to Table 135, Seat Eight – a slightly better seat but I find myself next to a guy wearing two World Series bracelets, one on each wrist. These symbols of poker-playing prowess are, I have to confess, pretty intimidating. Vulgar they may be, but you get a taste for vulgarity after a few days in Vegas. And these are more than mere wrist enhancements; they are awesome symbols of poker power. After a while I learn that their proprietor is a German airline pilot turned pro named Eddy Sharf; he's never got to a WSOP final table, he tells me, without winning the tournament. I think of the German who knocked me out of the media event and wonder if my homeland's sometime foe, now its European partner, will prove my undoing this week.

It's 3.40 p.m., and I've survived more of Day Two than I expected. Yet again I go all-in, this time with a pair of tens, and hope for a call from a grey-haired old-timer across the table in a New Jersey baseball cap. He thinks long and hard, then folds, flashing me an ace as he does so. I show him my tens – well, why not? I figure – and he nods sagely. I rarely show my cards when unchallenged; but I'm hoping the whole table will see that I don't go all-in with just *anything*.

When I go all-in again on the following hand, the young Swede next to me calls. I win, and double up, but the Swede gives me a hard look and says: 'You weren't looking that comfortable.' To which the old guy in the baseball cap muses: 'The really good players are good at not looking that comfortable.'

A compliment! But it comes, as it proves, from my nemesis. An hour or so later, we've lost almost half of today's field when I look down to see K-J suited. The best hand I've seen for a while, it looks positively lit-up. In late position I go all-in for the seventh time today, though it proves to be my ninth life. I'm called to the tune of $8000 by the same old-timer, who shows A-7 off-suit. The flop brings an ace and rags, and I stand up with a feeling almost of relief rather than the usual punch in the kidneys. It's hard work playing a short stack and it had to come to an end sooner or later. I shouldn't have let myself get that low in the first place. And I mustn't again.

The turn and the river bring no 'paints', or court cards, so I'm out of the World Series for yet another year. Calculations by experts, based on the giant scoreboard of Day 2-B, subsequently suggest that I bowed out in approximately 1137th place, out of a field of 5619. Respectably in the top 20 per cent but way off the money. I've got twelve short months to improve my game – by honing my skills on the new tournament circuit – if I'm going to do better next year.

In the subsequent TV coverage of this event, all-in moments like the ones I knew all too well are sponsored by a men's under-arm deodorant called Degree. I suppose it's because some TV-influenced players raise their arms aloft in triumph if they survive, and may not want to pollute the atmosphere, as much as they might wish to poison their opponents. But everything in poker is sponsored these days; the pocket-cam which sees the players' hole cards bears the name of a beer, Miller High Life. Even the chip counts are sponsored by Castrol.

The coverage shows me all sorts of things I never saw at the time, so huge and diverse was the tournament field. An armless man called William Rockwell was playing his cards with his feet. Another guy was doing mental arithmetic tricks – five-figure multiplications, square roots, that sort of thing – to entertain his table. Even the adverts bring surprises. 'You shouldn't gamble if you're lonely or depressed,' warns Garry Loveman, CEO of Harrah's, hosts of this very event.

Outside in the corridor, two brothers (both off-duty dealers) have set up a stall with a sign reading, 'TELL US YOUR BAD BEAT STORIES'. Bad beat stories are the nightmare background music to events like this, based on the old poker principle that losers always blame everyone but themselves. Anyone who can buttonhole you will bang on in excruciating detail about their improbable, wholly undeserved misfortunes. On all sides people are saying, '. . . so how could he possibly have called my raise with ace-nine *off-suit*?', while their interlocutors look desperately around, seeking any chance to get away. These dealer brothers are smartly seeking to capitalise on this syndrome. For $1, later upped to $2.50 through sheer volume of business, they will listen patiently and sympathetically to your account of how unlucky you were to exit the tournament and how badly the hand was played by the guy who knocked you out.

Phil Hellmuth is choosing, as usual, to tell the world. On Day 1-B up on the 'featured' TV table, Phil is (by his own confession) 'steaming'. A player called Jim Pitman goes all in with K-J and Phil calls with A-K. When Pitman catches a jack on the river to win the $15,000 pot, Phil goes nuclear: 'You guys can't even *spell* poker.'

He wanders over to his wife, who happens to be a shrink, for consolation. 'You gotta let it go,' she tells him. Then Phil goes walkabout round the room, getting anted away as he tries to come 'off tilt'. On his first hand back at the table, he gets A-Q against Paul 'Quack-Quack' Magriel's 7-7. Magriel goes all-in for $6725. 'That maniac put all his money in with two sevens,' rants Phil, gracious as ever in defeat. 'Worst players in the world around here.'

Is it all an act to win himself more 'air-time' and promote his lucrative 'poker brat' image? Hellmuth is perhaps the most successful of all the top poker pros in turning himself into a highly commercial brand name – and much of that has to do with the TV tantrums, which spectators love. Away from the table, he can be charm itself, though that giant ego does take very little time off. Howard Lederer told me that back in 1999, after Jack Binion had left the Horseshoe, he was standing in conversation with Erik Seidel, wondering whether or not it would be politically correct to play in the World Series, when Hellmuth joined them. 'Well, I have to play,' announced Phil, 'for history.'

Hellmuth's main rival in the mouthing-off stakes these days is Mike Matusow, nicknamed 'the Mouth' because of his non-stop attempts to psyche the other players, as well as his unseemly arrogance at the table. Only three months out of the nearby Clark County jail, on a drugs rap he insists was trumped-up, Matusow has just got a ten-minute time penalty for using the f-word. He repeats it to the floorman who gave him the first penalty, thus earning another ten minutes out of the tournament. By the time Mike finally shuts up, he's earned himself forty minutes in the sin bin, being blinded away in absentia.

I get bored with watching and decide to go play in a $100 satellite for tomorrow's $1000 No Limit Hold 'em tournament, the last chance this year to win a World Series gold bracelet. En route I bump into my old chum Jesse May, a former player who's pretty much given up the game these days to concentrate on presenting and commentating on its televised counterpart; in Britain Jesse is known as 'the Voice of Poker'. In the throes of making a documentary, he asks if I'd mind doing a stand-up interview, right there in the corridor, with rush-hour poker traffic swirling behind my back.

'Sure,' I say and the crew ready themselves. 'So, Tony Holden,' says Jesse, before moving the microphone my way, 'you're one of the people responsible for the poker boom in the UK.'

I am so dumbstruck that I can merely stutter: 'Am I?'

On Take Two things go better and with faux-modest charm I duly take credit for the fact that people tell me they read my book and took up poker. I've had people today coming up and telling me that's why they're here – here in Vegas, wherever they might call home. 'I suppose,' I conclude gloomily, 'I must have ruined a few lives as well.'

That's enough for Jesse, who lets me go play in my satellite. No doubt bucked by my own fifteen minutes of fame, I proceed to win it, and register for the next day's tournament. After a lively meal with some friends, I set off upstairs for a much-needed night's sleep.

At 4 a.m. the fire alarm wakes me from a vivid dream of which I remember little except a swirl of playing cards. A false alarm, it transpires, or maybe a drunk tampering with the system. Either way I find it hard to get back to sleep, so how will the exhausted players still in the main event feel about the siren call in the middle of the night?

During the first session of the next day's tournament, restless and a bit grumpy, I find myself drawn at the same table as Britain's best-known and most successful professional, Dave 'the Devilfish' Ulliott. Or, I should say, halfway through the first session, as Dave has taken to emulating Hellmuth's habit of turning up for tournaments fashionably late. What difference is an hour or so of being anted away going to make to the progress of a player of his calibre? And the Devilfish is looking pretty spruce too, wearing perhaps the only suit and tie in the card room, his hair still wet from the shower.

Now in his early fifties, Dave was raised in a tough working-class district of Hull. He had dropped out of school by the age of seventeen, when he relished a beating in a street brawl because it taught him that he was 'fearless'. Soon he fell among thieves and became an expert safe-cracker. After a few stints in jail, where he spent his twenty-first birthday, he turned pawn-broker before discovering poker, swiftly graduating from hair-raising all-night chases between games in London and the north-east to wins on the first series of the Channel 4's *Late Night Poker* and here in Vegas at the World Series. His name was really made when he won the $600,000 first prize in the tel-evised 2003 World Poker Tour event at Tunica, which he has since parlayed into a multi-million brand-name franchise, com-plete with website.

Dave's story, along with those of other prominent British pro-fessionals, has been vividly told in Des Wilson's 2006 book *Swimming with the Devilfish*. Ulliott hasn't won so many tourna-ments lately, but so what? 'Fortunately for me,' as Dave puts it, 'not many poker players have a character so despite not winning a big tournament in the past eighteen months, I'm still on the cover of magazines. This proves that having a character and being entertaining go a long way.'

Dave winks at me; we chat. I win a couple of hands off him – or, as he puts it later, 'I let you win a couple of little pots back there.' Much good does it do the Devilfish, who goes out before I do – or, as it turns out, me. By the end of the second session I'm still feeling restless – and, to be honest, a tad bored. This is the tightest of tables and I'm never seeing even remotely playable cards in the right position. After the thrill of the main event it's something of an anticlimax.

Soon after, the 'Cobra' arrives at the table, in the shape of my old pal Surinder Sunar. We are just in the throes of trashing Tony G – whose waistline, he concedes, is considerably larger than mine – when I look down to see a pair of sevens and go all-in against Sunar to the tune of $1600. The call makes little inroad into Surinder's huge stack and he rolls over a pair of eights. I give him a friendly pat on the back as I head off to see how things are going in the Big One. If I had to pass my stack to somebody, I'm glad it was Zapata. He'll make better use of it than me.

Back in the main event five hundred and sixty players, or 10 per cent of the tournament starters, are going to get paid for their week's work. Or at least get their entry fee back plus a small bonus. That's the point the organisers are trying to reach today, with players placed 501–560 receiving $12,500 each, $14,135 for those placed 451–500 and so on upwards to the top prize of $7.5 million. This means the worst place of all to come – known as 'the bubble' – is 561st. It's even worse than my own humble 1137th. You've played three fourteen-hour days, beaten more than five thousand of the world's best players and you've got nothing at all to show for it. You go home empty-handed. Not even for an amateur, let alone a professional, is that a good rate of pay.

By the end of Day Three, as this dread moment approaches, the rhythm of the tournament changes. Many players tighten up, and take as few risks as possible in the hope that the others will knock each other out and help them get into the money. With ESPN looking for 'heartbreak moments', the whole room has to grind to a halt every time an all-in player gets called. It is normal at this stage for the authorities to try to 'balance' the tables, to make sure they are in synch; but it is not normal for the whole room to wait while a camera rushes over to the latest dealer's cry of 'All-in and call!'.

Often the all-in hand wins so there is little of what TV would call drama, anyway. As a few do get knocked out, however, and the dread 'bubble' approaches, the pace of the action slows almost to a halt. For a sports-loving Brit, who hates the American habit of letting television dictate the pace and timing of sporting events, it's grim news that poker is its latest victim.

ESPN finally gets its man, a Swedish player named Carl Ygborn who goes out on the bubble in 561st place. Carl handles himself so well, and the attention makes it such a poignant moment, that the organisers promptly console him with a $10,000 free entry for next year's tournament. So the worst place to finish – the real 'bubble' – is now 562nd. And we've no idea who that was. He's already disappeared.

Or she. Some six hundred women were among the starters, but Britain's Tiffany Williamson (if Britain can claim an American lawyer now based in London, where she won her entry at the Gutshot Club) is the only one to have survived to the final three tables, the last twenty-seven in the tournament. Now we move en masse downtown to Binion's, in the heart of Glitter Gulch as the Rio card room is dismantled to make way for the North American Association of Synagogue Administrators.

Walking into Binion's I am ambushed by a surge of nostalgia for the days when I used to come here as part of an annual Boys' Outing, usually coinciding with my birthday in late May. With Al Alvarez, David Spanier and other members of our Tuesday Night Game, we used to have a wild old time, living and eating as Jack Binion's guests, playing poker for days at a stretch, often with little or no sleep. Now Alvarez no longer comes to Vegas. 'I love poker,' he has explained, 'have played it all my adult life and am glad that a whole new generation has fallen for its endlessly subtle fascination. But the sheer size of the game's success is harder to love. The World Series is now held in a conference hall as big as the biggest aircraft hangars . . . It is just a great anonymous sea of crowded poker tables crammed together under the hard lights, more like the mess hall of some gigantic prison than the setting of any poker game that I have ever played in . . . I am sure the games are as fierce and enthralling as they ever were and I look forward to watching them on television. But I wouldn't want to go back.'

So no Al. Poor Spanier has died and we can't even call this place the Horseshoe any more. The name has been bought by Harrah's. So what happens, I wonder, when some visiting suit notices all those horseshoes woven into that tired but oh-so-familiar carpeting?

The dear old place looks pretty beat-up, rendered only tackier by the overhead laser display outside above Fremont Street, introduced in the mid-1990s in a misguided attempt to revive the flagging fortunes of downtown Glitter Gulch as the Strip just grew and grew. I pause respectfully beside the photographic Gallery of Champions on the wall and the Poker Hall of Fame. Will these sacred poker relics outlive the new proprietors' determination to make this forlorn old place pay? The poker room that boasts them is a sorry shadow of its former self, with a few grizzled old-timers growling their way through low-stakes games.

This is where, until the late 1990s, Jack Binion used to pay ESPN to come and film the final table of the World Series each year. Now, for a fat fee, they've taken the place over. Upstairs in 'Benny's Bullpen', a bingo room converted for the next couple of days into a hot, crowded TV studio, I find myself sitting on the bleachers next to Mike Matusow's mother, Gloria, as the Mouth lives up to his name in a running row with another short-fused professional, Shawn Sheikhan. 'It's getting hot in here,' complains Sheikhan, to which Mike replies: 'Don't worry. You ain't gonna be here much longer.'

This time last year Matusow first rose to notoriety by bad-mouthing an unknown competitor called Greg Raymer, a patent attorney from Connecticut who had qualified online. 'Buddy, I got big *cojones*, you got little *cojones*,' Matusow taunted the unmoved Raymer. 'You'd better stop fucking with me,' the Mouth went on, with the TV cameras rolling (and luckily for him the 'f-bomb' penalty yet to be introduced). 'You fuck with me and I'll bust you.' Unfortunately for Matusow, things worked out the other way round. Minutes later he was out of the tournament, publicly weeping on the shoulder of his friend Phil Hellmuth as Raymer calmly added Mike's pile of chips to his own. The lawyer then went on to beat the entire field of 2575 to win the world title, complete with $5 million first prize. This year Raymer has been chip leader almost throughout the tournament and has only just gone out, in twenty-fifth place – a remarkable feat for a reigning champion that has won him public praise through even the gritted teeth of Hellmuth.

Matusow seems to have an in-built need to sink his own teeth into somebody, anybody, somehow. This time around he and Sheikhan have been verbally – and a couple of times almost physically – sparring all day. Sheikhan is visibly riled by Matusow's taunting; and maybe it finally works, because by midnight the Mouth has busted out the Sheik in eleventh place – just four better than Tiffany Willamson, Britain's (and womankind's) last hope, who has won $400,000 for coming fifteenth.

'What's happening?' Mike's mother asks constantly. 'I can't see.' Eventually the stewards take pity on Gloria and find her a better seat. One good enough to see her 'Mikey' make the final table – the last nine players – scheduled to begin at 4 p.m. the next day, the seventh and last of the tournament. It will, as it turns out, go on until 6.45 a.m. the following morning, becoming the longest final table in World Series history as well as the most lucrative. The nine players left to contest the title, all of them now dollar millionaires, come from four countries reflecting the power bases of the new, worldwide poker: the USA, Australia, Sweden and Ireland. My money's on the only one of the thirty-four Irish starters still standing, Andy 'the Monk' Black.

Born a Catholic in a Protestant area of Belfast in the summer of 1965, Black read law at Trinity College, Dublin, before discovering poker at the city's celebrated Merrion Club at the same youthful time as drink, drugs and all the rest of it. By 1997, when I first met him at the World Series, Andy had got his act sufficiently together to finish in fourteenth place in the year that Stuey Ungar won his third title in his own remarkable, if short-lived, comeback nearly twenty years after his first two victories, back to back, in 1980 and 1981. Within a year cocaine-addict Ungar would be found dead in a Vegas motel room at the age of forty-five, with just $800 in his pocket, leaving a wife and daughter to join the poker world in mourning the premature loss of the game's most instinctive genius.

Dissatisfied with his own performance in 1997 – he felt he was the best player apart from Ungar and should have finished higher – Black also underwent a radical, if less permanent transformation. After discovering meditation he became a Buddhist – a poker-playing monk (hence his nickname). Then a dramatic religious experience persuaded him to quit poker and retire to a Buddhist community for what turned out to be three years. Now he's back and playing as well as ever, but still a Buddhist. He finds that his Buddhist principles help his poker.

Earlier in this very tournament Black had got publicly upset when one of the players at his table failed to return from a ten-minute break, mistakenly believing it was the longer dinner break. In vain did the altruistic Black attempt to persuade the organisers to delay the restart, or the other players at the table to slow down their play, to save their opponent being blinded away too drastically. So he himself became distinctly unpopular by taking the maximum time allowed over every move. 'I felt for the guy,' Black told me later. 'The announcement he'd heard was for another tournament going on in the same room. It was an innocent mistake. He didn't deserve to suffer from it.'

Andy's spiritual dimension enables him to come up with gnomic poker truths like: 'A lot of people think the pain comes from bad beats, but in my experience the pain comes from not playing as well as you can.' Well, he's going to have to be at his best – and certainly at his most genial – against Mike Matusow, the best-known (and noisiest) pro at the final table and the only one of the nine still standing with final-table experience at the World Series.

Barely have I settled into the gallery before Matusow gets K♥-K♦ against fellow-American Scott Lazar's A♥-A♣. Steve Dannenmann, an amateur from Maryland who says he's not even the best player in his home game, has J♠J♣. With more chips than Lazar, Matusow declares himself all-in. Dannenmann, who's in for $250,000 but has another $5 million in front of him, folds. Lazar calls. 'It's up to them,' says the forty-two-year-old Californian pro, indicating the poker gods above, though the odds are 82–18 per cent in favour of his aces.

'That's about normal for me, right?' says Matusow, seeking consolation among his family in the crowd for finding his pocket kings up against pocket rockets. 'Yeah, about normal,' he repeats as the courteous Dannenmann shakes his hand.

The flop brings Q♥-8♥-K♦, giving Matusow a set of kings. He goes berserk, leaping up and down and throwing his hands in the air as if there were some poker justice, after all. 'Go, Mikey, go!' yells Gloria. But, as Mikey's brother presciently points out, 'It ain't over yet.'

'One time!' pleads Mike as the turn brings a 2♥. Lazar waits with dignity while Matusow walks away again – 'acting', to ESPN's Norman Chad, 'as if he'd just lost the hand'. The river brings the J♥, giving both of them a flush but Lazar the better one. Matusow is incredulous. 'This is brutal,' he says, hands on head.

'The best hand won, right?' Lazar understandably goads Matusow as they sit back down, while Mike's brother urges him to 'Focus, focus!' But Matusow is inconsolable. 'How does this keep happening to me? Am I the unluckiest human ever or what? First the cooler, then the miracle, then the [expletive deleted].'

He has lost a pot totalling $7.17m. 'Now,' declares the Mouth, 'I'm a steaming rock.' With the blinds at $50,000–$100,000, and rolling antes of $10,000, there's almost a quarter of a million dollars in each pot before the cards are dealt.

A few hands later Matusow makes an exploratory raise of $130,000, to a total of $280,000, with 9-5 off-suit. He has $5.5m in chips before the hand so plenty of leeway to play such tricks. Andy Black, then in third place with just over $8 million, immediately calls. He turns out to hold 10-J, making him 7-3 favourite to win the pot. When the flop brings J-6-5, an expressionless Black checks. Matusow bets $350,000 and Black immediately calls. The turn is a ten, giving Black two pairs. He bets a million. Matusow makes it two million. So Black goes all-in.

'I think I got you!' says Mike.

Black merely smiles.

'D'you want me to call?' Matusow asks him.

'Don't really mind, man.'

'Really?'

'Really.'

Matusow then does the old trick of looking like going all-in, moving his hand towards his chips while watching for any telltale signs in Black's response (of which there are none) – before folding. He has given Black more than $2.5m in this one hand.

With the blinds up to $60,000–$120,000, Matusow soon bluffs his way to a $1.59m pot after pre-flop calls from Dannenmann and Black. He shows them his 8-5 – Dannenmann had folded a pair of eights – and says, 'I'm sweatin' here, boys . . . It's the only way I'm going to get chips today because I'm not getting dealt anything and if I do I get coolered.'

Now Mike lies in sixth place with $2.66m, to Dannenmann's $2.56m, while Andy Black with $11.39m is breathing down the neck of chip leader Aaron Kanter's $12 million. Dealt A-J, Dannenmann raises $300,000. All fold round to Matusow who just calls with pocket tens. The flop brings 5-2-3 and Dannenmann decides this is the moment to go all-in. With a good read – he is 6-4 favourite to win the pot – Matusow calls. There can be no more betting, so the cards go on their backs. 'Was I right, was I right?' yells Matusow, waiting for Dannenmann to turn over his hand. 'I was RIGHT!' he exults, on seeing the A-J. Again Steve offers a handshake and wishes him 'Good luck.'

But the turn is a four, giving Dannenmann an unlikely straight. Again a stricken Matusow goes for sympathy to his family and friends in the gallery. 'What a read, huh? I knew I had him beat. There's no justice when I play great.' An ace or a six would split the pot for him; but the river brings a nine, and Mike Matusow – the most experienced player at the table, hot favourite to win – is the first of the last nine players to be eliminated.

'First bad beat I ever gave anybody,' quips Dannenmann, still smiling his way contentedly through every twist of poker fate.

'There never will be any justice in poker,' says Matusow, leaving the arena with a mere million dollars.

In the press room, soon afterwards, the Mouth really shoots off.

'Hey,' he rants, six feet away from my face, 'money doesn't mean a thing to me. You all know that. I played the six best days of poker in my life and when the TV comes out you'll see how great I played. I had a lot of confidence and a lot of chips.

'I knew I had a weak field. I was able to do what I wanted

when I wanted to. People started playing tight, which was really good for me. If you look at the chip position over the last few days, you'd see Mike Matusow's chips going up and up and up, but you never saw Mike Matusow in a pot. I was chop, chop, chopping away and never really risking any chips. That's what I wanted to do today. I wanted to chop away to get about twelve million and then get four- or five-handed, and then just rape them because these guys aren't short-handed players.'

Back among the supposedly non-short-handed players, otherwise known as the survivors, Andy Black has become chip leader with more than $15m after knocking out Brad Kondracki. This goes up to $17m after a win over Aaron Kanter. Soon it's up to $18.8m after another over second-placed Tex Barch, then $20m after he knocks out Scott Lazar. Andy's Irish support group is steadily going crazy.

All this time, however, there's been a quiet, watchful Australian at the table, a thirty-nine-year-old Lebanese-born chiropractor turned mortgage broker with a trim goatee beard named Joseph Hachem. Joe hasn't played many hands – as one of the short stacks, with barely $4 million in chips, he's had little room for manoeuvre – but he has made one great fold against Kanter. A televised rabbit-run later shows that had Hachem called he'd have been knocked out of the tournament. Even so he was soon down to just $2.45m – scarcely a dozen big blinds – after calling before the flop in a hand in which Tex Barch knocked out Daniel Bergsdorf. The cries of 'Aussie, Aussie, Aussie!' from the gallery are, for the moment, stilled.

During the dinner break, Hachem later told me, he went out for a walk around the block, his support group following at a quiet, respectful distance as he wondered how on earth he could claw his way back from here. 'I felt like I was drowning,' he says, dramatically placing his hand flat beneath his chin to illustrate his point. 'Something good had to happen, and soon!'

At the table, to all appearances, Joe remained very relaxed, chatting genially while biding his time, largely watching his opponents do battle. Soon he had doubled up with A-Q against Lazar's K-9. Then came a dramatic hand in which Black lost $8m of his $20m to Kanter when he failed to pair his ace against pocket kings. Whatever he was feeling inside, the genial Black smiled gently about it to the equally genial Hachem, who ribbed him: 'You gotta slum it with us [short stacks] now!'

Now Hachem is the one who gradually begins to advance while a chastened Black implodes. Another all-in, with A-10, doubles up Hachem again and Black loses two-thirds of his $12m to Dannenmann in one hand. Hachem suffers a temporary setback, going back down to $2.46m after folding a hand that would have proved a winner, then doubles up again when his all-in pair of sevens holds up against Dannenmann's A-J. Now Tex Barch is chip leader with more than $20m and Dannenmann is in second place with nearly $16m, to Black's $7.9m and Kanter's $5.03m, on a par with Hachem.

Then comes the demise of Andy Black, whose all-in pair of tens loses to Dannenmann's A-K when the turn brings a second king. Once a big chip leader, the Irishman wins $1.75m for fifth place. Next out are Kanter in fourth place, worth $2 million, and Barch with $2.5 million for third. After doubling up again, Hachem has won a huge pot in the hand that knocked out Barch. After Barch had gone all-in with A-6, Hachem's J-J was a 4-1 favourite against the 7-7 keeping Dannenmann in the hand. The pot was $17.3m as the flop brought 2-10-3. Hachem and Dannenmann checked it out as the turn came a queen, the river a nine.

So as the head-to-head begins – between two mortgage brokers, for heaven's sake – Hachem has a chip lead of more than two to one, with $38.74 million against Steve Dannenmann's $17.45 million. This, of course, adds up to $56.19 million, or the $10,000 contributed by all 5619 starters, including me –

now shared between just these two survivors. There is some determined jousting before the coup de grace comes when Dannenmann, on the big blind of $300,000, raises the pot to $700,000 with A-3. He should have bet more.

Hachem calls, of course, even with a mere 7-3. The flop comes 4-5-6, giving him an unreadable straight. Now 9-1 favourite to win the hand, Hachem checks. With his own open-ended straight draw, Dannenmann bets $700,000, which Hachem raises by $1 million. Dannenmann calls, to be rewarded with an ace on the turn. Now 97-3 favourite, Hachem bets $2 million at him. With his ace paired, and still on that straight draw, Dannenmann understandably raises $3 million more. Hachem announces, 'All-in!', and Dannenmann calls, making a pot of $44.9 million, the biggest in poker history.

The river brings an irrelevant four, and the world title is Aussie Joe Hachem's. His 7-3 off-suit has won him the $7.5 million first prize, soon to be doubled by internet sponsorship, while the still smiling, laughing Dannenmann shrugs and walks away with $4.25m – half of which he must share with Jerry Ditzel, a golf buddy from home who put up half his entry fee. 'I had all the fun,' says Dannenmann to those who point out that he did all the work. 'Jerry had no fun at all. He got ripped off!'

It's past 7 a.m. – and I don't know about those two but I'm pretty bushed. While Hachem and his Aussie pals party, I grab a cab back to the Rio and decide, after a few hours' dreamless sleep, that it's time to head back home – and return to what passes for real life.

For these guys, tomorrow will be just another poker game. For the rest of us, even if we'd rather join them, there's a living to be earned – if by rather more conventional and, yes, tedious means.

3

Minnie, Get Your Gun

The mystery of poker, and so its infinite fascination, lies in the element of chance, otherwise known as luck. The art of the game lies in minimising it.

Beyond the added element of bluff, that option unique to poker which has psychology making nonsense of the cards, the harsh truth is that the best starting hand does not always win – which in turn means that the winner of any given pot is not necessarily the best player, but the one chosen by fate to defy the odds in another's favour.

Just like life, really, as I've been saying for years. In common with most people in this cruelly indifferent world, I've had my ups and downs during the fifteen years since I was last on the pro poker circuit. More ups than downs, it may be true, both personal and professional, but maybe the downs were more numbingly negative than the ups were passingly positive. Life, after all, is not about breaking even.

The worst moment came in the summer of 2000 with the demise of my second marriage, when the Moll made a unilateral decision that she would rather be on her own. Having hoped to divide our joint lives between the UK and the US, I wound up living alone in New York, where my weekly poker game turned out to be one of the few remaining fixtures in my life to help me through a very dark period.

Cut off from family and friends back home in England, from my Arsenal pals and the Tuesday Night Game, from all the infrastructure on which any tolerable version of life depends, my only solace beyond the infinite patience of friends came in the shape of a weekly poker game hosted by Charles Simmons, the savvy novelist and long-time deputy editor of the *New York Times*'s Sunday book review, who gathered a group of simpatico chums and colleagues around his Upper West Side dinner table each Tuesday evening. Some of us would meet to eat first at an Upper West Side Italian as early as 5 p.m.

Occasionally Charlie would drive me up the Hudson to Yonkers, where the game was sometimes held in a lawyer's office. To me there was an especial romance about this, partly because I have always loved the name 'Yonkers' and partly because it felt wonderfully wrong to be playing poker in a lawyer's office. We would dine before the game in a local trattoria, again as early as five, then go beat each other up at the baize. Charlie and I had an understanding that whichever of us won more, or lost less, would pay the two-buck toll from US-9 back to the West Side Highway.

The game even came to the rescue on what I would now officially deem the worst day of my life – Tuesday 22 August 2000 – when I returned to Manhattan from a birthday weekend with the Moll at Cape Cod, convinced that she was not going to change her mind about ending our marriage, to a stinking review in the *New York Times* of my new life of Shakespeare, well enough received elsewhere. Publishers, agents and friends all rallied round – 'if that Michiko Kakutani hates it, then it *must* be good', etc. – but the power of the *Times* duly did great harm in the States to a book of which I was rather proud.

That evening seemed to offer a straightforward choice between poker and suicide. Given three sons to whom I am devoted, it was not, to be honest, too close a call; even so, it took a huge effort of will to show my face at the pre-game dinner, unable to tell my new pals of my private woes but cheered by their sympathy for my all-too-public one. From his years on the *Times*, Charlie knew just how low I was feeling. 'Come on,' said the others, amid more ritual trashing of Kakutani, 'the game will take your mind off things.'

Such placebos, of course, generally don't work in radical crises; but this one, miraculously, did – at least for that wretched evening. It's something to do with the degree of tunnel vision required in a game where the stakes are high enough and the dangers attendant upon letting your mind wander even for a moment, quite apart from the paradoxical camaraderie of a group out to get each other. As so often in adverse circumstances, I even managed to register a win.

Six weeks before, the day after Cindy had first told me she wanted a separation, I was committed to playing in a televised tournament in Cardiff – which, again, because (as far as I can tell) I was so focused, so intent on not weeping on national television, I won.

Not that I'd recommend this as a route to poker riches. The game may have therapeutic powers, but they are not curative. Do not, in other words, try this at home.

I had been introduced to Charlie's game soon after my arrival in New York the previous year by our mutual friend Walter Goodman, a veteran *New York Times* journalist penning acerbic TV criticism in his semi-retirement. Soon, out of nowhere, Walter got sick. Week by week he grew more gaunt. One evening early in 2002, while playing with his customary zeal, he suddenly fell from his chair and seemed unable to get back up. I rushed to help; and as I picked him up I was appalled to find that he was as light as air. All I could feel was skin and bone, little more than a skeleton. Just a few weeks later poor Walter died, which put my own passing problems squarely in perspective.

After one very happy year in New York, and two very unhappy ones, I finally decided it was time to return to the country I had so roundly denounced all over the front page of the *Observer* 'Review' – too soon, perhaps, after leaving it for a Fellowship at the Center for Scholars and Writers at the New York Public Library to research a biography of the Romantic poet and critic Leigh Hunt. Married second time around to an American and a passionate admirer of that country's constitution (if not always its politics), I had over the years spent many happy days in its hospitable arms. During my first marriage there were three years as a journalist based in Washington, DC, during my second a dozen summers of hazy, crazy days at Cape Cod; during both there had been numerous research and writing trips, book tours and vacations, and some twenty annual visits to Vegas for the World Series of Poker. This was the country, I thought, that could offer me everything I needed in life. This was where I would base myself for the rest of it, now that my sons were grown and out in the world, living their own lives. How wrong I turned out to be.

Whatever my continuing reservations about my homeland, it was now where my few remaining certainties lay. Like most great cities, New York can be a thrilling place to live when you're happy, grim and hostile when you're not. So back to London I reluctantly came in the spring of 2002, after taking the considerable risk of buying a bachelor loft via the internet. Unwontedly single, at least I now had a home; but otherwise nothing beyond my children and my friends. Not just no wife but no job, no car, little money, ditto self-esteem. It was time, in my mid-fifties, to pick myself up and start all over again.

Being something of a jack of all trades, I had frequently

stood in for the *Observer*'s various critics during the six weeks a year they each take off. Theatre, music, film, TV, even restaurants – I had covered them all and rather enjoyed it. The dilettante in me hoped I might just snag that as my dream job: thirty weeks a year of free seats at each of the theatre, opera, movies, latest smart eatery, etc., in exchange for a thousand or so judicious words and a modest stipend. But the editor of the *Observer*, Roger Alton, had different ideas. He had just lost his chief classical music critic to another newspaper. Over lunch one day to discuss what I might do for the paper on which I felt most at home, he asked me to take over for a while as classical music critic.

At first I was unsure. I have always preferred a roving brief to specialising in anything; and I may be a music-loving biographer, to the point of writing a life of Tchaikovsky in the mid-1990s, but I am far from being a scholar, let alone any kind of musicologist. As we talked, however, I could see a way of doing it – in the great British tradition of the enthusiastic amateur – that might be interestingly different from the others. Roger persuaded me to take on the job for three weeks while he and his arts editor looked for someone else. After three months they asked me if I'd like to stay on – and so, three years later, here I still was, the *Observer*'s unlikely music critic.

As part-time jobs go, it could be a great deal worse, entailing a few evenings a week at operas or concerts and a few hours at the end of it writing the column. So there was plenty of time to continue writing books by day. The pay was (and remains) distinctly part-time – it needs considerable further input each year, partly via tax-free poker, to keep my personal show on the road – but there were ample compensations. Single for the first time in thirty years, I soon discovered it was a great way to chase women. The lure of an empty seat beside me at Covent Garden or Glyndebourne proved a huge help in the rapid rejuvenation of my sad, lonely private life.

And it left, of course, plenty of time to play poker. Online poker was just catching on but my Tuesday Night Game was still in existence, if a pale shadow of its former self. Two long-time players had died; two had emigrated. The hard core came down to myself, two other long-standing regulars, one more recent arrival and a host of unfamiliar faces drafted in while I'd been away. It was not as much fun as it used to be; my attendance became fitful, not least because of my new job; and by the autumn of 2003 the game finally expired, after some thirty roller-coaster years of my own life and more like forty in those of some of my closest friends.

By then I had found a new game, also on Tuesdays (what is it with poker and Tuesdays?), in a private room above a restaurant off Knightsbridge, with such other chums as the playwright and screenwriter Patrick Marber, the inventor Sir Clive Sinclair and the advertising guru turned art collector Charles Saatchi, who would usually have spent the afternoon in the same room playing high-stakes Scrabble.

This was also where I had first got to know Matthew Norman, whom we last saw exiting the 2005 World Series on Day One. When not playing 'real' poker or writing one of his numerous columns, Norman is a manic online player – usually moaning about bad beats. The same goes for Marber. Before long, it went for me, too.

For quite a while I had resisted this new version of poker on the internet. It didn't sound like that much fun; and I didn't trust it. Was I really going to give my credit card number to an off-shore gambling outfit? Would I really trust a computerised dealer? But Norman, Marber and others banged on about it so much that eventually I felt obliged to give it a whirl. It did not take long to have me wondering why I had ever hesitated. Soon it was keeping me up all night.

By mid-2003 the *Observer*'s music critic was sending his paper an incongruous dispatch from this brave new poker world. In what now reads like a very wide-eyed piece, I made points that were then still fairly fresh, but are now commonplace, about the difference between online poker and real casino or home poker (now known as 'b&m', as in 'bricks and mortar'). For a start, online poker is of course available twenty-four hours a day, seven days a week – its biggest appeal (and, for the easily addicted, drawback). Given the clear advantage of being able to play at home, without having to travel across town to a casino or friend's home, even shave or get dressed if you can't be bothered, the web can be poker dreamland. But there are drawbacks.

Internet poker is the same as, yet subtly different from, the real thing. Part of the appeal of poker, part of its very nature, is the interaction between the players: the stares, the backchat at the table, the jovial or sometimes ugly interchanges that go on amid the dark looks, shrieks of joy and inevitable curse words. All that is recreated on the net, up to a point, by means of the chat-box, in which I can key in 'nh' (or 'Nice hand') to show Fatman I'm a good loser (or am pretending to be) or 'Up yours!' if I want to needle Stetson from Dallas in Seat Six. Some players are strong, silent types, who decline to get involved in all this and might come in for some ribbing at a real poker table. Here on the web, however, it's tough to get under anyone's skin, to rile them in the devious ways you would in real life.

Not being able to see their faces is the worst thing, on top of the hectic speed at which the game is played (which soon, once you get used to it, actually becomes a bonus). Much of the time it is all too easy to play hands online that you wouldn't at a real table. At first I made far too many calls I shouldn't have, hoping for the miracle card that never came, because no one could see me squirming with embarrassment when it didn't. Slowly, I imposed some self-discipline. These bad plays were costing me money I could ill afford.

There are some very good players out there in cyberspace

who have adjusted their games to random computer dealing – significantly different from random human dealing, for mathematical reasons way over my head – and the pervasive suspicion that some of the players are computerised 'shills', invented by the websites to fill up tables. These days you may also be up against a 'bot' – a poker robot, programmed to play expertly at low or intermediate levels, usually making its owner a modest profit while he or she finds something better to do.

The best online poker sites offer statistics on your play, histories of the hands and other useful data you don't get in real life. There are boxes to tick if you know in advance that you want to check, call, raise or fold. But you soon realise that even these can be 'tells' to the other players and adjust accordingly. If you play frequently there is a pad on which to make notes on the other players in case you come up against them again. When Fatman pulls the only card against you that can win him the hand, however, you inevitably wonder if it's a fix. At the felt there'd be a few 'Wow!'s, maybe even an apology or a discussion, sometimes an argument, even a fight; on the web you're on to the next hand before anyone has time to raise even an eyebrow.

For all the websites' reassurances about their 'poker police' roving cyberspace in pursuit of anything unusual, for all their pledges to investigate anything suspicious, there are many inevitable doubts and fears – some more paranoid than others. Maybe some opponents are partners sitting in the same room, clever enough geeks to falsify their location, working together to nail the other players? Or in touch with each other by phone or instant messenger, cheating the rest of the table by sharing their cards? Maybe that bad beat was the computer favouring one of its own regular players, measured by frequent player points? Maybe these offshore websites will just run away with all our money one day?

The persuasive answer to all of the above is: they're making so much dough, simply by taking a slice of the fortune exchanged by millions of players every day, that they don't have to. It's in their commercial interests to keep everything nice and straight.

The colossal impact on the game of online poker can be summarised in one terrifying statistic: a teenager anywhere in the world, unable to play (legally) in an American casino until he or she is twenty-one, can play more hands in six months than septuagenarian Doyle Brunson, the world's most respected player, has in his lifetime. And all too many are doing so.

Online poker is a very good way, in other words, to learn the game, then refine your skills with the help of the latest mind-numbing manuals. That's why so many smart twenty-somethings have recently emerged as world-beating players. But most online wizards, such as the guy with those pocket queens to my aces in the 2005 main event, have some difficulty making the transition to b&m poker across a table from real people. It's not just that aggression of that order is ill-advised at the start of a week-long tournament when the stacks are $10,000 and the blinds just $20–$50 or $50–$100. Real poker is much slower than online poker. You can stare down your opponent, maybe talk to him in search of a tell, before making your own move. This can unnerve online players making their debut at the felt, luring them into errors.

For the beginner, online poker is far less intimidating than the real thing. You're up against a bunch of faceless avatars who aren't going to be in your face as you make your decisions. Outside the voluntary chat-box, there is no talk at an online table. It can be a solitary business, playing in long-drawn-out online tournaments. But at least you have minimised the distractions – the casino clatter, etc. – which can give you the mother of all headaches in the real world of poker. And you can always have an expert mentor at your shoulder, giving you advice – which is not, of course, permitted at a live table.

Yet some of the game's essential skills are non-existent on the web. Watching your opponents' faces as they check their cards or as the flop comes down translates online into reading their betting patterns. Which is, needless to say, a useful skill to master. In the live game there are now much more informed responses to an unlikely bet, be it too large or too small or inconsistent with a previous round, than there were before the days of the internet. So some skills have been refined in a world of online casino lobbies much more helpful to would-be players than their real-life, b&m counterparts.

Just by clicking a few buttons before deciding which table to choose, you can learn the average pot size at any table, the number of players seeing the flop, how many hands they are playing per hour, the names of the players in each game, how many are on the waiting list and how many games of a particular limit are under way. You can take time, in other words, to pick the right spot for you and your bankroll – and there will always be one available pretty quickly.

Once you get to your table, some of the important chores of card-room poker are done for you, such as figuring out the size of the pot and the other players' stacks as well as your own. This is displayed for you, thus making it easier to calculate the pot odds and to weigh up your standing in the global scheme of things.

Online dealers don't make mistakes, unlike some real dealers (who don't do it often, but it can cost you). The 'rake', or money you pay to play, is much smaller per hand than in a casino, leaving more for you to win. And the lower-level players, on the whole, are less experienced. As are those on the smaller, lesser-known poker websites.

Online card rooms offer a wider choice of cash games and tournaments at all levels, with shorter (if any) waiting times, than casino card rooms. Another advantage of online poker is that you can get up and leave whenever you want to, especially when winning, without incurring the wrath of the other players.

One of the disadvantages is that it's generally much harder to bluff players out of a pot. It can be done; but the loss of the human interaction – the stares, the tells – makes it much tougher. Some players hungry for action, however, will be playing two, three, even eight different tables at once. Unless you feel this good about yourself – which I never have – you'll find that some of these players inevitably make mistakes, hurrying between one hand and the next in search of the best opportunities. Not, though, the more experienced.

One such is twenty-seven-year-old Oliver 'Olly' Chubb, a university friend of my son Ben, who now makes a decent living in Toronto from online poker. I asked him how come this was the career choice of a smart, well-educated young man?

'The transition from pastime to hobby to fully fledged obsession took no more than a couple of months. I started reading poker books, deposited a thousand dollars to try out the online scene and I've been playing off the proceeds ever since. I now play mainly on PokerStars, PartyPoker and Bodog, but I'm always looking for new sites and offers.

'It's only recently that I've been playing eight tables at once. I was comfortable with two tables quite early on but recently I've invested in an external LCD monitor which really helps. As long as the tables aren't overlapping onscreen, it's much easier to follow the flow of all the games. Online, I play 90 per cent of hands on autopilot so it's not too hard to move from table to table pre-action folding most pre-flop hands and playing strong hands in a fairly standard way on others. With the increased hands per hour this allows, I can earn fairly steadily just playing a solid game and not really worrying too much about adjusting to table dynamic or the individual playing styles of my opponents. In live play, with fewer hands per hour, I can devote more

mental energy to familiarising myself with my opponent's playing styles. I tend to see a lot more flops and really try to base my
decisions on the table dynamic and the state of mind of the
players in the current hand. I make more relatively in big blinds
per hundred hands in live play than I do online for these reasons, but with the huge increase in hands per hour of playing
eight online tables, it provides a much steadier income for my
day-to-day play.

'After graduating in PPE, I spent a year working in an office
in Oxford delaying the serious job-hunting for when my constitution could stand the stress. As poker was becoming a bigger
and bigger part of my life it became clear that, at least for now,
the job-hunting was going to have to take a back seat. I officially
abandoned the application process for strategy consulting
towards the end of 2003 and decided to go full-time with poker.
Having decided to give a year to playing, it occurred to me that
I had no reason to be based in the UK. I picked Canada as
somewhere with friendly immigration laws for UK residents
and, having a few friends over here, decided to give it a try. I
spent 2004 in Vancouver, within easy striking distance of Vegas,
and I moved out east to Toronto in 2005 – which proved a
pretty decent year: I earned more than all my consultant friends
in London and had a pretty good time doing it. So I've no plans
to revise my arrangement at the moment.'

When I myself first started playing online poker, in mid-2003,
some £6 million ($10.8 million) was being staked per day
worldwide. Within a year that figure had risen to £40 million
($72 million) a day – almost 10 per cent of that in Britain alone.
The online gaming industry's global turnover had grown to
£15 billion ($27 billion), with poker its fastest-growing segment.
Between 2005 and 2006 there was a further growth rate in the
region of a staggering 600 per cent. By mid-2006 one of the
leading websites, PokerStars.com, was dealing ten million hands

a day and had just handed out prizes celebrating its five bil-lionth.

This astonishing growth was achieved in under five years – despite what might have seemed an inauspicious start. PokerStars, now the world's biggest tournament website, dealt its first hand on 11 September 2001 – yes, *that* 9/11.

The first site to offer online poker was PlanetPoker in 1998, followed within a year by ParadisePoker. It was Paradise with its improved software and strong marketing campaigns that really lifted online poker to its next level, cemented in 2001 by the arrival of PartyPoker, PokerStars and UltimateBet.

After two years of steady growth, the scale of online poker was boosted beyond measure in 2003 by the arrival of poker on television. In Britain *Late Night Poker* (launched on Channel 4 in 1999) had already shown the game's small-screen potential. But when the *World Poker Tour* made its debut on America's Travel Channel at the end of March 2003, the face of poker was changed for ever. The show swiftly became the highest-rated in the channel's history, emboldening ESPN into a huge expansion of its coverage of the World Series and hundreds of thousands of new recruits to try to win their way there.

That year, 2003, more than eight hundred players partici-pated in the No Limit Hold 'em main event at the World Series of Poker, then the largest field ever, hugely boosted by internet entrants. The number more than tripled the following year – almost half of them qualifiers via online satellites. Even that massive field more than doubled in 2005. In 2006 they were planning to accommodate more than eight thousand, perhaps two-thirds of them internet qualifiers.

Both the 2003 and 2004 WSOP champions, Chris Money-maker and Greg Raymer, were online poker players who had qualified via PokerStars. The 2005 champion, Australia's Joe Hachem, paid his own entry fee – but was also swiftly signed up by PokerStars, which branded itself 'the home of champions'.

By 2006 almost every big-name player had attached his or her reputation to one online site or another: Chris 'Jesus' Ferguson and Howard 'the Professor' Lederer launched Full Tilt Poker with such other leading pros as Phil Ivey, Erik Seidel, John Juanda, Phil Gordon, Andy Bloch, Mike Matusow, Erick Lindgren, Jennifer Harman and Clonie Gowen; Lederer's sister Annie Duke, Phil Hellmuth and Antonio Esfandiari are sponsored by UltimateBet, as was Dave 'Devilfish' Ulliott before he launched his own website; WPT's Mike Sexton is an ambassador for PartyPoker; Doyle Brunson has opened his own online franchise with Doyle's Room; and Gus 'the Great Dane' Hansen has followed suit with PokerChamps. The ties between Hollywood and poker have also been cemented with the arrival of HollywoodPoker and CelebPoker, both of which offer the punter the chance to play poker with stars such as James Woods and Gabe ('Call Me Kotter') Kaplan.

Throughout the first nine months of 2006 the number of real-money (or dot-com, as opposed to play-money, or dot-net) online poker players was still increasing by as much as 25 per cent a month and showed no sign of peaking. Generated largely by the US, with Japan and the UK the next biggest contributors, the annual turnover of online poker was reaching the $10 billion mark. Despite PokerStars' dominance of the tournament market, the industry leader remained PartyPoker, commanding almost half the entire online business. Set up by a group of smart young Indian tecchies who had met at university, it was also the first online gaming company to go public, floating on the London Stock Exchange in 2005 for £4.7 billion ($8.5 billion) – a higher valuation than ICI and British Airways combined.

They haven't played a hand of casino poker in their lives, but former porn baroness Ruth Parasol and her husband Russell DeLeon have made more than £2 billion out of the game.

PartyGaming was Parasol's brainchild, as she looked to invest the small fortune she had built up after selling an online pornography empire – which, so legend has it, she started with a couple of sex phone-lines given to her by her father as a distinctly unconventional teenage birthday present.

Parasol used the cash to commission a friend of a friend, a computer engineering graduate from the Indian Institute of Technology named Anurag Dikshit, to create a programme for casino games such as roulette. In 2000, after seeing the success of ParadisePoker, they switched the focus from roulette and blackjack to poker. Thus was born PartyPoker, which went public a month before the 2005 World Series.

The previous year the company had shown a profit of almost £372 million on sales of £600 million. Its flotation also made very rich men of two Indians in their early thirties, both graduates of the Indian Institute of Technology: software programmer Dikshit (£1.7 billion) and marketing director Vikrant Bhargava (£592 million), who says he's never known a dull moment. 'None of us could have predicted what has happened. It has grown faster than we ever thought possible.'

In 2006 all four made their debuts in the 'Rich List' annually published in the *Sunday Times*, with Parasol and DeLeon leaping in among the wealthiest people in Britain at seventeenth place – compared with, for instance, the Queen, who comes 192nd equal with a mere £300 million. But they don't, of course, live or pay taxes in Britain. All four make their homes in Gibraltar, the offshore tax haven where PartyGaming is based. The share price has since wobbled every time the founders have cashed in more stock.

PokerStars, meanwhile, was the first site to introduce features that would soon became standard, such as multi-table tournaments, integrated game statistics, players' notes, personalised images, time-banks for tournaments and high-stakes cash games, satellites and multi-table 'sit-and-go' tournaments. By mid-2006 PokerStars had run more than twenty-five million tournaments, awarding well over $5 billion in prize money; the site boasted the world's largest poker tournament room, with six million registered players.

By February 2006 PokerStars.com became the first poker website to boast a hundred thousand simultaneous players. That watershed marked the next big development in poker history. Every week PokerStars started hosting its 'Sunday Million', the largest weekly tournament on (or off) the planet with a $1 million guaranteed prize pool. PokerStars now sponsors the year-round European Poker Tour (EPT) and the Caribbean Adventure each January. Each autumn it hosts the world's largest online tournament, the World Championship of Online Poker (WCOOP), which attracted 19,727 players in 2005, generating $12,783,900 in prize money.

Between 2003 and 2005, PokerStars sent more players to the World Series than any other source or website. No fewer than 1116 entrants (almost 20 per cent of the field) qualified to play in the 2005 WSOP via the website's satellites. The 2005 world poker champion, Joe Hachem, has been an active player at PokerStars since 2001. He joined Chris Moneymaker and Greg Raymer as the website's official representatives, thus fortifying its slogan: 'Where Poker Players Become World Champions.'

My objective over the coming year, after savouring the 2005 World Series, was to join them. My return to Vegas, after so many years away, had whetted my appetite for more. In an age when literally anyone could become world champion, more than likely an unknown amateur, surely I stood a better chance than in the old days amid the pros at Binion's, even though the field was now so much bigger? There was a better chance to get into the money, for sure, especially if I spent the next twelve months honing my online skills, to get inside the heads of all those cyber-challengers. In the meantime I determined to explore all the wacky offshoots of the poker boom, as manifested even here in little old Britain – in between, of course, getting on with the Job.

From Las Vegas to Glyndebourne is quite a journey, both literally and metaphorically. The idyllic country mansion-cum-opera house on the East Sussex Downs eased the otherwise brutal bump of my post-WSOP return to Blighty. Or it would have, if I'd managed to get there. En route to a Peter Hall production of Verdi's *Otello*, I ran into a vast, static traffic jam on the M25; after covering a mile or so in an hour, I had to call Glyndebourne to say I wouldn't be able to make it in time and ask them to hold me seats for the next performance. Such, at times, is the critic's lot; much more time, travel and effort usually goes into the job than the bland end-product might suggest. Reviewing just one out-of-town opera or concert can take a whole weekend out of your life.

This is especially bad news when said critic is also in training to be the next world champion of poker. The BBC Promenade concerts in the Royal Albert Hall, *Eugene Onegin* in Holland Park, *Boris Godunov* at the Royal Opera, Covent Garden: this was the scaffolding around a month writing a poker manual for beginners (called, like two other books published at much the same time, *All In*) and seeking out more poker practice. With Al Alvarez, these days a more regular visitor than me, I went back to our old haunt in Paddington, the Vic (properly known as the Grosvenor Victoria casino), to check out the action – and managed to lose a few hundred pounds at the fearsome £100 Pot Limit Hold 'em table before pleading (truthfully, as it happened) a dinner date. In the decade since I ceased to be a regular, the Vic has rarely been an especially lucky place for me; but I planned to be back there for a big tournament the following week.

Before that, though, there was a 'celebrity' event to celebrate the opening of London's latest card room at the glitzy Palm

Beach Casino in London's Mayfair. Here, thirty years earlier, I had piled out of a cab in black tie with a pal, somewhat the worse for wear after a Frank Sinatra concert followed by dinner at the Café Royal, only to be denied admission by the liveried doorman with a withering: 'Why don't you gentlemen just go home to your wives?' Now I was a 'celebrity' guest, given VIP membership and a chance to win a seat in a high-stakes tournament. Two of twenty starters in a media satellite would make it through.

After three or four hours it came down to the poker writers Elkan Allan, Matt Born, Phil Shaw and myself. Elkan was a friend dating back to my *Sunday Times* days in the 1970s; creator of the hit TV pop show *Ready, Steady, Go!*, then pioneer of the critical TV listings newspaper readers now take for granted, he was spending what passed for his retirement as a general poker factotum, advising websites and writing columns here and there. Phil, at the time, was editor of the glossy magazine *Poker Europa*, Matt a longstanding friend whom I knew to be as good a poker player as he is a journalist.

But Matt had a problem. Way ahead in the satellite, he was due at Heathrow within the hour to meet his wife. He had not expected to last this long or the hour to get so late. Once Elkan had been knocked out, Phil and I tried to take due advantage of Matt's anxiety. But the *Daily Mail*'s man could do no wrong; he just kept on winning. So we did a quiet deal for the two seats, slipping him a few Elgars (*see* Glossary), which of course provoked the poker gods' sour sense of humour.

We agreed to play the next hand at random so Matt could leave; without looking at our cards, he went all-in and I called. Matt promptly turned over two red aces to my K-Q. The board, of course, came 2-7-4 . . . Q-K. Those were two ridiculous starting hands, in the circumstances – the irony being that I would have beaten him and the odds without handing over those Elgars. Now the joke was on me.

The next day, playing in the tournament proper alongside sundry sporting and showbiz stars, my K-Q (again!) was this time beaten by a pair of tens, knocking me out in 38th place out of 140 starters. Top 20 per cent again; but still not good enough. The top 10 per cent – i.e., the money – must now be my target if this year's adventure was to prove profitable, perhaps even enable me to return to full-time poker.

At the Vic a few days later, I was playing my best poker for some time in a £300 super-satellite for the week's main event, the £3500 (or €5000) buy-in EPT London Classic. Nearing the final two tables where everyone would qualify, I made a mistake so elementary that I blush to remember it. Dealt A-K, I'd had just one caller for my big pre-flop raise; when the board of K-5-2 paired my king, I pretended to think for a while before lining up another huge bet. Meaning to say, 'Ten thousand', I misread the unfamiliar Vic tournament chips and said – clearly by mistake, given the scale of the pot – 'I raise a thousand.'

'A thousand!' laughed the surly opponent to my right. 'I'll call that with anything.' Verbal declarations being binding, I was obliged to stick to what I had said. The turn was a six and I went all-in; he called and rolled over 5-6 for two pairs. Such was the humiliating end of a really good day's work, which had so nearly got me into the big tournament at a 10-per-cent price. I mooched around the casino in a foul mood, really mad at myself, until cheered by a pleasant dinner with a group including the former England cricket captain Mike Atherton, a fellow-Lancastrian then in the throes of writing a book about gambling, including a chapter on poker – in which, a year later, I was thrilled to find myself described as a 'semi-respectable' figure.

But that A-K still haunted me; and A-K was to prove my nemesis all year. Generally rated the fifth best starting hand, after the four top pairs, it is nicknamed 'Big Slick'. But I'd come to prefer its latest name, Anna Kournikova – 'because it looks

good but always loses'. This was a line I'd be repeating ad nauseam in the year ahead – usually to my cost.

Next up, amid the rigours of the Proms in the sweltering Albert
Hall, was a heads-up 'speed poker' tournament staged for TV at
the Riverside Studios in Hammersmith, west London,
poignantly near the home I used to share with the Moll. Again
a score of journalists and celebrities had been invited to take on
the 2000 World Champion Chris 'Jesus' Ferguson and one of
the world's top female professionals, Jennifer Harman, for a
seat in the televised event.

After only four years playing in the World Series, Ferguson
made his name by winning the 2000 world title in a dramatic
heads-up against the veteran T. J. Cloutier, a former American
football pro proven by the statistics to be poker's most successful
tournament player of all time. It was Ferguson's dark beard
and long, straggly hair, cascading way down below his shoulders, and usually embellished by shades and a Stetson, that
inevitably earned him, then aged thirty-seven, the nickname
'Jesus'. He had ten times as many chips as the heads-up began;
but the wizened old Cloutier, then sixty-two, soon made significant inroads. Eventually there came a hand that dramatically
symbolised the old poker versus the new.

Cloutier was slightly behind in chips when he raised the pot
by $175,000. Ferguson reraised to $600,000, prompting
Cloutier to move all-in to the tune of some $2 million.
Ferguson, as is his way, sat in thought for a long time, his stig-
mata-free palms against his cheeks; clearly he was figuring that
Cloutier had the better hand, but this could prove his chance to
win the world crown. He was maybe a 2-1 underdog, yet that
might still make it a chance worth taking. Eventually Ferguson
called and rolled over A-9. Cloutier showed A-Q. Jesus had only
slightly miscalculated: in fact he was a 3-1 'dog'.

The flop and turn made no difference; then the river brought the Messianic nine that clinched it for Jesus. As Ferguson celebrated, the seen-it-all Cloutier merely shrugged and said, with the philosophical resignation of all chivalrous old-timers, 'That's poker.' But Ferguson has shown that his victory was no fluke, winning four more World Series events in the subsequent five years. If Cloutier can claim to be the most consistently successful tournament player of the twentieth century, Ferguson can lay claim to the same status in the twenty-first.

Jesus symbolises the new poker as one of its true intellectuals, a player who sits very quietly at the table, unusually taking more notice of his cards than his opponents. This is because he is a student of artificial intelligence who practises game theory, or a version of game theory he has run many times through computer tests to the point where he believes there is such a thing as the 'perfect' poker game. The son of a maths professor who taught game theory at the University of California, Los Angeles, Ferguson spent five years at UCLA, graduating with a computer science degree, then another thirteen years in the doctoral programme before being 'kicked out'; he left 'reluctantly', he says, but 'didn't go far' – only three hundred miles, in fact, to win the world poker title the very next year.

Ferguson is a student of the game theory pioneered in the late 1920s by the mathematician John von Neumann, regarded as one of the most brilliant men of his time, who played a seminal role in the birth of the computer and the atomic bomb. Neumann's idealistic inclinations led him to develop game theory, based on the perfect game of poker, in the hope of adapting it to diplomatic negotiations and the quest for world peace. The key to it was a theory of bluff: in essence that you should regularly bluff with the worst cards, with the result that you will eventually get called when you're holding the best ones. The trouble was that his theory depended on all players being equally proficient; throw a few amateurs, or 'fish', into the equation and it collapsed. It also worked better in two-player (or 'heads-up') poker than the standard multi-player game. But Ferguson's play against Cloutier was essentially based on a probability version of game-theory calculation; he got lucky, *very* lucky, but he would still have been in the game if he had lost.

Several of the new generation of top pros now share Ferguson's view that the heads-up game of Texas Hold' em will eventually be 'solved'. The MIT graduate Andy Bloch, for one, believes that the day will come when there will be a correct answer to every available permutation in a one-on-one Hold 'em game. Bloch recently discovered that his own computer-driven conclusions were the same as Ferguson's. Play at their level – which is the point, because few people do – and there will be an answer to whatever comes up. Only occasionally, as against Cloutier, will you need to defy the odds; even if you fail, however, the decision to call will have been the correct one.

The last time I had seen Ferguson, by way of contrast, he had been hiding inside a refrigerator, giving a player secret poker advice whenever he looked in for a fresh beer. It was a TV ad for Full Tilt, as weird as it was engaging. Now he is sitting opposite me and we both have $40,000 in chips, and a maximum of fifteen seconds each to make our decisions as we play just a dozen hands (to keep the proceedings short) – 'heads-up', as in game theory. But he won't – will he? – have the time he needs to make all those calculations.

At the other table two out of six players have already won all $40,000 from Harman as she plays fast and loose, maybe jet-lagged. With nothing at stake, why not? In his trademark Stetson and shades, Jesus has shown no such mercy; he has beaten every challenger yet. On the first hand I get half my chips in the pot with a paired ace which becomes two pair on the turn and Ferguson calls. When the river gives me a house and I go all-in, Jesus folds pretty quickly. He has to. Otherwise he would have been timed out – or knocked out.

The ensuing hands see little more than the ritual exchange of blinds; then, all too soon, comes the last of the dozen, in which I am again dealt an ace – and again go all-in, regardless of kicker. Ferguson folds. When we count the chips, for which there has been no time while playing at such speed, I find that I have won 17,500 (notional, alas) dollars off the former world champion. A satisfying result, one to bore the grandchildren with, although not enough to win that TV seat. I may have gotten the better of a top pro, a world champ, but I did not feel great about it; for a really satisfying start to my latest year as a poker pro, I should have won *all* of Jesus's dough.

The following Saturday I talked about it as a guest on the chat show of a new British cable TV station devoted entirely to poker, PokerZone. Hosted by the comedian (and poker player) Richard Herring, it consisted of three twenty-minute slots devoted, on this occasion, to the dashing player-writer Grub Smith, myself and Charles Ingram, the retired Army major who won a million pounds on ITV's *Who Wants To Be A Millionaire?* – only to be disqualified for receiving help from an academic friend in the audience, who was deemed to have coughed every time Ingram mentioned the correct answer. In the green room before the taping, Ingram and his wife Diana invited me down to Dorset to play in their home game. Before I could reply, they were whisked away to appear on the show.

As Grub and I watched the taping in the green room, Ingram spent a good ten of his twenty minutes protesting his innocence of the *Millionaire* charge – despite a 2003 court conviction for fraud – before Herring could finally get him round to poker. So what kind of stakes did he play for? Oh, said Ingram, well, technically he was bankrupt, so of course he did not play for real money. He played for cakes. His wife – he gestured towards the silent Diana, sitting loyally beside him on the sofa – baked cakes and they were his poker stakes.

'The hell with *that*,' I said offstage to a grinning Grub. 'I'm not going all the way to Dorset to play poker for cakes!'

'Oh, I dunno,' he replied at his most deadpan, 'look at it this way. Get the moll to bake you a pile of fairy cakes, in fact, fill the boot of your car with them – and it's the most you can lose.'

Was this the level to which I had sunk? Playing poker in England so often seemed just like so much dickering around – such small beer compared with the action across the Atlantic. The music job gave me only six weeks off all year, but maybe it was time I used one of them. As I mused upon all this, opera – of all things – gave me a timely kick in the pants.

Towards the end of September the Job took me to Covent Garden for Puccini's *La Fanciulla del West* – usually translated as 'The Girl of the Golden West', and the only opera, so far as I know, set in the Wild West. Its sole female character, Minnie, is naturally being pursued by both the bandit and the sheriff who's out to get him, respectively named Johnson and Rance. In my review I rechristened the work (rather wittily, I flattered myself) 'Minnie, Get Your Gun'.

At the end of the second act – i.e., just before the interval and a well-deserved drink – the wounded Dick Johnson is hiding in the rafters of Minnie's remote log cabin when Rance arrives to collar him. Our heroine is just protesting that she has no idea where Johnson is when drops of his blood fall from above on the sheriff, who promptly drags him out of his hiding place.

In desperation Minnie makes a bold suggestion: that they sort it all out over a game of poker. If Rance wins, he gets Minnie but lets Johnson go; if Minnie wins, she gets Johnson and they go free. The crafty girl knows that the sheriff is a bit of a gambler. So Rance agrees to this – foolishly, as it transpires, for Minnie conceals some aces in her garter, pretends to feel faint when she loses the first hand, then proceeds to fix the deck while Rance fetches her a brandy. The rest is inevitable – apart from the fact that Minnie and Johnson go free at the end, making her one of the few heroines Puccini does not kill off prematurely for the sake of a ten-Kleenex climax.

'*Una partita a poker*': when I saw the word 'poker' in the Royal Opera House sur-titles, a nanosecond before it was sung by the sultry American soprano Andrea Gruber, it was like the ghost of Hamlet's father turning up to remind me of my mission. Subsequent enquiries among expert colleagues confirmed that it is indeed the only time in all opera that the word 'poker' is mentioned. There is gambling, of course, in *The Gambler*, Prokofiev's setting of Dostoevsky, even card games in operas like Verdi's *La Traviata* and Tchaikovsky's *The Queen of Spades*. But the word 'poker' issuing from that diva's mouth floored me with all the force of a Shakespearean summons upon a guilty thing.

Poker-wise, it told me, I had been fiddling away the autumn while Vegas burned with action. If I was going to take this self-imposed challenge seriously, and mount a realistic bid to become the 2006 world champion of poker, it was time to get back on the road.

4

Brunson at the Bellagio

It's midnight in Las Vegas and the party's just beginning at Light, the New York-style nightclub inside my current home from home, the plush Bellagio Hotel. In just twelve hours' time, at noon, they'll be shuffling up and dealing the first hand in the Doyle Brunson Poker Championship, centrepiece of the World Poker Tour's North American Poker Finals. But who needs sleep? It's hip-hop time.

Feeling even older than my years, I enter the noisy, throbbing disco alongside Leonardo DiCaprio, the Hollywood heart-throb who is now just one more member of poker's growing showbiz community. But even he takes second place in the celebrity stakes tonight to a large, elderly, infirm man holding court in a cowboy hat beside the club's glitzy bar. As Leo disappears into the gyrating throng on the dancefloor, I pick my way over to pay homage to a poker legend.

Doyle Brunson is one of the few players still alive who remembers the old days of poker on the road, where a team of hustlers fleeced a bunch of innocents before swiftly moving on, hoping to leave town alive with their bankrolls intact. Today he's the *capo di capi* of living poker players, a multi-millionaire poker icon with his own website, Doyle's Room, which this party is being held to promote. In his early seventies, Brunson is clearly intent on seizing the crown of the late Johnny Moss as the greatest poker player of all time.

Born into poverty on a Texas farm during the Great Depression, Doyle was a star college athlete in his youth, a potential four-minute miler, until his right leg was crushed in an industrial accident. To this day he still walks with a crutch, if a tad more easily since a gastric bypass operation halved his four-hundred-pound frame.

A few years later, when Brunson was twenty-eight, surgeons found his body riddled with tumours. 'I was a big dog to live four months,' he drawls to all enquirers. Only weeks later, however, he was entirely cancer-free, baffling his doctors. 'Spontaneous remission, they call it. Why and how, I don't know, but somethin' miraculous happened.' Then his wife Louise developed uterine cancer; but as she was about to go into the operating theatre her tumour also mysteriously vanished. In 1975 their daughter Doyla was diagnosed with a serious spinal disorder. Louise organised a marathon prayer session and within three months Doyla's spine had somehow corrected itself.

But this, alas, proved the last of the medical miracles. At the age of eighteen, Doyla died from a heart problem. Did all these early traumas somehow contribute to her father's poker skills? 'Maybe so. All of that puts everything else into perspective and it was kinda liberating for my poker. See, you cannot be afraid to lose your chips. You have to be aggressive the whole time. And when you've been through all I've been through, you're not going to sweat over losing a pot, however big. All I know is, once I got over the cancer it all kinda clicked into place and I went on the biggest winning streak of my life.'

After his daughter died, Doyle found religion. 'I explored all the eastern religions but none of them made any sense to me.

So I'm a Christian. I don't go to church as much I should, but I do have faith.' Which prompts the question: does a belief in God, any god, bring a man more luck at the felt than mere faith in the poker gods? For those of us with no faith, some even militantly so, this is a bit of a poser. Brunson's winning example would seem to score one for the deists, leaving the rest of us landed with a host of mere superstitions. Me, I remain unconvinced. And there is very little help in this area in the manuals.

Half a century ago, after his accident ruled out a career as a pro basketball player, Brunson quit his job as a salesman for full-time poker – a game from which he could make more in a few hours than he earned in a month selling Burroughs business machines. For thirty years, in partnership with Sailor Roberts and Amarillo Slim, Doyle toured the saloons of the Deep South, hustling rednecks at stud and draw, then taking a chance on being pistol-whipped for his winnings on the way back to his car. Brunson lost count of the times he saw people shot, often killed for their money. 'On one occasion a guy walked into a game and just blew the head off the guy sitting right next to me. His brains wound up splattered on the wall.'

Fifty years on, after publicly wondering whether the sheer scale of the new poker world made it a young man's game these days, if only for reasons of mere stamina, Brunson has just added a tenth World Series bracelet to his collection at the 2005 world championships, matching the record of his fellow two-time world champion Johnny Chan, hard on the heels of a WPT win at the 2004 Legends of Poker. 'Winning those two titles was a great relief, 'cause the question in my mind was, Am I losing it? I thought, I'm seventy-one, maybe I can't play any more. I don't see any other seventy-one-year-olds out there.'

But perhaps Brunson's single most significant contribution to the game of poker was the publication in 1977 of a book that radically altered the way people played it. Within years of editing *Super/System* (originally published under the rather more vainglorious title of 'How I Won a Million Dollars Playing Poker'), he publicly regretted giving away his trade secrets in the section he wrote on Hold 'em – and those of the other leading players he commissioned to write chapters on their specialist games. 'If I had my time again, I wouldn't have done it,' Brunson told Al Alvarez five years later in 1982.

Yet the book sold more than half a million copies and Brunson has recently published an update, *Super/System 2*, to take advantage of the hundreds of thousands of new players joining the game every year – usually, at first, online. An immensely instructive, authoritative tome, *Super/System* translates complex theory into concise and readable English. 'I've always been able to express myself better writing than speaking,' he says, handing me a copy of his latest book, a guide to online poker.

We have barely skimmed the surface of all this, the brief continuation of a rolling, thirty-year conversation; but by now a queue of fans has formed to talk to the great man, or merely have their picture taken with him flanked by the scantily clad beauties laid on for that purpose. I retire gracefully to watch, smiling at the memory of Brunson's reply a few months before to my pal Matthew Norman, who took the chance during an interview to tell Brunson how he, Matthew, had exited the World Series main event. So what was the secret of being a great poker player? 'There are none. It's all about timing and situation. But one thing's for sure. You can't be folding A-K of hearts, like you did yesterday, and expect to win.'

So Doyle's a fan of Kournikova, then. And he himself, as it happens, has the distinction of being a poker hand: 10-2 is called a 'Doyle Brunson' because, as fate (or God) would have it, this was the hand with which he clinched both his back-to-back world titles in 1976 and 1977. Brunson was himself knocked out of this year's main event the day after Norman. But he, unlike

Matthew or myself, quit the arena to a standing ovation. He shrugged and told Matthew: 'This is what I do. It's what I've always done. And if I drop dead at the table in the middle of a monster pot, hell, I'll die a happy man.'

The odds would suggest that he probably will; it's where he spends most of his time – all of sixteen hours a day when in Vegas, even in his seventies. In 2000 David Spanier, poker journalist and author, suffered a fatal stroke at the poker table in the card room of his beloved Vic – 'as he would have wished', I had the temerity to say in front of his wife and sons in my address at his memorial meeting a few months later. To my relief, they didn't seem to mind. Another friend who died at the table was the Hall of Famer and 1982 world champion Jack 'Treetops' Straus, as he had so often said he hoped he would. But only Jack could have added that he also hoped he would be losing at the time.

Doyle Brunson, then, is the reason I'm back in Vegas. His eponymous annual tournament, held each October as part of the Bellagio's Festa al Lago, is the highlight of the North American Poker Finals, a World Poker Tour event that will draw a television audience of many millions in a hundred countries to see more than four hundred players compete for a prize pool in excess of $4 million, with a first prize of $1,060,050.

In the wake of the internet, the TV phenomenon that is the World Poker Tour has changed the face of poker yet further. There is a synergy here; the newfound popularity of poker on television has recruited more and more players for the web, just as the web created the appetite for as-live poker on TV. But the WPT has done more than spruce up ESPN's coverage of the World Series. It has turned poker, as its founder Steve Lipscomb hoped, into the latest television *sport*.

The WPT's first broadcast on 30 March 2003 has proved a landmark in the history of poker. It was the result of several years' planning by Lipscomb, then an LA television producer, now the WPT's driving force. He had worked out the idea and written a business plan in 2001, after making a documentary about the World Series for the Discovery Channel in 1999 – the first time, as he points out, that a TV programme was made about the WSOP without the casino having to foot the bill. Since 1987 Jack Binion had been hiring production teams to film the final table of the main event for ESPN; but despite the huge amounts of money involved, poker did not work on TV for the simple reason that you could not see the players' hole cards. Looking at nine men sitting around a table playing poker was about as much fun as watching grass grow or paint dry.

At the time poker was sagging as a casino game. When the internet began to kick in, card rooms were closing all over the country. Lipscomb could see the potential of live-looking tournaments as a TV phenomenon; but for a couple of years no one shared his enthusiasm. 'From 2000 to 2001 I pitched televised poker to any broadcaster I imagined might air the game,' he writes in a contribution to Brunson's *Super/System 2*, adding sarcastically, 'including most of the entities now racing to get in on the act'. Before the WPT hit the airwaves, 'they quite simply did not believe that poker could garner an American audience'. Their scepticism, he adds, 'was well-founded. The [WSOP] programs ran as filler in undesirable time slots and served as a constant reminder to all broadcasters that nine guys sitting around a table playing poker is not inherently interesting to watch.'

Undeterred, Lipscomb hired veteran pro Mike Sexton as an adviser in 2001, then secured player and entrepreneur Lyle Berman as his business partner. Their goal was straightforward: 'To establish poker as the next significant televised sport.' On 25 February 2002 the WPT went into business, negotiating deals with upscale destination casinos – which was why it attracted the otherwise unlikely interest of the Travel Channel. In early

2003 Travel made the WPT an offer it couldn't refuse – a weekly, two-hour prime-time slot, along with a commitment to 'establish Wednesday night as poker night'. That was exactly what Lipscomb was looking for: a dedicated time slot, known in the trade as 'appointment television'. He rejected ESPN's offer to put the show on the air without a specific slot and opted to go with Travel.

As of 1999, poker had already attracted huge audiences for the UK's Channel 4, with the under-the-table cameras revealing players' hole cards on the first series of *Late Night Poker*. Lipscomb refined this idea into the 'lipstick cam', or 'pocket-cam', hidden behind the hole cards and used his production expertise as much as his poker know-how to introduce other improvements: a maximum of six players at the table, for instance, filmed by sixteen cameras, rather than nine players by four, in an extravagant, neon-lit setting rather than some dull, unadorned casino card room; games would be edited down to two hours (at Berman's insistence) rather than just one; better graphics, showing not just players' names and their hole cards, above the flop, but their changing percentage chances of winning the pot, the current total of which would also be shown top-left of the screen; more experienced, informed commentators; and pop-up panels explaining any 'poker-speak' – which players were at first asked to keep to a minimum.

And there would be no deals – for years standard practice towards the end of tournaments, often refereed (and so enforced) by the tournament director. Deals by the few players left standing – to split the money in proportion to the chip stacks and play on purely for the trophy – are the norm in the modern tournament world. They are not considered unethical. 'After all,' as Berman put it, 'in poker tournaments the players pony up their own cash so why shouldn't they have a right to make a deal if they so choose?' But, in Lipscomb's view, if poker were to become another TV sport, viewers would feel 'ripped off' to learn that deals were being made behind closed doors and that the excitement of winning was faked. 'It is immeasurably exciting to see someone playing for a million bucks. For the integrity of turning poker into a mainstream sport, we cannot allow deals, just like other sports could not allow it.'

For several years Lyle Berman had also been vainly hawking around a similar notion: plans for a televised pro tour that would turn poker into the next PGA, NBA or NFL. When Lipscomb first approached him with his own version, Berman was playing in the World Series and had just lost a big pot. 'At that moment,' he recalls, 'I would have preferred to choke Steve, but, frankly, I was interested in what he had to say.'

So Berman got involved – persuading the board of his company, Lakes Entertainment, to buy 80 per cent of the WPT, leaving Lipscomb and his partners 20 per cent. Beyond the two-hour time frame Berman also saw the inherent viewer appeal, unique in TV sports, of amateurs competing against professionals, sometimes beating them. He also insisted on a minimum of twelve tournaments – in the WPT's fourth season, up to seventeen – 'so that the television industry, the advertisers and the viewers would see the events as a series, not a one- or two-part special or documentary'. He told Lipscomb to start shooting even before he had a TV deal and he would personally guarantee to get the programmes on air.

Above all, believed Berman, the timing was right. Gambling was no longer the 'taboo' word it had been in the 1980s, when he had first tried to persuade TV moguls to give poker a whirl. In the meantime, before the internet began to rob casinos of their customers, legalised poker had spread rapidly right across the country where for so long it had been the sole preserve of Nevada, New Jersey and, since the mid-1980s, California. Add the current craze for reality TV and, 'we had the ultimate "Survivor", a guy or gal that could outlast six competitors and take home a million bucks or more – all in two hours!'

In the future Berman can see interactive TV poker with play-ers at home choosing their favourite player at the table, shutting off all hole cards but his or hers and seeing whether they would play the hand the same way. Maybe, one day, you could even bet on it.

Lipscomb converted Mike Sexton's role into that of expert commentator, alongside the dashing Vince Van Patten, a former tennis pro who had caught the poker bug from the home games of his father, the TV actor Dick Van Patten. Vince got the job thanks to a reference from his then sister-in-law, Shana Hiatt, who had been hired to add a bit of glamour up front as host and interviewer. The first episode of the *World Poker Tour* – the Five Diamond Classic at the Bellagio, won by 'the Great Dane', Gus Hansen – took eight months to edit, reducing around 150 hands to thirty. 'Working ten to fifteen hours a day, seven days a week,' says Lipscomb, 'we invented a new language – graphic and oth-erwise – to translate poker into a televised sport.'

Sexton and Van Patten 'winged' the commentary, then waited alongside Lipscomb for the response. Three weeks after it went out in March, Van Patten heard the radio talk-show host Rush Limbaugh say on air: 'I just saw a great show called the *World Poker Tour*. It's fascinating!' He knew then, says Van Patten, that 'it was going to be big'. Two years later, in Lipscomb's words, the WPT series 'has captured the imagina-tion of the American television audience' – and has been much copied, as its ratings soared.

By the end of its first year the WPT leapt to the top of the Travel Channel's ratings, drawing audiences of five million viewers, which *increased* by 30 per cent on the reruns. Sports magazines and mainstream newspapers began to run awestruck features about the 'poker boom' sweeping America, attributing it directly to the WPT. Berman's favourite remark on poker's arrival as a 'cultural phenomenon' came from Kathy Redmond, now director of poker operations at the Venetian in Las Vegas, then still at Foxwoods, the Native American casino in Connecticut – one of countless card rooms around the country where the popularity of TV poker had increased business at the tables by as much as 30 to 40 per cent. 'People have been play-ing for so long around the kitchen table,' she said. 'It's a combination of America's pastime with the American Dream.'

Once Hollywood discovered poker and saw the giant num-bers behind its sudden popularity, a host of imitators followed in 2004 and 2005, some as sophisticated as Henry Orenstein's *Poker Superstars* for Fox, the *Heads Up Challenge* on NBC and *High Stakes Poker* (a cash-game show played for large amounts of real money), others as feeble as Bravo's *Celebrity Poker Challenge*. On this show I once saw the TV quiz host Bob Eubank try to fold Q-8 after a flop of 5-9-J – only to be told that there had been no bet, so he could stay in the hand for free. The turn brought a ten, and Eubank went all-in with his straight. Myself, I flipped over to another channel without waiting to see what happened and have strenuously avoided that show ever since.

How could it have taken me so long to get in on the WPT action? This is like a World Series main event every month. My bankroll being what it is, namely as slim as Amarillo Preston, I impose WSOP rules for the WPT, forbidding myself entry into the tournament unless I can somehow win the $10,000 fee rather than dig deep in my pocket for it. So I pay $1000 to enter a super-satellite with four hundred starters, of whom thirty-six will get into the tournament.

I last out the first couple of sessions okay. Then I call a raise with A-8 in position, to see the flop come A-8-9. I go all-in, to find myself called by a big stack holding 10-J. The turn brings a blank – then fifth street, of course, a queen. Rivered again, I sigh as I head outside for a cigarette. The odds were in my favour; I played the hand right. As Brunson says, 'You can't be afraid to lose all your chips.' But the other guy, in the least elegant of newish poker expressions, 'sucked out' on me. It happens all the time, to all sorts of players, but that doesn't stop it hurting. Hurting so much, sometimes, that you find yourself wondering why you bother. If I'm not going to play in this WPT tournament, why don't I just pack up and go home?

I'm dissuaded by a fellow Brit, John Gale, who has been at the same table. Now he offers a few words of sympathy out on the terrace of the Fontana Room as we watch the Bellagio's dancing fountains – quite a spectacle by night – reduced to their black tubular nakedness (while under repair) in the unsparingly bright light of the Vegas daytime. 'If you don't fancy another satellite,' says John, 'there's plenty of decent action over there in the card room.' That – and John's own example – is enough to start recharging my poker batteries.

Nine months before, in January 2005, John won the $900,000 first prize in PokerStars' Caribbean Adventure tournament at the Atlantis Resort in the Bahamas. Then a businessman from Bushey, Hertfordshire, he has since turned pro and made quite a name for himself on the tour. Gale is one of the game's true gentlemen, famed for hugging all his opponents in the Bahamas as, one by one, he knocked them out.

A fellow quinquagenarian, he is also living proof that poker life does not end at fifty – as even Brunson feared. But I've played several times at the same table as John, whose online training seems to have given him the aggressive style that is the hallmark of today's successful player. My own more traditional style of play, bred on the textbooks of Brunson, David Sklansky, Mason Malmuth, Mike Caro and others, is beginning to feel past its sell-by date. When I get back home, I must experiment more online. In the meantime, with the rest of the week still ahead of me in Vegas, I had better postpone my return to the felt and get back to the day job.

Up in my Bellagio suite I look morosely across the freeway to the red-and-purple monstrosity that is the Rio, where my adventure began in July and is due to end next summer. I've a long way to go if I want to have a shot at winning the world title there next August. Remembering that I have a more reliable income as a writer than a poker player, I punish myself for my poker ineptitude by settling down to correct the two sets of proofs I have brought with me, of two very different books reflecting both sides of my life right now: *All In*, my little pocket poker manual for beginners, and *The Man Who Wrote Mozart*, the story of Lorenzo Da Ponte, the womanising Jewish-born Catholic priest from Venice who would wind up as a grocer in New York after writing the libretti for Mozart's three greatest operas, *Le Nozze di Figaro*, *Don Giovanni* and *Così Fan Tutte*.

On page 163 I notice that I have said Da Ponte lost what little money he possessed playing poker during his two-month voyage from England to America in 1805. A quick check with the other book confirms my anxious suspicions: poker was not invented as such until those French sailors started landing in Louisiana in the 1820s. This potentially embarrassing error was wishful thinking on my part, I guess, while trying to spice up Da Ponte's departure for the New World, where he rose to become the first Professor of Italian at New York's Columbia University before winding up in an incongruous grave in Queens, with the jets into JFK roaring overhead. So what game *did* the old rogue play on that Nantucket schooner? We have no evidence beyond his own unreliable memoirs – which don't say. With great regret, I play safe by deleting the word 'poker' and replacing it with 'cards'.

Next day, still deflated by my poor performance in the satellite, I deny myself the temptation of a lesser tournament by mooching round the Bellagio's amazing art gallery, which originally housed Steve Wynn's extensive collection of Post-Impressionist work. Now it hosts a changing array of itinerant exhibitions, currently Van Gogh – not the kind of treat for which people usually flock to Vegas. The crowds are thinner than they would be at the Tate or National Gallery in London; in fact there's hardly anyone here at all, apart from two elderly couples and a small, for once quiet, attentive school group. You can actually lean right in and marvel at those great clomps of paint, tortured into agonised swirls, unique to this crazed creator. Why, beyond the merely aesthetic, do I love Van Gogh's tactile paintings so much? Because, I realise, he took such huge risks. It's time I got back to doing the same.

By my standards, anyway. On offer in the Bellagio card room is a No Limit Hold 'em cash game at a choice of several levels, from $2–$5 blinds (sit-down $200) via $5–$10 ($400–$1000) to $10–$20 ($800). There's a seat open at the $2–$5 table. I grab it and unpeel two hundred dollars.

No Limit Hold 'em is my game but I had never played it in a casino for cash – as opposed to tournament chips – before my visits here three months ago during the 2005 World Series, when it proved such a lucrative discovery. The principle behind it still seems to me, as I examine the other faces around the table, and note the size of their chip-stacks, pretty straightforward: you just have to be sure you double up the first time you go all-in, and take it from there. You can work your buy-in up to a thousand, then lose it and you've still only lost two hundred dollars. As it were. But the worst that can happen is that you take out another two hundred and start all over again.

For once Anna K does me proud and I manage to double up early on when a paired ace on the flop gets called by an ambitious pair of queens. Well, it is the weekend and the tourists are in town; at this low-limit table, by the standards of the room, some of these players are drunk and devil-may-care. My kind of fish. I run up a profit of $800 before some cocky late-night lawyers – here for a convention, I gather from their loud, dull, boozy exchanges – fill up the empty seats at the table. My ambition to win back my $1000 satellite entry fee is realised on the first hand when I catch a flush on the river after semi-bluffing an obviously made hand (which turns out to be the top two pairs) with A-7 suited. 'My little sister can play better poker than you,' declares the sore loser – clearly one of the many who has learnt his poker etiquette from TV – before I proceed to win $1500 more off him and his internet-trained pals. This should cover not just the satellite but the hotel room when I check out. Only when these drunken lawyers have had enough do I, too, manage to quit while still two grand ahead.

On my way out of the Bellagio card room around 3 a.m., I stop by the *salle privée*, named 'Bobby's Room' after Bobby Baldwin, and through its glass walls behold two tables of the great names of poker playing $4000–$8000 limit games across all the different disciplines: Brunson, Johnny Chan, Daniel Negreanu, Gus Hansen, Jennifer Harman, Lyle Berman. If I was tired enough to quit while ahead, these people (I catch myself thinking) must be *really* degenerate gamblers. Is this how they relax after playing tournament poker all day? Playing high-stakes cash games all night?

In later conversations, none of them deny it. 'Sure, we're all degenerate gamblers,' says Brunson. 'Especially those dumb enough to blow their poker winnings at other types of betting: craps, the horses, football, whatever. I used to do a lot of sports betting but I've tried to cut it all out in recent years.' At least one other player at that table, however, is likely to blow all his hard-earned winnings at the craps table he has to pass on his way out of the casino. This is known in the trade as a 'leak'.

Even in their time off from time off, true rounders like these relax by playing 'Chinese poker', a desperate variant in which four players are dealt thirteen cards each – the entire deck, in other words – of which they then have to make the best three poker hands (of five, five and three cards respectively). The game is played for points, which with these guys will add up to six figures.

How much, I wonder, do they win and lose in their sleep?

At the other end of the Bellagio's plush card room – widely regarded as the best in Vegas and so in the world (at least before the advent of its sleek rival at the Wynn) – there is a raised area for high-stakes games, its walls lined with expressionist portraits of the top players, many of them on display as their real selves in Bobby's Room. In the first few years of the twenty-first century, this was the scene of the biggest cash game ever played – as chronicled by Michael Craig, with whom I have a date for brunch the next day.

I'd met Mike at the World Series in July but only now was I really getting to know him. An engaging, garrulous connoisseur of the poker world, he started out as a lawyer with an obsession for poker. With a couple of legal textbooks to his name, he made his reputation as a poker authority with *The Professor, The Banker and the Suicide King*, which chronicles this biggest of all cash games in rich and scary detail. Rumours about the game had been swirling through Vegas and beyond for several years. But it took Craig's doggedness to piece together the definitive account, gleaned from sources notoriously reluctant to talk about such things.

In 2001 a billionaire Texas banker called Andy Beal challenged a team of pros put together by Doyle Brunson to play heads-up poker at limits of $10,000 and $20,000. The pros were used to playing at the highest levels, of course, but tended to peak at $4000–$8000. Beal's edge was to have moved even the world's biggest players above their 'comfort zone'; this game, said Brunson, could threaten nothing less than the entire 'poker economy'. His team to take on Beal consisted of himself, his son Todd, Todd's ex-girlfriend Jennifer Harman, Johnny Chan, Howard Lederer, Barry Greenstein, Chip Reese, Ted Forrest

and others. Beal agreed to this, thereby granting the professionals, collectively known as 'The Corporation', a considerable
edge.

But Beal is not just a gifted poker player. He is also a high-cal-
ibre mathematician, with a special interest in Fermat's Last
Theorem. At home in Dallas he wrote a custom-built poker
programme through which he ran literally millions of hands to
calculate (and memorise) the odds in any given situation. To
avoid tells, he attempted to eliminate his personality by donning
wraparound shades and headphones to shut out distracting
noise and all backchat. Then battle commenced, with the blinds
gradually escalating to an astonishing $100,000–$200,000.

It lasted, on and off, for more than three years. There were
sessions where Beal would win as much as $12 million, others
where the pros would win more. One of Beal's edges was to get
them to play at 7 a.m., not an hour favoured by many of the
world's top players. But most sessions would, of course, run to
marathon lengths, giving the edge back to the pros, who could
take over from each other while Beal played his lone game. In
the end, if not by much, he finished a loser; yet Craig's account
of his heroics makes him sound like a winner.

The next morning I tell Mike of my dismal performance in
the satellite, and wonder how he got on himself. After about half
the players had been eliminated, apparently, he got moved to
the same table as Mel Judah, who has two World Series
bracelets and a WPT win to his name. Low on chips, Craig
opened the pot by going all-in with A-6 on Judah's big blind.
Judah called with A-Q and . . .

I filled the pained silence with: 'You know that Mel used to
play in our Tuesday Game in London? We wound up kicking
him out – for being too good. So how is he doing?'

'Better, now that he's got all my chips,' fumed Mike. 'You
guys obviously didn't kick him far enough.'

*

As the big tournament begins without me – but with Doyle Brunson, of all people, on the WPT's featured TV table – I run into Mike Sexton at the entrance to the Bellagio's Fontana Room, which has been turned into a TV studio for the duration. Naturally, Mike does not tape his WPT commentaries until after the event, when the programme has been edited down; indeed, he tells me, it is illegal for him to know the players' hole cards while the tournament is still in progress. Maybe 25 per cent of the wit and wisdom he shares with Vince Van Patten makes it into the final cut.

I used to know Mike to say hello to when he was a journeyman professional in the late 1980s and I was briefly attempting to attain the same status myself. But it's unfair, in retrospect, to call Sexton a journeyman, as he was (and still is) far better than that; while never in the very top rank of professional players, he has a World Series bracelet to his name and several big tournament wins, including a European title and the first $10,000 buy-in event at Foxwoods. Here in Las Vegas, at the Orleans, he also started the Tournament of Champions of Poker – an invitational event designed to create an exclusive professional poker tour along the lines of those run by most other major American sports.

Mike seems gratifyingly pleased to see me – or maybe he's just glad to get away from the fans drowning him in bad beat stories (with which, nonetheless, he is infinitely patient). 'I dunno, Tony,' he says, 'I remember when guys like you and me used to scratch around all year for the $10k to enter the World Series main event. Now there's a $10k tournament somewhere every week.' Not to mention the $25k ones.

Mike's certainly making great money from the WPT these days and holds a stake in PartyPoker. But does he miss playing on the poker tour? 'Not really. I still get to play a few tournaments a year, but that's enough for me.' Sexton remembers all too painfully the hardship that can go with being a poker pro. 'Everyone gets bad runs as well as good. All poker pros worth their salt know what it's like to go broke every so often. People think it looks glamorous but it's a very tough life.' For the vast majority of itinerant players on the tournament circuit, there are all the travelling and hotel expenses on top of the substantial entry fees – which adds up to an annual budget well into six figures. Only the top 10 per cent get into the money in any given tournament, which means that 90 per cent don't. And few are adroit enough to cover their costs in the side games.

As Sexton recalls ruefully, it doesn't matter what level you play at; you still have to grind it out, to 'put the hours in'. And those hours are long and hard, often losing. 'I'm relieved to be spared all that these days. It's such a tough life. It can be so frustrating, so draining. You play your heart out, you play perfect, you get your money in with the best hand and *still* you get beat. You have no control over it.'

He may make a more reliable living these days, but Sexton has earned his crust. Nine months before PartyPoker launched, the founders asked him to go to India. They had been in the online gaming business for four years and now wanted to open the poker site. Six months into developing the software, they were looking for someone who could bring the site credibility.

So in January 2001 Sexton went to India, despite knowing nothing about computers, to find he'd be working with a software team who knew nothing about poker. They didn't even understand why the dealer button had to go round the table. Mike was there for two months, showing the team how to make the game work online.

Then he went down to the Dominican Republic for another four months, to train the customer support people. When PartyPoker launched in August 2001, it was Sexton's idea to embellish it with the announcement of a tournament on a cruise liner, known as the PartyPoker Million. The following year PartyPoker hooked up with the WPT and the whole thing took off – with Sexton lucky enough to have a foot in both camps. When Party was the first online site to advertise on tel-evision – strictly as dot-net – business quadrupled in a month.

Compare the Bellagio's card room, with some thirty tables, to the two thousand cash games available every night on PartyPoker. In commercial terms, it's no contest. But I still prefer the cut and thrust of real poker across a 'live' stretch of green baize – and head back there to check out the NLHE action.

The following day I awake at noon, having gone to bed at 4 a.m. another $800 to the good. This is one of the best feelings in the world: to awake, take a minute to work out where you are – and then remember, despite your dismay that there's no one in bed beside you, that you fell asleep last night a winner.

After a restorative brunch, again with Mike Craig, I decide to invest $500 of my winnings in today's Bellagio tournament – and last all of an hour until my all-in pocket queens are called by pocket jacks and pocket kings, making the board of 10-10-9-4-A academic – to me, at any rate. So my spirits sink back through the floor. Had I *really* expected to get anywhere in that tournament? You've got to start thinking like a winner . . .

The truth is that my tournament confidence level is low. I seem able to do fine in the cash games, where you know that you can always fish in your pocket for more money if you suffer a bad beat. But the extra discipline required in tournaments, where the ele-ment of luck is so much higher and one mistake can see you knocked out, is making me play much too tight against all these internet-trained belligerents. And my mind is too much on the other worlds I inhabit – writing, music, my football team, my love life – when expertise at poker demands tunnel vision. I still love the game as much as ever, not least because you see something new every time you sit down, finding out more about the human race with every session you play. But do I love it enough to grant it the exclusive attention needed to succeed in the obsessive, hugely com-petitive world of today's top players? Maybe, as yet, not.

Feeling the need for a break, for some exercise and fresh air (as if there were such a thing in this city), I sentence myself to the cruel and unusual punishment – in Vegas terms – of a long walk: at first from the Bellagio to Caesar's Palace, home of Amarillo Slim's Superbowl of Poker last time I was on the circuit, now without a card room (but fast building itself a shiny new one). Thence, by way of Frank Sinatra Avenue, to the Mirage, scene of many happy memories, whose card room is as bustling as ever. Then across the freeway to the Venetian, which improbably reminds me that I've still much work to do on the proofs of my book about Da Ponte, a Venetian no one here will have heard of.

The Venetian, too, has no card room – but is also, I am told, in the throes of constructing a huge one. Suddenly downcast by the new poker and all its works, I jump in a cab downtown to Binion's, where the biggest game on offer is a derisory $2–$5 Limit Hold 'em. And even that's short-handed. I wolf down a hot dog before crossing Fremont Street to the Golden Nugget, also awash with memories, to discover that it *does* these days boast a card room. Impulsively, I plonk down $200 to enter its evening tournament. With forty-some starters at five tables that means a first prize of $4000. Which, soon after midnight, I win.

The advantages of positive thinking. What, this time, did I do right? I have no idea. At least that's the air fare covered now, as well as the hotel. Okay, it was only a small tournament, but how did I manage to win it? All I can think of is that the spectre of Eric Drache must be stalking me. The Nugget is where I first met Eric, then manager of its card room as well as tournament director of the World Series, back in the mid-1980s. Once the world champion at seven-card stud, his character and career are all but defined by the story that a magazine later ranked him the seventh-best stud player in the world, adding sourly: 'His problem is that he only likes to play with the top six.'

And I am meeting Eric for dinner the following evening. Maybe I needed to have some positive news for him, recalling those good old downtown days, and an excuse to remind him of that magazine's canny judgment, which always makes us both laugh. 'I know, I know, it's true,' Eric smiles with a note of wistfulness, as he has since seen hard times while many of his friends and contemporaries have gone on to cash in big-time on the poker boom. At the end of the 1980s, when Steve Wynn built the Mirage, he moved Eric there from the Nugget to open one of the few card rooms on the Strip. Smack in the middle of the gaming floor, to draw curious tourists into the depths of the casino, under Eric's direction the room proved more successful than most. Usually he would be sitting up in its top left-hand corner, playing high-stakes stud with his back to the room; even so, you could tell that he was in touch with everything going on behind him. All would go well, I was told by one Wynn-watcher, 'until the day Steve figures Eric out' – Wynn was apparently fascinated by Drache's mercurial, enigmatic character. But fate intervened in the shape of the Internal Revenue; Drache was prosecuted for unpaid taxes and lost his gaming licence.

There followed a dark period during which he lived in his car in Los Angeles, making furtive visits to Vegas (where he owed a lot of money) to see his partner, Micky, and their two young daughters. Once, in the mid-1990s, he failed to make a meeting we had planned with Alvarez because he couldn't afford the air fare from LA to Vegas. Eric had hit skid row.

Then two poker bigwigs came to his rescue. The first was Larry Flynt, owner of *Hustler* magazine, who sought Eric's advice while building a Hustler casino in southern Los Angeles and then in recruiting the right players for the high-stakes poker game he still hosts there. The other was Henry Orenstein, inventor of the under-the-table camera which has revolutionised televised poker, who retains Drache as a consultant on his various TV poker initiatives. 'I'm Henry's eyes and ears in

Vegas,' Eric tells me, urging me to go see the great man at his home in New Jersey.

That day, as it happens, brings 0.93 inches of rain, the highest single-day rainfall in the history of Las Vegas. 'That's amazing,' says Eric, the prototype Vegas man, who never ventures outside. 'I didn't think it *ever* rained here.'

Dinner for two in the Bellagio's Circo restaurant, including two bottles of pricey wine, comes to $480. We split it, and Eric leaves a $100 tip. Such, in Vegas, are hard times.

Back at the Bellagio, after four days and nights of play, a Vegas pro named Minh Ly finally bested Dan Harrington in the heads-up for the $1 million first prize in the WPT's Doyle Brunson North American Poker Championship.

Not until a few months later did I realise that maybe it was a *good* thing that I had failed to qualify for it. Beyond my handsome profit in the side games, in which I might not otherwise have played, participation would have involved my signing the WPT's release form, already the subject of heated debate among the professionals and to become more so as the year progressed. As the tournament began I looked on while Full Tilt's Andy Bloch registered strong objections to the terms of the release form he was required to sign before playing. The paragraph to which so many pros objected, leading to a boycott by Howard Lederer, Annie Duke, Chris Ferguson, Phil Gordon and Bloch, plus the reigning and last world champions, Joe Hachem and Greg Raymer, reads as follows:

[Player's name] hereby irrevocably grants to WPT the right to film, record, edit, reproduce and otherwise use [Player's name]'s photograph, likeness, signature, biographical information, appearance, actions (including without limitation, revealing Player's hole cards), conversations . . . and/or voice . . . in, and in connection with, the Programs

and/or the 'World Poker Tour' . . . and any and all deriv-
ative, allied, subsidiary and/or ancillary uses related
thereto (including, without limitation, merchandising, commercial tie-ins, publications, home entertainment, video
games, commodities, etc.), in whole or in part, by any and
all means, media, devices, processes and technology now
or hereafter known or devised in perpetuity throughout
the universe.

'By any and all means . . . in perpetuity throughout the universe': by the end of my year back on the circuit this would be
the target of an anti-trust suit by the players unwilling to sign
their images away to Steve Lipscomb's voracious marketing
machine.

Such, in Lipscomb's mind, was by now the power of the
WPT. Yet Doyle Brunson, intriguingly enough, was among
those who did not at first have faith in it. Becky Binion's World
Series was another, declining Lipscomb's invitation to join the
WPT – as did her brother Jack, whose advice was sought by
Brunson and Chip Reese when Lyle Berman approached them
to sink a million dollars each of their own money into the proj-
ect.

This was before Berman had gone to the board of his own
Lakes Entertainment, about whose reaction he admits he was
apprehensive. 'Our board is not as aggressive as I am with start-
ups and new ideas, and many times they have said to me, "Lyle,
we love you, but we just don't think this is a good business for us
to go into. Let's stick to our roots."'

Berman turned out, of course, to be wrong. His colleagues
were all enthusiastic – to the tune of $8 million. But not Jack
Binion, even to the tune of one. 'Man, that's a lot of money,'
Berman reports him as saying. 'I don't know who's going to
buy it, and I'm not sure anybody's going to watch it on television. Nah, I don't think I'm in.'

Binion then talked Brunson and Reese out of it, too – costing each, according to Berman, $45 million over the following three years. Both, obviously, later had their regrets, Reese confessing to his on his website: 'When Lyle Berman . . . offered me a chance to buy in [to the WPT], I was so gun-shy from failed investments that I turned it down. Life's strange. Here I am, all my life taking shots at shaky investments having nothing to do with poker. Many of those shots are doomed from the get-go, and here's one with the right people behind it, with the right vision, at the right time, involving the right game – my game – and I turn it down. Yeah, life's strange, and so are the choices that people make in life.'

Brunson seems to have regretted it even more. Back in July, right in the middle of the 2005 World Series, he had created a huge buzz in the poker world by launching a $700 million bid for the WPT, which six months later – just after my return to the Bellagio – resulted in an investigation by America's Securities and Exchange Commission (SEC).

Brunson's offer was around twice the size of the California-based company's market value at the time. The stock's value had shot up in frenzied trading, then slid rapidly back down again when the offer expired, without further action, four days later. In its suit the SEC said Brunson's offer 'caused WPT's stock price to rise sharply. But, soon after publicising the offer, Brunson and his attorneys abruptly backed off it, refusing even to respond to WPT's requests for more information. This caused WPT's stock to nosedive, costing investors tens of millions of dollars in lost market value.'

'On its face,' the suit alleged, 'this conduct implicates possible violations of the anti-fraud provisions of the federal securities laws.' The lawsuit says the agency would seek to discover why Brunson made the buyout offer and 'whether anyone connected to Brunson or the offer improperly traded WPT's stock'.

Brunson's offer for the WPT, which had gone public in

August 2004 at $8 a share, was valued at about $34 a share. The stock jumped from $17.75 on the day before the offer to as high as $29.50; it then started sliding, falling below $10 a share by September. Six months later the price remained stuck down at $7.09. When the agency subpoenaed Brunson's testimony in the matter, according to the SEC, 'he invoked his Fifth Amendment right against self-incrimination'. And there, for now, the matter rests.

5

From Yale to Walsall

In the middle of the window of the Yale University book-shop – yes, *that* Yale, in New Haven, Connecticut – sits a large pile of *Busting Vegas: The MIT Whiz Kid Who Brought the Casinos to their Knees*, Ben Mezrich's bestseller about a big-time blackjack scam by a group of savvy student geeks from, er, another university not that far away.

So that's what Ivy Leaguers are studying these days. On either side of it are novels by Zadie Smith and Umberto Eco, the kind of extra-curricular Eng. Lit. I might myself have been reading at Oxford forty years ago. Oh, and the latest offering from Salman Rushdie – who, come to think of it, is a bit of a poker player himself, with an exaggerated view of my own abilities. Every time I approach Salman at one of the literary dos where we occasionally meet, he holds out his arms as if to fend me off, with cries of: 'No, no, I *won't* play poker with you.' Ah, the price one pays for once having even masqueraded as a professional.

Wandering around the store with Michael Craig, I embarrass us both by wondering a bit too loud why on earth there is a huge, wall-size poster of the dread George W. Bush in this mighty (and supposedly liberal) institution. Ah yes, of course, the American President partied away his youth here at Yale. Silly me, I'd quite forgotten. Besides, by now we've reached the biography and religious studies departments, between which is a table groaning under the weight of several stacks of books about poker, with a large pile of Craig's in the centre. And some of Alvarez's. But none of mine.

Usual, I sigh to myself, story. Mike meanwhile rushes around in high excitement, introducing himself to the staff and offering to sign all his books, as I would naturally have done myself in his situation. In the old scribblers' motto, 'A copy signed is a copy sold.'

Craig is the reason I've come here to Yale, en route to another WPT tournament, the World Poker Finals, at nearby Foxwoods. This afternoon he is to give a lecture on poker at the university he insists on calling 'YAY-EL'. Mike is incapable of saying the name except in the capital letters that symbolise both his pride and his disbelief at being invited to talk here. As if to prove to himself that it's true – that he's going to give a talk about poker at 'YAY-EL' – this alumnus of Michigan University buys himself and his family a lifetime's supply of Yale mugs, sweatshirts and other memorabilia.

After lunch, during which he promises to give me a mention (well, I have come a long way to support him), we head over to Branford College, where the talk will take place over a Master's Tea hosted by Steve Smith, political philosopher and Master of Branford. Smith tells us they have already entertained such august poker writers as James McManus, Andy '*Poker Nation*' Bellin and Brett D. Fromson, author of a history of Foxwoods. Suddenly the room is full of students, and an excited Craig is off and running before he's even been introduced.

Craig's on a high. He has just spent twenty-four hours with his friend Mike 'the Mouth' Matusow, whom he visited in jail

several times earlier in the year. Matusow had just atoned for his
World Series exit by winning the $1 million first prize at
November's WSOP Tournament of Champions; he might have
missed the final table, had Craig not tiptoed into his house and
woken him up a few hours before it was due to start. Today
Craig is even wearing a Full Tilt baseball shirt – number eight,
as in Matusow – for, yes, this, the finest hour of his life so far
here at 'YAY-EL'. The students promptly offer to purchase it for
$1000. But Mike regards it as beyond price.

Craig is the kind of guy who talks a lot even when no one is
asking him questions. The students have trouble getting a word
in, but it soon becomes clear that they are interested less in
poker strategy than personalities. They want to hear inside stories, and Craig has no trouble changing gears. In fact, they
come pouring out. Meeting eyes with Doyle Brunson for the
first time, before Doyle knew of him or his book project, and
receiving a disapproving glare ('The man's still got it,' Mike
told the students). How did Ted Forrest lose the Lincoln Mark
VIII that Craig describes in the introduction of *Suicide King*?
Forrest repossessed the car of a gambler who owed him and
others more than a million dollars, then felt bad about leaving
the guy without a car, so he gave him his own. Having Daniel
Negreanu tell him how easy it is to lose five million dollars.
How the pros lie about the size of their losses, just like every
losing sucker in a home game.

Barry Greenstein, Craig tells his rapt audience, has to date
given $4m to charity; although far from rich (contrary to
received wisdom) when he left the computer business, his net
worth is now some $10 million. Howard Lederer's is between
five and ten. Yes, Craig agrees, guys like these are '*very* lucky to
have come good in the unprecedented era of celebrity and
internet poker'.

To the question 'So what do they think of each other?', Mike
gives engagingly candid answers. He could go on all night, but

all good things must come to an end. After more schmoozing over drinks we are taken off to dinner at Mory's, the campus restaurant with comely female 'glee singers', who serenade us as we tell tall poker tales. Craig is still stunned to have given a lecture on anything, let alone poker, at Yale, as indeed am I to have witnessed it. We log it as yet another index of the remarkable rise of the new poker, so much of which breeds on college campuses – even, it seems, in the Ivy League.

Next morning we are heading for another specialist corner of the new poker world – a Native American casino, as exemplified by nearby Foxwoods.

Since the Brunson event at the Bellagio, I had been back in Blighty for a while, letting my poker slip by concentrating more on the Job. But the game kept butting into what passed for my normal routine. Two female friends who are fans of *The Archers* told me that now they were playing poker even on this long-running, super-safe BBC radio soap opera supposedly about 'the everyday life of country folk'; some bloke down at The Bull had apparently lost all of a hundred grand. The once venerable *Times* newspaper, these days shrunk to a tabloid, began to devote a whole page to poker every Saturday. And none other than Doyle Brunson started writing a weekly poker column in the po-faced *Sunday Telegraph*. Who would ever have believed it?

Or that a book I wrote twenty years ago could have moved a Japanese teenager to murder her mother? This was the news that leapt off the page of my newspaper in early November. Under the headline, 'Japanese Girl Poisoner Inspired by UK Serial Killer', I read in the *Guardian* that a seventeen-year-old Tokyo girl had admitted poisoning her mother with the heavy metal poison thallium. A promising chemistry student, she apparently recorded her mother's deterioration in her weblog, along with photographs taken as the poor woman lay in a coma.

'She had been inspired', the report continued, 'by Graham

Young, who was convicted of killing three people and poisoning dozens in the 1960s and 1970s. During a search of the girl's bedroom police found and took away a copy of Anthony Holden's book, *The St Albans Poisoner: The Life and Crimes of Graham Young*.'

One of the few books of mine that has been translated into Japanese, and indeed filmed (as *The Young Poisoner's Handbook*), my 1974 treatise on Graham Young was written when I was a cub reporter on a local paper in rural Hertfordshire, for which I covered Young's trial for multiple murder. It was bad enough with *Big Deal*, the forerunner of this book, which turned out to possess the potential to ruin at least as many lives as it left where they were. Maybe it was dumb of me, but not even the possibility had crossed my mind as I was writing it. Now I was in demand on Japanese TV as the author of a book that had inspired a horrifying copycat murder.

'Marvellous,' emailed my novelist friend John David Morley, a Japanese specialist, whom the news had reached at his home in Munich. 'You should feel highly honoured. To move a reader to admiration is as far as most writers aspire. To move a reader to murder is the highest accolade granted us here on earth. Congratulations!'

That was not quite how I saw it myself as I packed my bags for Connecticut. 'Know that we're proud of you,' Morley went on, still in defiantly dubious taste. 'To have Japanese girls killing their mothers in your name . . . You could become the leader of a cult. I think it might be Tokyo, not New York, to which you should be headed.'

The following May, the girl (who could not be named 'for legal reasons') would be convicted and sent to a juvenile correctional facility 'for treatment'. It was not, I managed to persuade myself, my fault; but I could not shake a feeling of guilt by proxy.

*

Japan was still on my mind, post-the Master's tea at Yale, as Craig's rented roadster sped up the I-95 from New Haven to Foxwoods. Through the beautiful, auburn-tinged forests of the New England autumn we cruised, until we rounded a corner near the small town of Ledyard to confront the most unexpected, almost unearthly sight.

In the middle of this idyllic nowhere someone had built a huge Walt Disney castle, its blue ramparts and red towers a gross offence to the eastern Connecticut countryside. Who on earth had granted planning permission for this act of architectural vandalism? No one, it turned out, for we were on self-governing Native American territory, in the heart of the Mashantucket Pequot Tribal Nation.

Native Americans have occupied this area of south-eastern Connecticut for more than ten thousand years. In the early seventeenth century, just before the arrival of European settlers, the Pequots had approximately eight thousand members inhabiting 250 square miles of Mashantucket. But the Pequot War (1636–38), the first major conflict between the colonists and an indigenous New England people, proved devastating. It took more than three centuries of slavery and oppression – at the lowest point, in the early nineteenth century, there were only thirty to forty Pequot tribal members still living on vastly diminished territory – before a resettlement programme in the 1970s emboldened the tribe to file suit against neighbouring landowners to recover land sold by the State of Connecticut in the middle of the nineteenth century.

In 1983, after much arm-twisting, the Connecticut Legislature petitioned the federal government to grant the tribe recognition as such and so settle its land claims. With help from the Connecticut delegation in Washington, the Mashantucket Pequot Indian Land Claims Settlement Act was finally enacted by the US Congress and signed into law by President Reagan on 18 October 1983. It gave the tribe federal recognition, enabling it to repurchase and place in trust the land covered in the Settlement Act.

Now the reservation is 1250 acres, used at first for such (none too successful) commercial enterprises as the sale of cord wood, maple syrup and garden vegetables, a swine project and the opening of a hydroponic greenhouse. Once the land claims were settled, the tribe purchased and operated a restaurant, and established a sand and gravel business. In 1986 it opened a bingo operation, followed in 1992 by the first phase of the Foxwoods Resort Casino.

This has now brought the Pequots the economic security they had so long sought. And then some. The tribe also owns ship-building and pharmaceutical companies, and several inns and hotels. But it is thanks to the Indian Gaming Regulatory Act of 1988, authorising Native Americans to open casinos on their autonomous reservations, that the Pequots' future is looking decidedly rosy for the first time in nearly four hundred years.

That's the official version, anyway, as gleaned from the Pequots themselves. The true story of years of political intrigue and lobbying, of a handful of Pequots struggling to prove that they did indeed constitute a tribe, of political manoeuvring that saw off the opposition of Governor Lowell Weicker and a local challenge from none other than Steve Wynn – all this and more has been expertly told in Brett Fromson's fascinating study *Hitting the Jackpot: The Inside Story of the Richest Indian Tribe in History*.

Despite its downbeat ending, amid the usual tales of crime, drugs and violence attendant upon big-time gambling, this is the remarkable tale of how the tribal leader Richard 'Skip' Hayward delivered on his promise to make every Mashantucket Pequot a millionaire – a lot of them (including, of course, himself) many times over. Some see it as a quintessentially American tale of greed and ambition, lobbyists and lawyers, others as the Pequots' just reward for centuries of oppression.

Either way, as Fromson concludes, 'What makes the Pequots so remarkable is that they have achieved the American dream by redefining themselves as an American Indian tribe. Led by talented lawyers, they managed to leverage the barest trace of Indian descent into a fortune akin to the Rockefeller family.'

'No one will come all the way out here in the woods for bingo,' people said when the Mashantucket Pequots decided to build a high-stakes bingo hall on this spot in 1986. They couldn't have been more wrong. Nearly twenty years later, it has grown into the world's largest casino – or casinos, to be precise, six beneath the same roof, with 340,000 square feet of gaming in a complex covering nearly five million. By 2007 it will be seven million, after a $700 million development under way during my visit that, while upping the number of employees to 13,500, was due to boost the number of poker tables from 76 to 114.

When Mike Craig and I passed beneath the glass-domed entrance into the Grand Pequot Tower, the smartest of Foxwoods' three hotels, we were gratified to find ourselves ushered to the VIP check-in where staff told us that we were both to be 'comped' for the week by the World Poker Tour. This was a very pleasant surprise. As I had flown out on air miles, this had all the makings of a trip whose expenses it would not be hard to cover. They would barely exist.

I checked into a large, handsome room with a stunning view out across the great Connecticut forest, before heading straight back downstairs to attempt to register for a tournament. First, I was told, I would need a Wampum card. What the heck was that? It's a frequent player card, apparently, that rewards your investment (i.e., losses) with prizes from iPods (no, thank you) to plasma-screen TVs (yes, please).

'Welcome, Mr Holden,' said the obsequious man in charge of this transaction. 'Are you related to our own Michael Holden?' No, I told him, I didn't think so. We Lancashire Holdens don't have much Native American blood. 'That's a pity, sir. Mike's a tribal elder, in charge of our bingo operations.' I began to wish I had said yes.

My main purpose in coming to Foxwoods (via, as Craig kept reminding me, YAY-EL) is to make my debut on the Seniors Tour. I figure the players may be just as good, but they're older and there aren't as many of them – and the entry fee is cheaper. When I turn up at the registration desk with my $500 buy-in, I am thrilled that the clerk asks me for ID. Does he really believe I don't look fifty? This is a good start to what feels like being a very good week in Native America.

Three months into my adventure, I confess, my poker confidence could do with a boost. In nights off the Job, or after a night out doing the Job, I've been playing plenty of online 'sit-and-gos' and winning or cashing in quite a few; but this was already my main area of expertise, now in urgent need of expansion. What is it within me that, despite my advancing years, is driving me on to the impossible dream of tilting at the world title? The money would come in handy, obviously, but I've realised that it is just as much a matter of pride: if you're going to claim expertise at something, you want to be regarded as the best. And I know I'm not. That's my problem. So let's start with a realistic assessment of how good I am in my own age group, the over-fifties.

The tournament, for reasons none of us old-timers can grasp, starts at the ungodly hour of ten the next morning. Why so early? No one seems to know, beyond the fact that oldsters don't sleep much – at conventional hours, anyway. As with every event I enter all year, there are a record number of starters: 471, of whom forty will get paid, with a first prize of $75,000. Deal me in.

I go into training with a couple of cigarettes in the smoking zone right outside the tournament area, glad to see so many other seniors here asserting their constitutional right to smoke.

Then it's back to my seat as the master of ceremonies, 'Oklahoma' Johnny Hale, introduces the oldest player, a guy of eighty-one called Paul something. It happens to be Veterans Day, so – American or not – we all stand for the Pledge of Allegiance. Amid a sea of Veteran and Vietnam caps, I decide this is not the place to voice opposition to the war in Iraq. Besides, it's time to shuffle up and deal.

Even God is playing in this tournament. Well, there's a guy at my table who looks just like him. I'm at Table 25, Seat Five. In Seat Eight is this serene old man with a long white beard. And he wins the first hand with Q-K over Q-8, when the board comes Q-Q-A-rags. Soon he's all over the table, calling a pre-flop raise of $200, then betting $600 with pocket sevens after a flop of A-K-10. God seems to know what he's doing; the other guy, who lamely folds, must have been pushing his luck pre-flop.

It's 10.25 a.m. On my small blind I call $50 with 8-8 and the flop comes 8-4-2. Seat Seven bets $200, Seat One calls, I raise $500 and they both fold. I make a note of the name of the dealer, Khamphoui. It's a thing I have.

Having started with $2k, I am up to $2745 by the first break. No one in the room has more than $3000, so I feel in reasonable shape. From the rail I get an encouraging thumbs-up from my friends Donnacha O'Dea and Willie Tann, two of fifty alternates still waiting for seats. It's reassuring that players of their stature, both winners of major tournaments, are as keen as me to get into this geriatric game.

There are plenty of rugs around today (on men's heads, that is), much evidence of Grecian 2000, numerous Zimmer frames, a few motorised wheelchairs and dozens of crutches and sticks. The wily Oklahoma Johnny, mastermind of the Seniors Tour, has even come up with the bright idea of the 'piss' chip: 'Suppose your turn comes to take the blind in the tournament – instead of using the regular tournament chips to post your blind, you could use your pissin' chip. That way, if you needed to go to the bathroom or take a quick nap, you get a free round.'

It's a smart idea but not yet in use – a pity, because the men's room is indeed busier than usual. Some players can't hear what you say, others can't see the flop. A few are proving Johnny's slogan that, 'Seniors don't take breaks, they take naps' – even at the table. Still, there's little or no taunting, bad-mouthing or other disrespect. On the Seniors Tour, it seems, everyone may be a bit slower but they're also a lot friendlier. There's a pleasant sense of camaraderie in the air.

I am still going fine at 12.10 p.m., when I get pocket aces under the gun. The blinds are now $50–$100 so I make it $300 to go. And get one caller. The flop brings a pair of tens. I bet $500 and he folds. Another 220 hands to go before *that* happens again.

12.20 p.m.: I get A-J and, with the blinds still at $50–$100, again make it $300 to play. The flop comes K-Q-10 – all diamonds. I bet $300 and the guy on my left makes it $750. Neither of my cards is a diamond. I think for a long time before . . . folding. Now I'm down to two thou, back where I started. There is much discussion of this particular hand at the table, with Grecian 2k to my right telling me I should have reraised: 'It would have been hard for him to call a raise from you, even if he'd flopped a straight.' Lefty, who bet me out, seems pleased with himself. Should I have checked his stack more carefully before putting him on diamonds, even a diamond draw? While thinking, he had made much of counting the chips he had left – rather more, I could see, than I did. Which should maybe have given me pause before betting into him.

12.30 p.m.: I am dealt 7-7 and the flop comes A-K-3. I bet an exploratory $250 and everyone folds. This is beginning to feel easier than a regular tournament.

12.45 p.m.: I am moved to Table 3, Seat Four. There are twenty-five tables left, i.e., 225 players, less than half the field. So I should have more than twice as much as I started with. But I can boast only $3k.

1.10 p.m.: Up to $3750. Thanks to 8-8 on my big blind (now $200), with a flop of 7-8-9, including two hearts. Out of position, first to act, I bet $500 and get two callers. The turn brings a third heart. I go all-in for $1250 and get a caller, who turns out to be drawing to heart flush. For once the river is a blank and I take down the pot.

By 1.15 p.m., with half an hour till lunch, we are down to two hundred players, by 1.30 p.m. down to 180. I am dealt J-J but wind up putting it down because I'm out of position. The guy before me makes it $600 to go so I feel like I made the right move. Soon there's only a minute or two left before lunch, with time for one more hand while elderly stomachs rumble. How glad I am that I took the precaution of treating myself to a cooked breakfast in my room this morning. My next move, however, goes wrong; I'm trying to steal the blinds, $100–$200, by making it $500 to go. Everyone folds to me – except the old-timer on my right, who raises another $500 to $1000. I put in an Oscar-winning display of agonised indecision before folding. But I've lost a thou in the last half-hour.

At the break I have $2750 – still less than the average – and now we discover it's not the lunch break, after all. Those rumbling stomachs are now grumbling. Dinner, we are told, will not be served till 5.30 p.m. 'Someone should have told us that earlier,' moans a snow-haired guy at the next table as he heads off in search of a burger.

1.55 p.m.: We resume. There are 180 players left. The blinds are still $100–$200 but now with antes of $25 a hand, so each round costs $550.

2.15 p.m.: Down to 160 players – we've lost two-thirds of the field.

2.25 p.m.: Down to 150 players, but I'm as low as $2k again. The cards have gone completely dead on me. I've played only one hand – which I lost – in the last twenty minutes.

2.45 p.m.: I steal the blinds to climb back to the heady heights of $1500.

2.50 p.m.: I go all-in to the tune of $1500 with A-Q against the chip leader, who calls me with 6-6. The board brings no paints at all. My tournament's over. I come 138th out of 471. Top third of the field. Not even top 20 per cent, let alone top ten and the money.

It's been fun, but a disappointing start to my career on the Seniors Tour. I had thought I might fare better without all the twenty-somethings, the super-aggressive Swedes, the iPodded hoodies. But these over-fifties know what they're doing, and all I've really managed here is to re-register in my psyche my medi-ocrity as a tournament player. At least I get a consolatory handshake from Oklahoma Johnny himself. That, for now, is all I'm going to get – beyond the uneasy feeling that I've done nothing to *deserve* to win a tournament like this. I'm a poker dil-ettante, a recreational player with no right to think he can hold his own with the pros. I've got to put in the hours.

Upstairs the huge Foxwoods card room feels like one giant, enticing home game, as cash games always do after the intense discipline of a tournament. This can be dangerous, so I decide to leave it till later and allow myself a satellite for this week's Big One, the $10,000 buy-in World Poker Finals. At my table is Steve Dannenmann, the genial, ever-smiling gent – a local here-abouts – who came second to Joe Hachem in the main event at this year's World Series.

I play rather loose – as usual after the strict discipline of tournament play – and exit in fourth place. Over I go to sign up for another, only to find that they've closed them down. Apparently they've run out of room for tomorrow's tournament. That's a bummer; I am consoled by a well-wined dinner with Mike Craig, his publisher Colin Fox of Time Warner and Des Wilson, who is high on 'winning' a tournament in the US, *any* tournament in the US.

In truth, as Des bashfully explains, he got to the last table of a $100 buy-in event as the short stack, then used his silky public relations skills to persuade the nine other players to carve up the money equally, to the tune of a handsome $800 each. So he can go to his grave boasting that he won a poker tournament in America. Not bad for the guy who founded Shelter, ran Friends of the Earth and the Campaigns for Freedom of Information and Lead-Free Petrol, was president of Paddy Ashdown's Liberal Democrats and a bigwig at such sporting organisations as the England and Wales Cricket Board, while knocking off a couple of novels and finally making himself some money at the airports company BAA. When I reel off this list of achievements by the New Zealander who came to England as a journalist in the 1960s, has gone poker-mad in his retirement and is now blushing and telling me to shut up, our American friends begin to see Des in a whole new light.

Later, fuelled by Dutch courage, I take a seat at the $5–$10 No Limit Hold 'em table where you can sit down with a minimum of $300, or a maximum of $500, rather than the strict $500 elsewhere. At my table I recognise Olga Varkonyi, wife of the 2002 world champion Robert, whom I then spot at the next table. Within a couple of hours I've won all of $2000. Maybe I should just stick to cash games? It's nearly 3 a.m. and it's been a long day, so I take considerable pleasure in quitting while ahead.

The next afternoon I manage to repeat the feat, achieving my private target of another $2000 profit in three hours or so, some at the same table as Robert Varkonyi. Towards the end of the session the former champ thinks long and hard about my raise of $1000, out of position, and asks if I want a call. 'That's a matter for you,' I hear myself saying, sounding (to me) very English – i.e., worried – with an internal prayer that he won't. Varkonyi thinks some more, then shows me a pair of tens as he folds. I show him my pair of pocket jacks as I haul in a hefty pot. Damn, turns out I did want a call, after all.

The main event is proceeding without me, so I decide to take my winnings to Manhattan, where Charlie Simmons has been lining up a special reunion of his Tuesday Game. Of late it has begun to falter. Another player, Harold, has died since I left town; others have grown too old or lost interest; it is often difficult to find a quorum. Which again proves true, alas, on my latest flying visit. Charlie is raring to go, but he can't fill the table. We content ourselves with a good, old-fashioned dinner at Sardi's, alternating memories of favourite books with favourite poker hands.

The next afternoon I take myself off to the new movie about Truman Capote, with the uncanny impersonation that would win Philip Seymour Hoffman the Academy Award. As I stand in line to buy my ticket, I notice a sign saying the admission fee is $7 (rather than $11) for over-fifty-fives. When I arrive at the desk, I tell the young man behind it that I am over fifty-five. Unlike my hero at Foxwoods, he does *not*, alas, ask to see my ID.

Self-esteem sinks again. But I am cheered by a matinée of Neil Simon's *The Odd Couple* with Nathan Lane and Matthew Broderick, which of course boasts one of the funniest poker games in all drama, and the Monty Python musical *Spamalot*, starring Tim Curry as King Arthur, soon to be replaced by my friend Simon Russell Beale. However, my real reason for coming to New York, apart from seeing Charlie and other friends, is to leave for JFK Airport by way of Verona, New Jersey, to visit the remarkable Mr Henry Orenstein.

Octogenarian Orenstein has played a central role in the poker revolution. Before hearing that story, though, you have to get your head round the dire details of his early life. Before coming to America to make a considerable fortune, Henry was very lucky to survive his teens.

Born in Poland in 1923, the second-youngest son of a wealthy Jewish family, Orenstein was sent to no fewer than five Nazi concentration camps. His parents were put to death, as were a sister and a brother, but Henry and his two other brothers survived – to his own continuing amazement – by signing on to a project named 'Kommando', in which Jewish mathematicians and scientists were recruited to help German scientists develop a gas that could paralyse enemy tanks. The work involved, though personally approved by Himmler, was meaningless. 'I was no mathematician, nor were my brothers,' says Orenstein, who believes it all to have been a ruse by German academics to avoid call-up to the front. (Documents appearing to support this theory have been discovered only recently.)

Even so, Orenstein was among those being marched towards the Baltic, one of thousands of Jews about to be put on ships, sailed out to sea and sunk, when rescued by Soviet troops after the demise of Hitler. Orenstein has described his experiences, including several brushes with very unpleasant forms of death, in an exceptionally graphic and moving memoir entitled *I Shall Live*, praised by luminaries from George Steiner to the late Simon Wiesenthal.

After coming to the United States in 1947, twenty-four-year-old Henry began by loading bales of cotton for eighty-five cents an hour, then got work stitching dresses. Soon he had made enough money to buy a grocery store; having paid $600 for it, he sold it six months later for $6000. Then he moved to Verona and a job selling Libby's canned foods.

But Orenstein was never comfortable as a company man; his entrepreneurial spirit soon had him 'tinkering'. He invented a doll whose eyes opened and closed magnetically, then another whose hair grew when you twisted her arm. Each sold four million. Soon, thanks to his ingenuity as an inventor, the patents were pouring in. Henry got the franchise for spin-off merchandise from Sesame Street – upmarket, educational toys, such as 'Walking Letters' to help children learn how to spell. Next, in the 1960s, came the 'Johnny Lightning 500' race cars and track. When Al Unser won the 1971 Indianapolis 500 in a 'Johnny Lightning' car, Henry Orenstein rode around the track with him on his victory lap.

These and other toys are scattered around Orenstein's modest Verona home, along with the one that really made him serious money – one even I bought for my children in the 1980s: Transformers, 'robots in disguise' that could become cars or planes. In 1984 alone Transformers grossed $115 million, soon spinning off into cartoons, comic books, lunchboxes, even a Spielberg movie. Today sales still reach at least a hundred million a year and are nearing a total of two billion in little more than two decades. 'From grocery stores to toys, you name it and Henry's been around it,' says George Greenberg, executive vice-president of his next stop, the Fox Sports Network. 'He looks at things and thinks, How can I make it better?'

In the mid-1990s Henry began making poker better. A lifelong chess wizard, he had never played the game until his mid-sixties when he took it up at his wife's suggestion after chess started giving him headaches. By then a wealthy man, of course, he sought out the high-stakes games in Atlantic City and began playing in tournaments against some of poker's biggest names. Watching ESPN's coverage of the World Series one evening, Henry thought it 'incredibly boring. You couldn't see the hole cards. They played hand after hand but never showed the cards.' It was so dull that he switched it off – and began to think of a way to make it better.

Within six months Orenstein had invented the under-the-table camera, the secret behind today's pocket-cam and all other variants that reveal the players' hole cards. Again Henry took out a patent; the copy he gave me shows that it dates from 1995. It took him several years to persuade TV executives that it would not rob the game of its mystery, and players that it would not rob them of their secrets. In all that time he never lost confidence; the players, he knew, would all want to be on TV.

It took the UK to prove him right. In the late 1990s a version of his sub-table camera, which read the cards through a glass panel round the edge of the table, was first used in Channel 4's *Late Night Poker*, then by the first Ladbrokes Poker Million. When the World Poker Tour was launched in the US in 2003, using the pocket-cam that relies on his invention, Orenstein made another fortune. His patent meant that everyone, from the WPT's Steve Lipscomb to Matchroom's Barry Hearn, was obliged to pay him royalties. Now poker can be seen on several cable channels every night in the UK, as well as on occasional terrestrial coverage, and in the US on the Travel, Bravo, Game Show and ESPN networks, even NBC. All of them have to pay Henry.

In the meantime he was becoming no mean poker player himself. Orenstein has even won a World Series bracelet: in 1996, after he had invented the hole-card camera but failed as yet to sell it, he came first in the $5000 WSOP Seven-Card Stud tournament, earning $130,000 by beating such respected professionals at the final table as fourth-placed T. J. Cloutier, third-placed Cyndy Violette and runner-up Humberto Brenes. Orenstein had already twice finished in the money in the

$10,000 WSOP No Limit Hold 'em main event, coming twelfth in 1993 (the first time he played in it) and eighth in 1995. He later placed seventh in the $2500 Seven-Card Stud event at the 2005 United States Poker Championship

When the pocket-cam took off, Orenstein naturally started inventing new types of poker programming to make the best use of it. At eighty, he himself was the oldest competitor in the first National Heads-Up Poker Championship, an idea he sold to NBC, and won his first round against Chip Reese before losing to John Hennigan. With his poker 'ambassador' in Las Vegas, Eric Drache, Orenstein also came up with the popular *Poker Superstars* TV tournament in which big names put up substantial amounts of their own money to play for prizes he boosts. The structure of the tournament – a series of heats before a final – is based on Orenstein's belief that the all-in move should be strategic (i.e., aggressive rather than passive) and not terminal if you lose. You may be out of this heat but you still live to fight another day.

In 2005 Fox made thirty-five hours of *Poker Stars III* before the NBC network showed the final on Super Bowl Night, immediately before the game. Never has poker received such high viewing figures or indeed attained such corporate respectability – and all thanks to the ingenious Henry Orenstein.

When I arrived at his Verona home, to be shown in by his British-born wife Susie, Henry had just returned from the therapist, two years after breaking his back in a car crash. He had been returning (in a chauffeur-driven car) from the Saturday night high-stakes stud game in which he still plays in Atlantic City every week. As I was making my way out, after a few hours of lively conversation, he showed me a handsome bronze bust of his hero Winston Churchill, then revealed that he had made it himself back in 1968. This is quite a guy.

I asked him his secrets for successful poker and he gave me his four top priorities. 'There are more things you need to do well in poker than in chess and fewer people know how. First is reading the other players; second, finding tells; third, remembering everything that has happened, in this and previous games; fourth, money management.'

Doyle Brunson, ten years his junior, has said of Henry Orenstein: 'He's an inspiration for everybody.' As his chauffeur drove me to JFK, I was feeling pretty inspired myself.

Back in Blighty, Orenstein's precepts still in mind, I meet up with Alvarez for a trip to the Midlands, specifically Walsall, where we've both been invited to play for a team of ten so-called 'professionals' against ten students who have won their way here via online tournaments. From Yale to Oxford, where Al and I both got through our degrees without playing a single hand of poker, the boom is sweeping across university campuses to the point where you wonder how students get any work at all done these days. This is the biggest event yet staged by the UK's new University Poker League, which has grown out of the Oxford Cup and is run by the same guy, now a graduate, Joe Barnard.

At the time of the first Oxford Cup, contested in the hallowed debating chamber of the Oxford Union in 2002, club president Barnard declared Alvarez and Holden the 'honorary patrons' of the Oxford University Poker Club. As we stumped up our £20 entry fees that year, I made some remark to Al about being sure to let the students knock us out. That, I said, is what we were here for. That's why Barnard had just bought us an expensive dinner – as compared to the pint of beer I had just about managed to buy Al in 1968, as president of the Poetry Society when he came here to give a reading. That evening had proved the beginning of a friendship now almost forty years old – and so close enough to accommodate the occasional disagreement. 'Bullshit,' he snapped back. 'I'm planning to win this thing.'

And Al did indeed get to the final table – at which I volunteered to act as dealer, purely in the hope of putting a hex on his tilt at the title. This thing should be won by a *student*, for chrissake; they've come from all over the country to lift the trophy. Al went out in third or fourth place, worth £100 or so, and the first Oxford Cup was incongruously won by Stacia Xanthos, wife of the British semi-professional Charalambos, popularly known as 'Bambos'.

This year Al and I had got the start time of the Oxford Cup wrong. Expecting the event to start at 2 p.m., we fetched up at 1.30 p.m., only to find it had already been in progress for two and a half hours. With just three hands left in the rebuy period, tournament director Roy Houghton managed to find us both seats and I won the first hand I played, to the tune of 300 to add to my 2000 in chips. Then came an add-on, or double-up, so I started the afternoon session with 4300.

The first hand saw one player at my table knocked out, his A-K against 5-5 destroyed by a flop of A-K-5-x-5. Another player went on the second hand. On the third I got K-K, a guy raised into me, I reraised him all-in and he called before flipping over aces. Which – no doubt because they were his, not mine – stood up. I'd come all this way to play six hands. And lose a 'last-longer' bet with Al of £100.

As he played doggedly on, I was challenged to a £50 heads-up match by Adam Matusiak, a Cambridge graduate who had been working for the website Betfair. After much back-and-forthing, my K-10 beat his J-J. All along the winner had been challenged to a double-or-quits repeat by spectator Phil Shaw, the former editor of *Poker Europa* who had by now turned semi-pro. Eventually I went all-in against Phil with 9-9, which stood up against his A-K, and won the £100 I owed Al.

In the years since the first Oxford Cup, the poker boom has seen the birth of the nationwide University Poker League, complete with its own website – host of today's event. When we arrive at the Village Hotel, Walsall, Al and I discover that this is to be a heads-up contest, between two teams of ten, likely to be disrupted by a simultaneous tournament at the casino next door, the Midlands Masters. In fact our captain, Dave 'El Blondie' Colclough, has yet to arrive because he is still trying to become the Midlands Master.

I am reminded of the time I myself was still playing in an Omaha tournament in Binion's at the start of a media event for which I was also registered; for a while I dashed from table to table, playing in both at once, if neither very successfully. And of Des Wilson's story about Dave 'the Devilfish' Ulliott, who was reminded in the middle of the $10,000 buy-in London Open tournament at the Vic that he had double-booked himself: he was due right now at Hamley's, the giant toy store in London's Regent Street, to market his 'Devilfish' cards, chips and other merchandise to a waiting group of excited youngsters. To universal astonishment, Dave promptly got up and went off to Hamley's, leaving his chips to be blinded away in his absence. And according to Wilson, who went with him, Ulliott was sweetness and light to the children, putting in a 'surprisingly impressive performance', as if nothing important were going on elsewhere. By the time he got back to the tournament the Devilfish had lost $7000 of the $37,000 chips in front of him when he had left – 'and never recovered his momentum, being knocked out early on the second day'.

But soon Colclough shows up and takes charge of a motley crew of so-called pros, including two genuine ones, Lucy Rokach and Pascal Perrault, along with the likes of 'Mad' Marty Wilson (fresh from back-to-back tournament wins in the north and Midlands), Tony 'Tikay' Kendall (Colclough's then partner in the poker set-up known as 'Blondie'), Malcolm Harwood, Alvarez and Holden. The format is a twenty-match shoot-out of heads-up No Limit Texas Hold 'em. Players will start with a notional 10,000 in chips and blinds will start at 100–200 on a fifteen-minute clock. The tournament director is our old friend Roy Houghton, brimming with enthusiasm about a new card room he is planning to open in London, the Loose Cannon. 'Which team', as Joe Barnard asks in his subsequent report on the UPL website, is going to 'take the title, lift the UPL plate and crack open the champagne?'

There are ritual TV interviews before battle commences and we (the pros) are 6-4 up by the time I play the first of my two matches, against Will Smith, a qualifier from Scotland. Rokach and Perrault are anxious to get back to the tournament across the road; amazingly, Lucy lost her first match to a student called Ben Woods but there were then double victories for Perrault and Malta's Joe Grech, putting us 5-2 ahead, before Lucy atoned by beating Joel Burman. Our skipper, 'El Blondie' himself, then lost to an American maths wizard called Tony Bendinelli and 'TK' to Jack Prevezer. So the pros' 6-2 lead has shrunk to 6-4.

I'm doing okay against Smith until a flop of 6-7-8 turns his 9-10 into a straight against my all-in pocket queens. Now it's 6-5 to the pros, which becomes six-all when Mad Marty goes down to Mike Piper. Alvarez claws one back against Alex Roseman, promptly lost by TK to make it 7-7. The next two are shared: 8-8. Then Marty loses again, to Milan Peric, before Colclough beats Richard Hawes to bring it back to 9-9.

This is closer than anyone was expecting. By the time Malcolm Harwood loses for the second time, to Alex Roseman, we are approaching the denouement I have been dreading. Yes, as fate would insist on having it, it's all down to me. We're losing 10-9 and I have to beat the maths whiz from Harvard, Tony Bendinelli – the man who has already beaten Captain Colclough – to level the scores and take it to a tie-break between the skippers.

A crowd gathers around the table and the hitherto noisy room suddenly grows hushed and tense. During the third level

(300–600), I get a flush to pull back to an even chip count; but the other Tony is an aggressive if cerebral player, and I'm playing rather tight to avoid making a fool of myself in front of my teammates and the cameras. So I'm back down to 5000 (to his 15,000) when I try to double through again with a ten paired on a flop of K-10-2. To my horror, he's paired his king. The students have won 11-9.

At the end of November 2005, when Joe Barnard posted his match report on the UPL website (while 3944 student punters were in play at 597 tables), it began: 'What a perfect conclusion to the UPL's UK Student Poker Tour 2005,' and ended: 'What a performance! The rest of the poker-playing world . . . beware!'

The previous year thirty-two-year-old Ashley Revell of Kent, a professional gambler and poker player, had sold all his worldly goods via auctions and car-boot sales, right down to his clothes, and taken £76,840 to the Plaza in Las Vegas to wager on evens at roulette. At the last minute, when the wheel was already spinning, he decided to go for red. And up it came, red, so he walked away with £153,680.

For our 'pro' team today, Revell has again been walking on water. His streak of cards has included turning a straight flush and flopping quads when all-in against poor Richard Hawes. Revell, Perrault and Maltese Joe are the only pros to have won both their matches. Alvarez, Colclough and Rokach have each won one, lost one. Like Harwood and Marty Wilson, I myself have lost both my matches and let the side down ignominiously.

My November has begun and ended in university settings, on opposite sides of the Atlantic, on high and low notes respectively. Walsall feels like the lowest point of my poker year so far. Then I suffer two bad online beats while leading a multi-table tournament with just five players left – a back-door flush beating my flopped set and a full house rivering my flopped flush, costing me a quantum leap in prize money.

It makes me glad to be leaving 2005 behind and getting on with 2006, the year in which I plan to be crowned world champion. But right now I feel like I stand less of a chance than most of these students.

6

The All-Out Move

One Saturday night in early 1994, in the bar of London's Barracuda Casino, the Moll and I fell into conversation with a genial, forty-ish guy with a mid-Atlantic accent – waiting, like us, for the start of a poker tournament. In those days the Barracuda had a thriving card room, run by the ubiquitous Roy Houghton.

Introducing himself as Randolph Fields, the mysterious stranger said he had taken up the game after reading my book *Big Deal*. So the least I could do was buy him a drink.

'And what do you do,' I asked him, 'when you're not playing poker?'

'I start things,' said Fields. As self-descriptions go, it sounded as evasive as any I had ever heard in any bar in any casino the world over. And I'd heard a few.

'Start things?' I repeated. 'What sort of things?'

'Companies. I start companies.'

'I see,' I said, dubiously. 'And would I have heard of any of these companies you've started?'

'Have you heard', he asked, 'of Virgin Atlantic Airlines?'

Had I heard of Virgin Atlantic? I felt like I'd spent half my life on Virgin Atlantic. During the year that wound up as *Big Deal*, I virtually lived on it. And teenagers being what they are, refusing to travel on any airline but Richard Branson's flying fun palace, the Moll and I were then buying seven Virgin tickets to Boston each summer to take the family on vacation to Cape Cod. 'Yes,' I replied through seriously gritted teeth. 'I've heard of Virgin Atlantic.'

'Well,' said our new friend, 'I started it. And then I fell out with Richard Branson. As part of my settlement I got free first-class travel on Virgin for life, for myself and two friends, as often as I want. Maybe you'd like to come to Las Vegas as my guest – Upper Class, of course – for this summer's World Series of Poker?'

It was an offer I couldn't refuse. As I drove home that night, however, I began wondering about this guy Fields. Could he possibly be on the level? Or was he, like so many of the people you meet in the bars of casinos, just another stylish con artist? 'Forget about it,' said the Moll, usually a shrewd judge of these things. 'You'll never see him again.'

A few days later, I came home to a message on my answering machine. 'Hi, Tony, this is Randolph Fields. Would Friday 6 May be convenient for you to travel via LA to Vegas? Give me a call.'

Friday 6 May was certainly convenient – the very day, as it happened, I had been planning to go anyway. So that day I duly turned up at Heathrow – feeling naked, in those pre-electronic days, without a ticket in my pocket, and still unsure whether I was actually going to get airborne. But there on the red carpet beside Virgin's Upper Class check-in desk stood Fields, cheerily waving two tickets.

Via Branson's VIP lounge we were ceremoniously escorted to the Virgin 747's Upper Class cabin. 'Hey there, Randolph,' said the stewardesses, 'good to see you!' Fields was on first-name terms with them all. For he jetted to or from the States on Upper Class virtually every week, with a couple of clients or chums.

A busy international insurance lawyer, then up to his elbows in corporate claims against Lloyd's of London, Fields certainly made the most of his Virgin privilege – to the tune, he reckoned at the time, of £300,000 worth of free flying each year, or some £3 million over the ten years he had been using it.

The following May I travelled again to Vegas as the guest of Randolph, by now a close friend, along with our mutual friend Al Alvarez and the poker player and writer Paul Spike. We were all suitably grateful and relished a lively in-flight poker game with some other passengers on the oval table that in those days graced the Upper Class bar.

Then two months later disaster struck – for Fields and his business, not to mention his fortunate, freeloading friends. On 16 August 1995, after booking seats to take his niece to summer camp in California, with his mother and a poker buddy along for the ride, he received a fax from Virgin effectively down-grading him to economy.

For ten years Fields and his flying friends had been entitled to Upper Class seats as available at the time of booking. Henceforth, said Virgin, his deal would be honoured only on a space-available basis on the day. He would have to wait until all the other passengers had checked in, and the flight closed, to see if any upgrades were available.

It amounted, as Fields saw it, to 'a declaration of war'. He took Virgin to court to defend his contractual right to fly first class, with a couple of guests, for life. The writ he served alleged that Virgin's action was causing him 'damage and loss of reputation and esteem'. The downgrading, in short, was degrading. 'My pride', he told me at the time, 'is at stake.'

But so was Branson's. As Virgin's lawyers refused to budge, Fields declared that pending the court case he would be flying first class on other airlines and sending Virgin the bill. So off he flew to California with his niece – first class, of course – on Air New Zealand. Virgin ground staff saw him and called out: 'Hey, Randolph, why aren't you flying with us?' He could only shrug, catch his flight and send Branson the tab.

'The Virgin staff were upset, and so was I,' he told me. For the next six weeks, Fields was abnormally UK-bound. 'At £3000 a trip, it was hurting.' Then on 5 October he won a summary judgment in the High Court. Branson had, after all, signed the contract. 'Airline Founder Wins Right To Fly First Class For Life' was the headline in the next day's *Times*. Said one of his lawyers: 'Some of the points raised in the case may seem unusual. But for an international businessman like Mr Fields, they can be very important for the effective conduct of his work.'

And his play. For as well as being a successful international lawyer, Fields was a formidable poker player – a winner of major tournaments on both sides of the Atlantic and a figure feared at the big-bucks tables from London to Las Vegas. That first time we went to Vegas together in May 1994 was also Randolph's first visit to the world capital of poker. He promptly proceeded to come close to the money in the very first tournament he entered. Later that year he won the £10,000 first prize in a British championship event at London's Victoria casino. Now he had his sights set on the $1 million world title.

A less independent spirit might have been content with the lucrative life of an LA lawyer, which had been Fields' lot in the early 1980s, fresh out of law school. Born there in 1952 of American parents who separated before he was born, he was one of the few lawyers to have qualified at both the English and Californian bars.

Living in England but employed in America, with dual citizenship and a parent on each side of the Atlantic, Fields was making so many long-haul flights that he had thought it might be cheaper to start his own airline. With the collapse of the no-frills Laker Airways in 1982, he seized the moment to found British Atlantic, designed as an 'entertainment-oriented' airline with a business section named 'Upper Class' in the upstairs cabins of its 747s. Among those he approached as potential investors was Richard Branson, who was immediately enthusiastic. Within two weeks they had announced the change of name to Virgin Atlantic and by June 1984 they were airborne. But within a year they fell out over Fields' 'abrasive' management style and parted by mutual agreement, with Branson buying out Fields' 25 per cent holding for a little over £1 million.

In lieu of a handsome severance settlement, Fields negotiated a nominal pay-off and his 'dream ticket' – free first-class travel for life, for himself and two companions. He also won the same perk for his mother, who had lent him £5000 to start the company, and any wife or children he might one day have.

Within two years of his £1 million pay-off Fields had lost it all in a vain attempt to start another airline, Highland Express. But the legal business generated by the problems of Lloyd's, along with his expertise in insurance archaeology, soon combined to make him a wealthy man again. As his fortune grew so the inveterate gambler in him became increasingly addicted to poker.

Despite several more attempts by Branson to revise their agreement, Fields and his friends flew merrily on, often to the casinos of California, usually corralling other passengers into a poker game en route. A mite worried about his 'hopeless obsession' with poker, Fields consulted a psychotherapist as to whether he might be 'addicted' to the game. 'No, Randolph,' came the reply, 'you're addicted to 747s.'

At the time of the court case I wrote an article about all this for a Sunday colour magazine, which naturally involved ringing

Branson for comment. He wouldn't speak to me. But his spokesman said: 'The real problem is that so many of the friends Randolph Fields takes on Virgin Upper Class are poker players who get our other first-class passengers drunk and then fleece them at poker.'

'Yup,' I replied cheerily. 'I'm one of them! That's me!'

So you can imagine how intrigued (and surprised) I was, ten years on from all this, to be invited to Richard Branson's palatial home on the edge of London's Holland Park for a mini-tournament to launch his Virgin Poker website.

I arrived, appropriately enough, jet-lagged, after returning from Foxwoods and New York (on British Airways, this time, thanks to the air miles) and full of fond memories of poor Randolph – who had died of kidney cancer in February 1996, six months after the court case, at the age of only forty-four. I travelled down to his funeral in Jersey with the Moll and, among many others, Jamie Palumbo, founder-owner of the Ministry of Sound nightclubs, who had been best man at his wedding to fellow barrister Fiona Harvie-Smith. Just two months before Randolph died, she had presented him with a son, Randolph Jr, who will no doubt haunt Virgin for many a year.

Beside my bed, to this day, sits a wonderfully vulgar Las Vegas ashtray, inscribed 'Tony's butts', given me by Randolph despite his own detestation of smoking. How he would have loved this moment!

And the first person I saw, by some sort of serendipity, was the Moll herself, still an occasional visitor to the London poker circuit, ready to take her seat at one of the half-dozen tables arranged in a marquee in Branson's back garden. The Virgin boss was not there, to my disappointment; I'd love to have seen how he responded these days to the name of Randolph Fields. But many of the usual suspects were, from Grub Smith to the *Times*'s poker correspondent Howard Swains, who had drawn the seat to my right. Also at my table was the former *EastEnders* star Michael Greco, nowadays a formidable poker player.

There was one interesting hand, when I went all-in with Q-Q only to be called by Swains with K-K; we watched the board come 6-7-8-9-10 and contentedly (on my part, anyway) split the pot. I didn't last much longer; a combination of jet lag and disinterest in the prize, a weekend for two at some Virgin hotel in Morocco, saw me make an early exit and join Grub in the Branson living room, where some uncouth journos were making notes of the titles of the books on his shelves.

The Moll made it to the final table but not to Morocco (which she would devoutly have wished). Once she was eliminated, we made polite excuses and headed off for an overdue dinner, during which I was able to tell Ben's stepmother the exciting news that he and Salome were about to get married – on an ocean-side cliff-top in Carmel, California, with no one there but the requisite judge. No parents, not even a witness. It was the most romantic thing we had ever heard.

On 25 November 2005 my youngest son and his lovely bride did indeed plight their troths, had a sandwich, got into their Mini Cooper and drove to San Francisco for a weekend's honeymoon. There would be a big celebratory bash in London in six months.

Over Christmas, a time of year for which I don't much care, I had killed too many hours playing poker online, though not without some success. With my eldest son, Sam, staying on Christmas Eve, prior to Christmas lunch at his mother's with the visiting newlyweds, our joint efforts won us second place in some PokerStars tourney, netting a few hundred bucks to ease the Christmas spending pain.

'Who are these sickos, playing poker at midnight on Christmas Eve?' I asked Sam while scooping a monster pot.

'You, Dad,' he replied shrewdly, 'are one of them.'

Late on Boxing Day I won another $3000 in a thirty-starter tournament – but in a manner of which I was far from proud. On what turned out to be the final hand of the heads-up, which I started with $25k to my opponent's $5k, I set him all-in with A-J and he called with A-6. The flop came A-3-6, giving him two pairs. The turn was irrelevant. I'd resigned myself to a long, hard struggle for the $3k when the river brought a jack, giving me two better pairs and the first prize – and no time to commiserate with my gallant opponent as the table closed down before I could hit the chat-box.

'That's poker,' someone would say if something like that happened at a real table. 'That's online poker,' I muttered to myself moodily, regretful that I hadn't had the chance to offer the unlucky loser my apologies, whoever he (or she) may have been, for that freak river card. Still, I had started with the better hand.

Off to bed I went, nonetheless, a disgruntled, dispirited winner.

It was also over Christmas that Steve Lipscomb, founder of the World Poker Tour, sent a long, defensive letter to 'the poker community', in which there had been growing discontent all year at the way he and the other WPT bigwigs were enriching themselves at, as the players saw it, their expense. Where were the freerolls? Where was the subsidised prize money? Why should they sign their names and images away without financial remuneration? In what other game or sport on earth is the prize money paid by the contestants, most of them unsponsored?

The holiday season, to Lipscomb, was the appropriate moment to 'challenge' the poker community to be 'very cautious about accepting misinformation without looking further'. After dealing with complaints about those 'release' forms –

which were 'industry standard', he insisted, and would not cost any players endorsement opportunities – he got to the issue of money. 'Another rampant misunderstanding in the poker community is that the World Poker Tour or WPT Enterprises (WPTE) is making massive profits and is somehow the evil empire that refuses to spread the wealth. Nothing could be further from the truth. WPTE has been in business for four years and has yet to turn a profit.'

How did this square with Lyle Berman's assertion in his autobiography, *I'm All In* (published earlier that same year, 2005), that had Binion, Reese and Brunson chosen to invest each would now have received a 45-1 return on their million-dollar risk?

Lipscomb wasn't saying. The WPT, he went on, had launched and funded the first player management company in history, as well as the first professional poker league in the sport, 'giving $2.5 million dollars away prior to securing a broadcast deal'. As yet it had received no return on that investment.

And it was the World Poker Tour, its staff and casino partners that had made this poker boom possible. 'Every player that commentates on a rival TV show, every player that wins a million-dollar first prize, every player that participates in or endorses an online poker room, every player that sits down in a packed poker room full of new players benefits from the World Poker Tour. Some people seem to forget that just three years ago you had to wait a year to get a shot at a million-dollar first-prize tournament. Poker rooms were being shut down across the country and industry leaders were holding conferences seeking ways to save a dying business. People forget that the biggest five- and ten-thousand-dollar buy-in events had thirty to sixty people in them – not the six to nine hundred players you see today.'

In the next section, headed 'A Land of Opportunity', Lipscomb continued to hand the credit for the poker boom to the WPT and the other poker shows it has spawned. 'Poker rooms across the country are making money as they never imagined they could or would. Online poker has exploded from a two-hundred-million-dollar market to a three-billion-dollar market by associating with the WPT and other television shows. And, whereas no one wanted to put regularly scheduled poker on television in the US in 2001/2002, at least fifteen shows are currently airing in the US – copying the WPT format.'

Then he took credit for the internet boom. 'There are a lot of people making money in the poker market today. Most of those opportunities did not exist prior to the World Poker Tour. The founders of PartyGaming cashed out over a billion dollars from their business this year. Estimates are that Full Tilt Poker, owned and launched by A-list poker players, is making hundreds of thousands of dollars a day, millions of dollars a month. Poker players are being paid for appearances, endorsing products and poker sites and even beginning to crack the difficult layers of legitimate corporate sponsorship. Freeroll television shows totalling millions of dollars in prize money are being announced monthly and new poker interest shows are being produced as well.'

The WPT was 'excited' by all of this. No one was happier than Steve Lipscomb or his business partner Lyle Berman when players did well and managed to cash in on the boom. 'But, with all the money being made, the poker community should be aware that the guy who put up millions of dollars to change the poker world – Mr Lyle Berman – has, to date, not made a cent. He has never drawn a salary and, as of today, he and [his company] Lakes Entertainment have not sold one share of World Poker Tour stock. Their investment has appreciated, but I cannot imagine that poker players or the poker community begrudge him that – any more than they would expect PartyGaming's investors or the Full Tilt players to redistribute their profits.'

Lipscomb didn't mention, let alone detail his own earnings, but he said that he himself had sold 'less than 20 per cent' of his stock. When the WPT began Berman had made a $10,000 bet with another player that it would turn a profit within five years. 'To date, he has not been able to collect on that bet.' The WPT was still making a loss. For anyone who didn't believe him, all its files were open for inspection.

Again this did not square with Berman's own account – that the guy with whom he made that bet 'owes me ten big ones'. Undeterred, Lipscomb concluded: 'Together we have managed to change the face of poker for ever. Together we have managed to dispel the perception that poker could never be a sport.'

Hmmm. For now, I think, I'll stick to British-based Ladbrokes, the world's biggest bookmaker, which has generously invited me as a 'celebrity' guest on its annual Caribbean poker cruise – held in January, when the main point of the British weather is to get as far away from it as possible, preferably in the direction of the sun.

The unusual thing about Ladbrokes, the betting and gaming division of Hilton Group plc, is that it has no American customers. Hilton apparently had the prescience not to wish to get involved in the increasingly ugly arguments about the legality of online betting in the United States. Instead it boasts what it proudly calls 'a poker community' spreading right across the rest of the world. And six hundred of them were currently converging on – ironically enough – the United States, specifically Miami, to climb aboard a ten-day poker cruise promising as much as $50 million in stake money once the ship had sailed out into the legal no man's land of international waters.

With an anticipated prize pot of $2 million and a first prize of $750,000 up for grabs in the No Limit Hold 'em main event, players such as 2005's Poker Million champion Tony Jones and (according to the press release) 'legendary' poker writer Anthony Holden would be joining such stellar company as World Darts Champion Phil 'the Power' Taylor, comedian Norman Pace and pin-up Leilani Dowding aboard 'one of the world's most luxurious liners', the 682ft, 45,000-tonne MV *Zenith*.

I kept a daily diary.

FRIDAY

On the eleven-hour flight to Miami Ladbrokes' poker manager Albert Tapper tells me of the twelve months and more of preparation that have gone into this, the biggest ever gathering of non-American poker players. Some six hundred poker players and guests will be aboard Celebrity Cruise's *Zenith*, with five hundred more to deal, feed and generally serve them. The surreal atmosphere begins as soon as we arrive, with Dave 'the Devilfish' Ulliott being told by the US Customs man to take his hands out of his pockets while talking to him, thus missing Ulliott's declaration that he's carrying somewhat more than the legal limit of $10,000.

At a welcome party at the Miami Airport Hilton Devilfish tries to buy the entertainer's guitar to serenade us on board, but Tapper declares it too steep an investment for Ladbrokes at $4500. Lesser mortals among poker people are meanwhile meeting for the first time the faceless avatars and wacky aliases against whom they tough it out in cyberspace. When Jesse May meets his online 'nemesis', he declares himself dismayed at what a nice guy he turns out to be. Mad Marty Wilson is already telling his legendary stories – all the madder because he gave up smoking two weeks ago.

This is a first glimpse of the poker community of which Ladbrokes is justly proud. With no Americans here, it is generally agreed, there seems likely to be less unpleasantness at the tables.

SATURDAY

Late arrivals (because, ironically, of 'computer failure') are still flying into Miami as the ship prepares to depart. It sets sail minus a few who have turned up at Heathrow without the machine-readable passports required for entry into the US since 9/11; they must now get themselves to our first port of call, the British Virgin Islands, if they want to join the poker party.

After dinner, at a welcome party in the Celebrity Show Lounge, Tapper and his colleague Greg Amoils endear themselves to the four hundred players on board by announcing a $20,000 reunion freeroll online when the cruise is over. In the meantime there will be no 'juice' on the $5000 main event and cash-game rakes will be capped at the lower of $5 or 5 per cent. 'I would have settled for twenty!' cheers 2004 Poker Million champion Donnacha O'Dea.

When the siren sounds for the ship's entry into international waters – the signal for the action to begin – the unusual winds which greeted us in Miami turn out to be the tail-end of a tropical storm. Amid heavy weather and choppy seas, Night One turns out to be 'Vomitgate', as dealers in the late-night super-satellite for tomorrow's main event drop as fast as the players. One dealer invents a new poker term – the 'all-out' move – by throwing up on the player in seat one.

SUNDAY

Day One of the $5000 main event, with 392 starters. I find myself drawn in the overflow room downstairs at the same table as the reigning champion, the affable septuagenarian Eric Dalby. So my first objective is to survive long enough to make it upstairs from the Rendezvous Lounge to the main on-board card room, the Fleet Room.

This I achieve by mid-afternoon, during the fourth level, only to find myself on the left of the Swedish pro William 'Il Capitano' Thorssen, a massive chip leader bullying the table. I manage to last to the sixth level, and dinner-time, before going out in 150th place, just better than halfway, when my all-in J-J loses to A-8 as the flop (of course) brings an ace. The day ends after twelve rounds with a hundred players left, but the side-action continues all night in high-stakes cash games unusually fuelled by drink.

In the adjacent bar the most popular cocktail is a chocolate martini. I opt for one without the chocolate. 'Just look at the stacks those Swedish kids have got in there,' says some unknown, resentful middle-aged Brit. 'Three hundred, four hundred thousand. That's three times the size of my mortgage.'

The Swedes are but the most numerous and enthusiastic of the Scandinavian players now tightening their grip on the European poker scene, challenged only by the Brits and the Irish. One of the effects of the internet is to have taken poker to parts of the world it had never previously reached – parts of the world where, according to the usual, jokey, politically incorrect generalisations, there is little to do all day but play poker. Especially in countries where it's dark more than it's light. Still, there's no denying that something in the Swedish temperament suits the new game's aggressive tactics. And the piles of chips in front of them in these cash games are potent evidence indeed.

Which brings us to the hoary question: if people are winning that kind of money online, who is losing it?

The answer, I hate to tell you, comes from the horse's mouth: 5 per cent of online poker players are winners. A sobering 95 per cent are losers.

MONDAY

All day at sea. For those who haven't made it to Day Two of the main event, today holds Day One of a $500 No Limit Hold 'em tourney. Mine is one of the first tables to be broken and I find myself moved to the same table as the Devilfish, who promptly commits suicide with 6-7 to go play in the cash games. At one point I get an all-in call holding Q-Q and the flop brings Q-x-x-x-Q.

But this is not to be my day, either. Again around dinner-time I go out on A-J, beaten by pocket sixes. No ace or jack on the flop for me – is this divine victimisation or what? – leaving me eightieth out of 192 starters. Still not good enough. At least, for once, I have a decent excuse: I busted out, I persuade myself, because I am due as a guest for dinner at the table of the ship's captain, Xenofon Livianos. Other guests include the lovely Leilani and my old friend Donnacha O'Dea, whose son Eoghan (pronounced 'Owen') is still going well upstairs in the main event. Leilani endears herself to me even further by telling me she's dating an Arsenal player, Jérémie Aliadière.

TUESDAY

Zenith arrives in Tortola, British Virgin Islands, at noon (actually 11 a.m., but the clocks have gone forward an hour during the night). With sixty hours of poker logged by now, most players are ready to get ashore and check the messages on their mobile phones, which don't work at sea. The hundred-plus Swedish contingent squares off at beach volleyball while others stay aboard to sleep off three days and nights of play. Like most, I settle for a Caribbean swim and some gentle shopping. The ship's departure at 6 p.m. signals the start of a $200 NLHE tournament, with one rebuy and/or add-on. This time I last till 2 a.m., but deny myself the cash games to try to catch up on sleep.

WEDNESDAY

I wake late to find we've already docked in St John's, Antigua.
When I try to go ashore, the ship's security machine makes an
ugly noise and I discover I've got the wrong 'sea pass'; last night
when I bought a drink during the tournament the waiter must
have given me back the wrong one. As I wait for a new one at
customer services on Deck Five, I overhear the guy next to me
is moving rooms because he's fallen out with his girlfriend.

When I finally get ashore, a visit to the internet café reveals a
rave review in the *Sunday Times* of my life of Da Ponte – published while I'm here at sea, four thousand miles away. But there
aren't many people around here who are going to be too interested in that.

As dusk falls and we sail away from Antigua, an online bad
beat story from TV comedian Norman Pace kicks off Jesse
May's Poker Jamboree in the ship's snazzy theatre, the highlight of which is side-betting on a swimming race filmed ashore
that day between Mad Marty and friends. There follows the
final of the $200 tournament, eventually won by the 10-1 out-
sider, a charming Canadian woman whose husband and
nine-month-old son agonise in the audience throughout. At
the same time, ironically, a Ladies Freeroll goes on upstairs
alongside Day Three of the main event. Unless, that is, you're
one of the few foreswearing poker for the poolside seventies
disco party on Deck Eleven beneath the full moon escorting us
to . . .

THURSDAY

. . . St Maarten, which lies outside my stateroom window when
I wake. The ship's programme calls today a 'rest day' but few
around here are the type to obey orders; the guy beside me at
the internet shack in the capital, Philipsburg, is playing multiple
hands on, er, PokerStars.com. The beach bars and restaurants

can scarcely believe their luck as punters crowd ashore with bundles of hundred-dollar bills to squander. Tonight we get an extra hour in bed (or not, if you're still playing) as time goes back again. On my way to my cabin, Mad Marty catches me smoking. With the zeal of the convert, he insists I meet him in the gym at 11 a.m. tomorrow morning.

FRIDAY

11.10 a.m.: Marty lets me off with ten minutes on the treadmill, listening to his Walkman. Well, Day One of the $1000 tournament begins at noon. I break one of my superstitions by arriving at my table with two bottles of water, as if confident of lasting long enough to get through both.

Today I'm varying my play, taking a more aggressive approach, which pays off in the first few rounds with some decent pots. Then I am dealt K-K in late position. With blinds at $50–$100, I raise $300 before the flop. Everyone folds but the big blind. Then the flop brings K-3-6. I trap-check and he bets $500. I raise him all-in and he calls. The turn brings a seven, turning his 4-5 off-suit into a straight. The river does not, as I need, pair the board. How the hell could he have called that all-in bet?

But that is the very nature of the new poker. These people are prepared to commit ritual hara-kiri as the price of a potential advance. I have a few hundred left, which I lose to the same guy just two hands later, when my A-8 is beaten on a flop which adds a queen to his Q-4. On deck that afternoon a player called Charlie from the same table commiserates as Norman Pace presents Roy 'the Boy' Brindley's poker trivia quiz beside the pool. One of the prizes is a signed copy of *Big Deal*, which I narrowly avoid winning when my sixty-eight points is just one behind the first-prize winner. So I miss out, dammit, on a signed Leilani calendar.

I devote the evening to lively sit-and-gos, at which I clock up a tidy profit, winning two and finishing in the money twice more. In one case the table started with three Brits and seven Scandinavians – and all three Brits (including me) take the money, while a Brit team also manages to beat a team comprised of the all-conquering Scandies.

SATURDAY

During a day ashore in Labadee, Haiti – on a private beach with a brick wall blocking access to the rest of the island – news arrives that my football team, Arsenal, have been beaten by my nephew's, Everton. I recover in time to read an extract from *Big Deal* onstage in the showroom during a break in the $1000 final.

SUNDAY

After the final table of the main event (won by a Nord), Norman Pace hosts a terrific talent show featuring Bruce Atkinson and his cousin as Elvis and Kenny Rogers, Devilfish singing the blues (and cursing his 'inadequate' guitar), and comedians Lucy Porter and Roy 'the Rapper' Brindley, before a Geordie streaker provides a hilarious descant to the suave 'House of the Rising Sun' of Ladbrokes' Terry Sherring. The Tyneside Adonis is forgiven until he does it again during the curtain-call. Someone quotes David Niven protesting about a streaker at the Oscars 'exposing his shortcomings'. Apparently he's still at it in the bar later on; I wouldn't know, as I'm busy mopping up in an impromptu ring game.

MONDAY

The last time I came on a poker cruise, with the Moll in the late 1980s, there were only enough card sharps to corral a corner of one of the biggest liners afloat, the *Norway* – to the bemusement of other passengers, who received flyers beneath their doors offering 'Free Poker Lessons!' in an effort to draw them into the card room and relieve them of their hefty bankrolls. These days there are more than enough poker players to take over an entire ship – and the crew love it too, because they say it's more fun than an average cruise out of Miami, with geriatric Floridians forever complaining about everything. All these poker players – well, most of them – seem *happy* and having a great time.

Not least, I guess, because in nine days at sea, six hundred players and their guests have sunk no fewer than ninety thousand bottles of beer and fifty thousand cans of Red Bull – now, it seems, the official drink of poker. They've also munched their way through ten thousand burgers.

Back at Miami it's up early for reluctant disembarkation and sad farewells. Everyone is pledging to be here again next year. For me it's been useful tournament practice but further evidence that I'm still not up to the standard required to get into the money, let alone win the world title this coming summer. All I can think of is to book myself into a poker camp, to polish my skills with the experts, after the next two expeditions I am planning: a trip to Monte Carlo, to check out the action on the European Poker Tour, and another visit to the States for a poker writer's tournament in Atlantic City.

For now, however, it's back to London, the Job and *The Marriage of Figaro* at Covent Garden, in celebration of Mozart's 250th birthday this month. The only poker on my immediate horizon is a new 'home game' I have started with my pal Joe Saumarez Smith, managing director of BetUK.com, and other refugees from the second Tuesday Night Game in Knightsbridge, which seems to have followed the first into oblivion – after barely forty months, rather than forty years. Thanks to the Job, I have gone along with universal pleas that it be held on a Friday, for the benefit of those (unlike me these days) with real jobs, wives and young children.

'The Friday Night Game': it'll take a bit of getting used to.

7

The Kid Who Broke the Bank

There are 1326 different two-card starting hands you can be dealt at Texas Hold 'em. Only 5 per cent will be the seven so-called premium hands, i.e., pocket aces, kings, queens, jacks, A-K, A-Q or A-J. So, with ten players at the table, the odds are that one of your opponents will hold one of these top-seven starting hands every other deal while you will receive one only one deal in twenty.

It's the rest of the time – the other 50 per cent when no one at the table, including you, holds one of the top seven – that's when the real poker is played. Given the widespread expertise at playing and/or reading those top hands, it is these marginal pots where the subtlest poker moves are made and the most significant money is often won and lost. Half the time, that is, or every other hand.

Try telling that to my new Friday Night Game. There are people here who call every hand, raise every hand, fold every hand. It's lousy practice for my tournament regime. We're playing the same game – but, of course, it's completely different. A round of Hold 'em every so often, amid dealer's-choice bouts of Omaha, stud, high only and high-low, is a quite distinct animal from the non-stop Hold 'em marathons to which I've grown accustomed. It's tough to maintain the proper discipline when you know there are going to be only seven or eight hands before we move on to razz. It is tempting to call with any old starting hand, to pay more than you should to see the flop.

I *know*, for instance, that Hugh is bluffing; if only I had the cards to come over the top of him. I *know* that Matthew is pushing his luck; oh, for a hand to inflict his come-uppance. I *know* that Patrick holds what he's representing; what a relief to fold. The same, on the whole, goes for Joe and Richard. As for Al . . . well, who knows? I know him too well to know any more. The amounts of money involved are serious enough but not life-threatening; losing is a cause less for concern than embarrassment. What the heck, I call.

This, unlike the hard grind of tournament poker, is supposed to be fun – a social occasion where friends get together for a few drinks, a few laughs, some gossip and some cards. Even so, everyone takes it pretty seriously. There is pride at stake here.

Home poker is what I was weaned on in the late, much-missed Tuesday Night Game; this year it's pleasant relaxation from the rigours of the professional circuit (and the Job). But the growth of poker on TV and the internet has somehow combined to make the home game less devil-may-care than it used to be. In the old days we were pioneers, raising intrigued eyebrows in our other social circles by playing a game rarely seen outside the movies. There was something rugged about it, something manly, something romantic. Now we're just playing the same universal game even our children are playing with their pals, the same one hundreds of thousands of other people all over the country, nay millions around the world, are playing as we speak – a game which the poker boom has somehow robbed of its mystique, its derring-do.

But it's still the best game on earth. Deal me in.

The Job, meanwhile, goes on. At the London Coliseum, on the first night of English National Opera's new staging of Vaughan Williams' *Sir John in Love*, I take some pleasure in telling my friend Hugh Canning, music critic of the *Sunday Times*, that I'm off to Vienna the next day. His reply is just as expected.

'Oh, lucky you!' cries Hugh, his face lighting up. 'What are you going to see?'

'I'm going to see the inside of a casino.'

Hugh's face falls.

Waiting for me the next evening at Vienna International Airport, after I've survived an all-nighter writing my column, is a smiling blur of red: my middle son Joe, with big red hair and a big, bushy red beard. Joe lives in Berlin these days, and it's a few months since I've seen him. I've managed to schedule a reunion in Vienna on my way to Monte Carlo, to celebrate his birthday on Monday. He's insisting on spending at least three hours of it doing *The Third Man* tour, to scope out the scenarios (with especial reference to doorways, ferris wheels and sewers) of a movie we both love, Carol Reed's version of the Graham Greene novella set in post-war Vienna. But first, poker.

It's nearly midnight by the time we arrive at the Starlight Suites in the heart of the Austrian capital, but the restaurant next door is still serving Wiener schnitzel and delicious, chilled white wine. The plan is to check out the city's celebrated Concord Casino before this week's Austrian Open tournament – which drew us here under its original name of the EWSOP, or European World Series of Poker event, now dropped for mysterious 'legal reasons'. The Concord's host is Thomas Kremser, a familiar figure throughout Europe these days as the director of many televised poker tournaments, dating right back to 1999 and the daddy of them all, *Late Night*

Poker from Cardiff, which made his name. Ten years ago the tall, suave Kremser was a humble dealer; now he is the owner of the Concord, as well as a professional player with tournament winnings of more than $80,000 and Europe's most respected, in-demand tournament director.

Kremser's organisational skills, aided and abetted by those of his dealer wife Marina Rado, have given the Concord a reputation as one of Europe's premier card rooms. So it comes as something of a surprise to find it tucked away beneath a motorway in one of the less salubrious areas of the city. 'Being on a business park is not the most attractive location. Culturally and architecturally, I felt somewhere between Walsall and Luton,' was the verdict of the poker pro turned columnist Ashley Alterman, an old chum from the Saturday-night tournaments at the Vic in the 1990s. 'But at least I could understand what they were saying in Vienna. And the facilities were good. The food was mediocre at best but if you've ever eaten in the casino in Luton you'll be familiar with this sort of experience.'

Joe's birthday present from me is his €500 entry fee for a lesser tournament the night before the Austrian Open. Like both his brothers, he's a solid player; but Joe is perhaps more ruthless, certainly more devious, than either Sam or Ben. He's got all the qualities required not just to do well, but to win things.

Trouble is, the casino is closed in the mornings. To my pleasant surprise, Joe says he is more than willing to escort me to the Mozarthaus, newly refurbished for this 250th anniversary of the composer's birth, and close to my heart not just as a life-long Mozart-lover; I feel like I've spent the last year living with him while writing the story of his librettist Da Ponte. The last time I was here, on a research trip for that book, the smart Viennese house in which the Mozarts lived in a first-floor apartment, since turned into a museum, was closed for refurbishment. Now it has reopened as an elegant, high-tech shrine; but it is all so sleek that I find myself curiously unmoved, at the end of the tour, to stand in the very room where he and Da Ponte together wrote one of the greatest of all operas, *Le Nozze di Figaro*.

As we leave and head off in search of a pre-poker lunch, I am waylaid in the street by an Indian fortune-teller, who tells me I'm going to be lucky and will live to be ninety-two. (If I were you, I'd sell on that one.) For this intelligence he wants €150, and gets ten. His rampant optimism fills me with pessimism about this evening.

Over a drink at the Concord before the tournament, I ask Joe what he will do if we're both drawn at the same table. 'I'll be utterly ruthless and do my best to take all your chips,' he replies. 'Isn't that how you raised me to play?'

'It sure is and I know you'll expect the same treatment from me. Winner buys dinner?'

'I'm figuring that we'll both last way beyond dinner and meet at the final table.'

I'd like to think so, I tell him, but first we've got three hundred or so of these internet geeks to dispose of. Joe detects a curmudgeonly tone in my voice towards the new generation of players his own age. He's got a point. 'Like you,' I tell him, 'they're all better than me with computers, as well as mental arithmetic, so they can play eight screens at once, which means they can get years of experience in just a few months as Doyle Brunson has in a lifetime. Which also means many of them are pretty good. But they're cocky, with it.'

'Is that an admission that poker is a young man's game today?'

'I'm beginning to think so, if only through sheer weight of numbers – all those students with laptops, etc. Brunson and Chan may still be winning WSOP events but not the main one. Given the stamina involved in getting to the final table – seven or more consecutive days at fourteen hours a day – Brunson himself has said that no one over fifty is going to win it again. I'd say forty. So now's your chance!'

Then things turned a tad more metaphysical, with Joe wondering: 'Physical stamina aside, don't you feel the oldsters still have the edge when it comes to that gut instinct for the game cultivated over decades of taking down big pots?'

Again he had a point. 'With years of experience at life as much as poker,' I mused, 'oldsters can still smell weakness, inspire fear, play with more – what? – *insight* than these spotty youths with pocket calculators built into their heads. Some of them are very good players but it's their cockiness that gets me. The way they tell you how badly you played a hand – especially if you just won it. The cool body language learnt from TV. The hoods and back-to-front baseball caps. The shades. Mind you, if you or one of your brothers came home a poker millionaire I wouldn't be moaning like this.'

'I expect', countered my son, 'that you're also relieved none of us wound up as degenerate gamblers, living on skid row, always touching you for cash?'

'Of course, though I wouldn't have minded being bought a house or a car, like some poker parents.'

'I still could. Give me time.'

We were saved by the public address system, which now announced: 'Players, take your seats, please. The tournament will begin in one minute.'

We start with €3000 in chips. My table is quiet, with tight, untalkative players – unlike Joe's where there are two all-ins in the first five minutes. Yes, this is a rebuy tournament but Joe and I have seriously handicapped ourselves by pledging not to rebuy, let alone 'add on' when the time comes. This is a budget trip for me, en route to Monte Carlo; and self-denial is also a way of imposing more self-discipline.

For the first two levels I cruise along contentedly, holding my own against a table of players half my age. Towards the end of the third level it's my A-10 versus a Scandinavian skinhead's K-K. I bet €1000; he goes all-in; I call and flop an ace, doubling up to €5600. A few tables away Joe has €2600. During the first break we discuss tactics, which is fairly pointless as we both know what is required of us. 'Hang in there' is scarcely the most profound advice a father can give his son.

Of 135 starters, half were still alive when we reached the end of level three and the break for dinner – which turned out to be free, laid on by the Concord for all tournament players. But the survivors did not, alas, include Joe. He was jet-lagged because of a flight back the previous day from Los Angeles, where he had been researching a megabucks Hollywood biopic, and maybe a bit homesick for his new life in Berlin, working for the international, non-profit initiative droppingknowledge.org. Still, he wasn't making any excuses. Over dinner my son told me candidly: 'I think you wasted your money, Dad. I don't care enough about winning. I'm just not hungry enough.'

He meant that last remark about poker, as a means of building a bankroll, not the dinner, which he was destroying as if there were no tomorrow. We congratulated ourselves on avoiding any rebuys and rising above the add-on, though it saw me at something of a disadvantage when I returned to my table. To make matters worse, the guy next to me had a mobile with a 'Blue Danube' ringtone, which was really bugging me (well, this was the music critic's week off), as was the fact that they were building the final table alongside us as we played, all ready for TV, with a dreadful racket of drills and vacuum cleaners.

Or maybe, like Joe, I just wasn't really in the mood tonight, whatever that fortune-teller may have said. I should really be doing this for a living, not just for fun; then I might play as if my life literally depended on it. Soon I am dealt A-9 suited and raise three times the big blind. Seat One calls all-in with A-5 and the flop comes A-K-Q-J-9. In other words, I rivered him out of what was looking like a split pot. By the fifth level, with rolling antes of €25 added to the €100–€200 blinds, I am up to six thou – as if I had purchased the add-on. Dealt pocket jacks, I bet €700 and get a call from the tightest player at the table. When the flop brings a king, he bets €1200. I think for a while, knowing that I'm going to believe him and fold, which eventually I do.

Before too long at this level I am down to €4000. Then the blinds go up to €150–€200, with the antes still at €25. After a raise of €1200 in front of me, I fold K-J, but he gets a caller, so I'm appalled to see the flop come K-Q-J. All-in and call . . . the bettor turns over A-J, the caller Q-Q; then the flop brings a ten, giving the first hand top straight. I would have come third and been out of the tournament.

Ten minutes later I am. I raise with that magical A-J, Seat Two calls and the flop brings A-K-x. I go all-in; he calls, showing the accursed Anna K, which always seems to work for everyone but me. Rags, of course, ensue and I am out in thirty-third place.

A solid performance, I suppose – top 25 per cent – but still overcautious, unimaginative, cumulatively dispiriting. Years of playing a 'solid' game are still making it hard for me to adapt to the super-aggression of the online generation. I'm beginning to wonder if I ever will.

Over the next two days I eschewed the €2000 Austrian Open to spend my son's birthday with him, much of it trudging happily through the Viennese snow on *The Third Man* tour. To Joe's dismay (and my relief) we were spared the sewers, which were 'closed for repairs'; but the quest for the celebrated cafés, doorways and sewer entrances otherwise corresponded to a remarkable degree with the Mozart tour of Vienna I had undertaken the previous year on that research trip for Da Ponte.

Exhilarated and exhausted, we capped things off with dinner at one of Vienna's best restaurants, Plachutta. However pricey the tab (and slow the service), I figured it was better spent than handing over €2000 to those young sharks at the Concord.

When we looked in there later to check out what we'd missed, Ashley Alterman confirmed my suspicions. 'As it turned out I fell on my sword during the second level of the [second] day when blinds had increased to €300–€600.' He had 'sunk without trace in a sea of young aggressive barracuda', which had him musing: 'When you see a group of hooded youths on the street, you may feel uneasy if they behave in a loud, obnoxious way but they are much more dangerous at the poker table. They are more likely to be internet millionaires than itinerant and the fearlessness they display is a result of their experience rather than their machismo.'

Back at our hotel, for our last night together until his brother's wedding celebrations in a couple of months, Joe and I were again in meditative mood. 'Since poker is an endless lesson in sizing up situations, calculating risks and seizing opportunities,' he said, 'it could be said to be a skilful parenting tool, teaching life tactics any father would wish his sons to learn. But I was brainwashed at an early age, so of course I would think this.' He expected, he told me touchingly, 'that my brothers and I will go on playing together for the rest of our days'.

Then he asked me why I was still playing after nearly forty years. 'Not, for sure, because I'm much good at it – by today's standards, anyway', I reflected moodily. 'Because I love it, I suppose, as an escape from the grind of everyday life, of keeping the show on the road, etc. And because, you should be relieved to hear, I think it gives a good workout to the dark side in all of us – i.e., playing poker regularly all these years has stopped me, among other things, taking it out (unduly, anyway) on my family and friends.

'And I still believe that poker is also a metaphor for life, in much of which (both personal and professional) I still relish taking risks – if only the most calculated of risks.'

Before we part Joe asks affectionately after his stepmother Cindy, alias the Moll, reminding me that they played a game of heads-up poker on the first day he ever met her, back in 1986. 'I was holding A-x and, at age nine, didn't really know what I had – though I suspected an ace was worth something. You told me to bet everything I owned. So I did. Cindy bet her record collection. I won the hand. That may have been the moment I realised I liked Cindy – and also this new game.'

I had only the haziest memory of this charming moment. Little did I know how soon I would have a chance to check it out.

The journey from Vienna to Monte Carlo proved the most quixotic of my slender bankroll's long year. Fifteen euros got me from the hotel to a bus stop on the edge of Vienna. Ten euros then got me a bus ride from Vienna to the airport at Bratislava – in another *country*, for heaven's sake – whence, in these days of budget Euro-travel, my flight to Nice cost all of €0.01. Unsure how to get from one place to the other, and assuming it would be a complex if enjoyable train journey, I had merely Googled 'Vienna–Monte Carlo' and up popped this Air Euro miracle. But the de-escalating cost of the whole thing was then ruined by the €100 cab ride for the few miles from Nice to Monte Carlo.

I had come to Monaco for the grand finals of the European Poker Tour, sponsored by PokerStars.com, and planned to apply my own private version of WSOP/WPT rules by allowing myself a satellite or two for the €10,000 entry fee. Just before leaving home I had emailed Lee Jones, card room manager of PokerStars, to tell him I was coming. I have known Lee since the late 1980s and cemented our friendship in 1994 by supplying an enthusiastic jacket quote for his book *Winning Low Limit Hold 'em*. He has since become a major figure in the modern poker world.

And it was Lee's book that changed his life. A self-styled geek with degrees in computer science and electronic engineering from Duke and the University of Maryland, Lee had just taken on a new job in Silicon Valley in 2003 when he received a call from PokerStars, who had tracked him down on the strength of, yes, his book. They offered him the job of the fledgling website's card room manager – but it would involve moving to Costa Rica where the site was then based. Newly remarried with two school-age stepsons, Jones felt obliged to turn them down. To his surprise and delight, however, they rang him back, rearranged the details, including the location – and the job was his.

Lee loves to recall a seminal moment that summer when PokerStars had sent all of thirty-six players to the World Series of Poker, one of them Chris Moneymaker. In Las Vegas for a meeting of tournament directors, Jones was playing poker in the card room of the Bellagio when the famous hand between Moneymaker and Humberto Brenes came up on the TV. Moneymaker went all-in with 8-8, trapped by Brenes with A-A. At his apparent moment of triumph when he flipped over his aces, Brenes wagged his finger at Moneymaker as if to say: 'You fell for it, sucker!' The flop came down J-7-3. Then the turn brought a third eight. 'My job', agonises Jones, 'was drawing on two outs.'

That moment was the making of PokerStars, now online poker's largest tournament site. As the 'Moneymaker effect' kicked in, its business went berserk. Other sites have anonymous or composite card room managers but Lee Jones is flesh and blood, a cult figure to online players. And, boy, has that book sold well.

Within minutes of sending my email to Lee's formal work address I was pleasantly surprised to receive a cheery reply from the man himself, asking if I would be playing in the tournament. Well, I replied, I hoped so; but my bankroll was slender and it would depend on success in a satellite. Inside twenty-four hours, after transatlantic consultations, PokerStars had offered to stake my €10,000 entry fee for the main event, the Grand Final of the European Poker Tour, if I were willing to wear their logo while playing. It seemed a small price to pay for not even having to try to win a satellite.

Sponsorship! This was something I had not anticipated, let alone factored into my financial calculations, when embarking on this adventure. If they're prepared to sponsor me, I thought, they'll sponsor anyone these days. They're making so much money that they seem to be all but giving it away. 'I'll try to do you proud', I wrote Lee by way of thanks. 'Maybe I can even win the damn thing.'

'You don't understand, Tony,' he replied. 'You've *already* won. You're playing in a poker tournament for which somebody else has bought you in, and they don't even have a piece of your action. You have reached, my friend, poker nirvana.'

Literally, it seemed, on checking into the swanky new Monte Carlo Bay Hotel, the first European resort I have known to boast a touch of Vegas about its decor and landscaping. It turned out that I had also been upgraded to a huge suite possessed of more rooms than my London apartment, two giant plasma-screen TVs, and a balcony commanding a majestic view of Monte Carlo and its spring-sunlit bay. This *was* poker nirvana. On heading downstairs to check out the poker action, I ran straight into the other man behind all this, John Duthie.

John's poker name was made when he won the first televised Poker Million event on the Isle of Man in 2000. A television director at the time, born in Yorkshire in 1958, he had just won £18,000 in a third-place finish at the Vic and had a premonition that he would win the Isle of Man event. His wife Charlotte didn't want him to go – she had a dinner party lined up for that weekend – but John insisted. And his premonition came true when he emerged the winner from a final table including two formidable British pros here in Monte this week: Tony 'the

Lizard' Bloom and Barny Boatman of the Hendon Mob (a genial group comprising Boatman, his brother Ross, Joe Beevers and Ram Vaswani, who travel the world playing as a team, pooling their wins and losses). 'It was just one of those days', John recalls modestly, 'when I was in the zone.'

Ten years earlier Duthie had been making cups of tea as a runner on *The Young Indiana Jones*, the TV version of the Steven Spielberg–Harrison Ford movies. Soon he had graduated to second unit director on *Kavanagh QC* and later fully fledged director on such award-winning programmes as *Hollyoaks, Silent Witness, Clocking Off* and *As If*.

The rest of the time John was still playing cards, making three appearances on UK TV's *Late Night Poker* – eventually outlasting a field including Surinder Sunar, Julian 'the Kid' Gardner and Dutch maestro Marcel Luske to qualify for the Series Six Grand Final. In the wake of his Isle of Man triumph, he has also come second to Mike Sexton in the 2003 European Heads-Up Championships in Paris and finished in the money three times at the World Series of Poker, with tournament winnings to his name in excess of $2 million.

When Steve Lipscomb's World Poker Tour took off in 2003 Duthie's combination of poker and TV know-how prompted him to explore the idea of a European equivalent – the European Poker Tour. 'The idea', he laughs, 'was the easy part. We had a very hard time finding venues. You could not, for instance, then film in UK casinos; but the Vic got the British Gaming Board to say yes.' Barcelona, too, said no, but Duthie 'didn't take no for an answer'. He also fixed Dublin and Baden, Austria. Then he started meeting with poker websites in search of a sponsorship partner, finally opting for PokerStars 'because it was the biggest tournament site. They would bring more players.'

Duthie's next dilemma was whether to direct the programmes himself. Never having worked in TV sport, he eventually decided against and brought in the independent production company Sunset and Vine. He showed some WPT tapes to S&V's Geoff Foulser, the deal was done and the EPT was launched – on the smallest of scales at first, with only 220 starters in a €1000 event at Barcelona, but growing as rapidly as everything else in poker nowadays. In this, only its second season, the EPT has attracted more than two thousand players, generating a total prize pool of nearly €10 million. This week three hundred starters are expected at €10,000 a head for the EPT Grand Final, the biggest event in the history of European poker. Next season there will be nine EPT tournaments around Europe – Barcelona, London, Baden, Dublin, Copenhagen, Deauville, Dortmund, Warsaw and back here to Monte Carlo.

At this point the EPT's tournament director – guess who, Thomas Kremser, whom I had last seen yesterday in Vienna – interrupted us in search of some prize money. 'Yeah, I suppose you might be needing that,' growled Duthie, who has a pathological aversion to 'admin'. He went off in search of the dough and Lee Jones finished the story.

'John came to us with the idea and we thought, Yes, this could be big. Also, in Europe it was a great relief to find that there are none of the problems you get in the States with the Chinese walls between dot-com and dot-net.'

PokerStars has recently relocated to the Isle of Man. None too convincingly, Californian Lee Jones – who this time *does* have to make the move – tries to argue a case for the island's 'spiritual' qualities.

Back up in my room – sorry, suite – a bell-boy arrives with two smart black dress-shirts for me to wear in the tournament, each emblazoned with the PokerStars.com logo. *Two* shirts? They must think I'm going to make it to the second day.

With 298 starters from twenty-five different countries, that might be a tall order. Among my emails is one from my Friday Night cohort Joe Saumarez Smith, passing on the tournament odds as quoted by his website, BetUK.com. Erik Seidel and Gus Hansen (are they here? I haven't seen them) are quoted as 33-1 favourites, closely followed by such familiar European names as Devilfish Ulliott, the Hendon Mob and Marcel Luske at 40-1, Surinder Sunar, Tony Bloom and Willie Tann at 50-1, and John Gale at 66-1. Down towards the bottom, alongside other poker writers at 150-1, I am amazed to find my own name.

Pleased to be on this select list but outraged at his lack of faith in me, I ask Joe to put £20 on myself for me. If the worst happens I'll pay him back next time I see him. If I win the first prize of a million or so euros, however, another £3000 will surely come in handy to tip the dealers and buy a round of drinks.

As the 2 p.m. start approaches, I find myself standing behind reigning world champ Joe Hachem in the queue for seat assignments. I don't want to wind up at the same table as him, so I step aside for a while to let the random process take its course without me. When I step back in I get Table 16, Seat One, dammit, next to the dealer again, a restricted-view seat from which I cannot see the players obscured by the dealer. But that cuts both ways.

I have drawn the same table as Victoria Coren, who proceeds to run all over it. Her 7-3 pairs the three on the river. Her K-5 turns into a straight when the board brings 3-4-6-x-7 (and Vicky is playing her 'rush'). After ninety minutes, at the first break, she is up to €17k and I'm down to €9.6k. I defer to her as 'table boss' when telling the blogger from London's Gutshot Club, Steve Bartley, that Vicky is playing a blinder. By the time we resume she tells me she's had several support calls from London as a result. Who are all these people with nothing better to do than follow a poker tournament happening halfway across Europe?

During the break I reminisce with Micky 'the Legend' Wernick, top of the all-round European rankings after forty-three years in the game. The genial John Gale wanders over to give Micky some genial shit. Andy Black is here with his sister. Everyone is joking, smoking, enjoying each other's company. The whole thing seems much friendlier, less ferociously competitive, than it would be in America – where the new poker players seem to have learnt their table manners, as well as their playing style, from the worst of those grandstanding for TV air-time.

When play resumes, moreover, only eight players per table means there is room for each one of us to have a table beside us for glasses (of water) and other clutter. Compared with Vegas or Foxwoods, this all seems so civilised – European and elegant – apart from the cards I'm getting, which have yet to show a spark of life. With the blinds now at €50– €100, my A-J is beaten by 10-10 with a flop of A-J-10. Luckily, my opponent did not bet on the end. It sinks my stack to €8k. 'It could have been a lot worse', Vicky rightly observes. She wasn't involved in the hand; but she's been watching the whole thing, eagle-eyed, like the smart player she is.

During a ciggy break halfway through the level, John Duthie tells me that former world champion Carlos Mortensen and top British pro Julian Gardner have both been knocked out already. As always this gives my ego an absurd, completely irrelevant little boost. It also renews my determination to give my sponsors some value for their money.

As the third level gets under way, with the blinds at €75–€150, an A-J actually stands up for me. So I decide to play my rush, *à la* Coren, when the next hand brings J-6. I am out of position but the flop brings J-6-4 – and I get two calls from Vicky before she senses that I mean business here.

Then comes the dread A-K, both spades. Again in early

position, I make it €350 to go and get two callers – Vicky again and an elderly American chomping on an unlit cigar. The flop comes A♥-7♥-4♥. I bet €500; Vicky folds, he calls. The turn brings the 3♥. I check, he checks; but any heart in his hand would now give him a flush. When he bets on the end, I feel obliged to play safe and fold. Like a true gent, he flashes a heart at me as he throws the dealer his winning hand.

At 6.45 p.m. our table is broken. I bid a fond farewell to *la* Coren as I move to Table 3, Seat Eight, with only €6.6k of my €10k left. With thirty minutes until the dinner break, I immediately get pocket aces, then pocket nines. No one calls either of my pre-flop raises. They're still sizing me up, knowing that any reraise might see me pot-committed. As it is, I just collar the blinds and make only a modest advance to €7.5k.

During the dinner break I ask the Hendon Mob's Ross Boatman how I can play in the tournament and watch Arsenal versus Real Madrid on TV in the European Champions League at the same time. We are 1-0 up from the away leg and this game really means a lot to me. Ross says he's a Spurs fan so he doesn't care. My mind is at Highbury as the fourth level begins, the blinds now €100–€200. With only €6.8k I'm going to have to make some moves before too long.

At 9.10 p.m., forty minutes into this level, my pocket fives are beaten by pocket threes when the first card on the flop is a three. My Danish is non-existent but the conversation at the next table suggests that Arsenal have done enough, with that first-leg lead, to win on aggregate in a 0-0 draw. That's some compensation for my bad beat; and I celebrate by going all-in with pocket nines, get one caller and a flop of J-9-x-x-x. My five thou has doubled up to ten – back where I started.

'You're doing us proud, Tony,' says Lee Jones when I'm still alive at the last break of the day – during which I then get the shock of my poker year. That blonde over there in the bar, talking to one of the dealers. That can't be the Moll, can it? Looks suspiciously like her from behind.

I head over to find that it is indeed my estranged wife (yes, technically, we are still married), who had hitherto been hiding from me. She knew I was coming to Monte Carlo – well, I'd told her over dinner the previous week – and decided to head down here for old times' sake after a weekend visit to Paris. Cindy always loved 'the poker life' – on the road, living out of a suitcase as you hustle your way round the circuit – and she couldn't resist revisiting it. She had got here earlier today, hadn't played in the tournament herself – not at that entry fee – but was worried about distracting me. During the previous breaks she'd been hiding herself away. But now that she could see I was doing okay, she had decided to take the risk of letting me find her.

In the absence of any other talismans, mojos or lucky charms, I was more than glad she had. Now she could come and sit at the rail, like the Moll of the old days, and bring me some much-needed luck.

Which, as play resumes for the last session, she immediately manages. I go all-in with A-9, get a caller and double up when the flop comes x-9-x-9-x. Then my all-in A-K actually beats J-10. I'm back up to around €15k when Anna Kournikova strikes again, this time halving my stack by losing to an all-in pair of fives. At 2 a.m., when for some reason a snatch of Vivaldi heralds the end of the day's play, I'm hanging in there with just €5250. Half the field has gone but there are only seven players below me.

Yet the Moll is pleased. She'll have something to watch in the morning.

After a lazy breakfast in the Monegasque sun on the balcony of my suite, by which the Moll is suitably impressed, Day Two begins with the blinds at €150–€300, with rolling antes of €50, and my short stack sitting alongside another, belonging to none other than 2004 world champion Greg Raymer.

There in front of the genial Greg is one of the fossils he uses as a card protector, earning himself the nickname 'Fossilman' when he took the $5 million first prize in the World Series. The following year, as one of the 5618 beaten by Joe Hachem, Raymer put in one of the best performances ever seen from a reigning champ, leading the field into the penultimate day and finishing twenty-fifth.

Greg played nickel-and-dime poker in his college fraternity but didn't get serious about the game until he became a patent lawyer in Chicago. During law school he had made extra money as a blackjack card-counter in the Native American casinos of Minnesota; in Chicago he could find no blackjack, and stumbled across a $3–$6 Hold 'em game. 'I liked it and decided to become a winning poker player for extra spending money.' He read a bunch of poker books and slowly advanced from $3–$6 to $20–$40 and eventually to $150–$300 at Foxwoods, near his Connecticut home.

Good company as well as a strong player, Raymer has always waxed modest about his world title win, saying that his poker was the best he has ever played – and he got lucky. 'There was a hand on the TV table where I raised with 10-8 off-suit to steal the blinds and got reraised from the big blind by John Murphy. I felt sure he thought his hand was the best – and it probably was – but also weak enough that he simply wanted to win it right there. He'd been pushing me around a bit that session and I wanted to back him off. So I reraised all-in. He looked unhappy but folded fairly quickly. I showed him my cards. I don't know if it made any difference or not later on but that was my intention.'

At the final table there were a couple of hands where Raymer got the kind of luck you need to win these things: his pocket tens flopped a set to beat pocket aces and his A-10 against A-K turned into a queen-high straight on the river. 'These were the only bad beats I remember inflicting on anybody.' He adds: 'There were a few hands where I was in really bad shape and caught a miracle card, but never one that would have made a big dent in my stack.' He still doesn't understand, he says, how he managed to stay so calm and focused over a whole week of play. 'If I did, I'd be doing it every tournament.'

He doesn't seem to be managing it in this one. Raymer starts Day Two with barely €7000 – not much more than my own meagre €5250. A big table-talker, he's amusing about the familiar syndrome where everyone at the table wants to knock out a player with a face now as famous as his. There are ceiling-high posters of him around the room, which can't help. 'Everyone wants to take a crack at you – either to say they've beaten the world champion or to say it was the world champion who knocked them out. It's a good story to take back home to their friends. It means people call you with the craziest hands. That's great, of course, but it does add another layer of pressure.'

At the moment he's telling me that he and I are in the same boat here: we're both, as the short stacks, 'one move' players – i.e., all-in or nothing, shit or bust. Greg's first ambition is to double his way back to being a two-move player – all-in or maybe just raise. While he's waiting for his moment, I get mine. All-in with A-J, I get a call from an A-9. The Moll stands up from her seat on the rails as the flop brings 9 . . . 6 . . . J. The turn and river are rags. I have doubled up to €8.5k – more than Raymer. Soon he goes all-in with pocket jacks, only to come up against pocket kings. The kings hold up and Raymer is eliminated in 120th place.

'If you can lay down jacks there,' he says, 'you're either a genius or a moron.' I step back to let the cameras capture the moment, then step forward again to shake his hand as he leaves – an image I later see immortalised on television. Hey, I think, who is that guy with the bald patch? I don't remember

him. But that black PokerStars shirt does look familiar . . . oh
hell, it's me. Thank God I can't see myself from behind – except
on television.

At the time the bald patch was the least of my worries. At
least Raymer and others were getting playable hands, even if
they are going out on them. Me, I haven't seen a hand since the
last one, a good half-hour ago. Yet again I'm playing the art of
the short stack.

People are getting knocked out on all sides, so it does feel
right to wait for some cards rather than taking unnecessary
chances. This reluctant patience is at last rewarded – on my big
blind, too – when I get K-4, the best hand I've seen in a while.
The small blind just calls and I'm tempted to raise, but rein
myself in. When the flop comes K-9-4 rainbow and the small
blind checks, I go all-in again. To my amazement – well, he
doesn't have *that* many more chips than me – he calls and rolls
over 8-9 off-suit. The turn and river are harmless, so I double
back up to just over €10,000. With two-thirds of the field gone,
only a hundred players left, it's barely a third of the average
stack – but it's something. Now I'm at least a two-move player
again.

Come the second break, the Moll has booked herself a massage.
She seems to feel that she is leaving my fate in safe hands. I'm
not so sure.

When I run into the Gutshot blogger Steve, whose overnight
reports I have been reading, I remonstrate with him that he
has called the music announcing each interval 'Beethoven'.

'It's not Beethoven, Steve,' I tell him, probably the only
person in the room who either knows or cares. 'It's Vivaldi. *The
Four Seasons*. I'm a music critic, man. My reputation's at stake
here!' That, too, naturally goes into the blog, with the punch-
line: 'It's important to be accurate', and a picture of me looking
pretty fed up with my short stack.

The blinds are now €400–€600, the antes €75. At €1200 per round, I have ten rounds' worth, €12k. No need to panic yet. I'm still a two-, maybe even three-move player. It is galling, however, to watch the only stack shorter than mine double up with pocket aces. Why can't that happen to me, is the kind of self-pitying thought you start having at times like this. He gets an ace on the flop as well. Where's the justice?

Twenty minutes later I'm dealt A-9, the best hand I've seen in quite a while. In early position I raise the bet to €2000, like the coolest two-move player, and get one caller behind me. When the flop brings A-10-7 I go all-in, another €5300. He calls with alarming speed and shows A-Q. Uh-oh. The turn brings a four, the river a two. Yet again my bid for glory is over.

At least my chips went to a Brit – one of the top British players, none other than Paul 'Action Jack' Jackson. We shake hands and I am consoled by blogger Bartley. 'Well, a man's gotta do what a man's gotta do' I go down in history as having told him, with all the originality available at such moments, choosing to add: 'Better than Ace-deuce, anyway.' Why the hell did I say *that*?

Steve's next act, I discover later, is to immortalise all these banalities, including the hand, in his Gutshot report – alongside a gilt-edged portrait of the great Vivaldi captioned: 'Tony Holden – Italy'.

Very droll.

With the Moll still enjoying her massage, I wander off for a consoling glass of wine in the late-afternoon Riviera sun. That sudden feeling of deep tiredness descends, after all those hours of concentration, and I find myself having downbeat thoughts. If I were a government minister, suddenly pushed out of office, for instance, I'd be pitched out of that sponsored suite now. Then Lee Jones wanders by to reassure me that there'll be no night of the long poker knives.

After a quiet dinner with the Moll, followed by killer nightcaps in the hotel's svelte cocktail bar, my best night's sleep in a long time sees me unusually perky at breakfast and raring to go for more. This is to be the Moll's moment; she is determined to beat me in a sit and go so that I will have to admit as much here in print.

Lee Jones joins us for the first, a €250 buy-in, and bosses the table effortlessly, gleefully quoting the wit and wisdom of Andy Bloch: 'Poker is a godless game full of random pain.' As poor Cindy soon finds out. She is the second to go, her all-in K-10 beaten by a K-Q when the flop brings K-Q-x-x-x. Nonetheless, it's a wild enough game for her and other departees to enjoy hanging around to watch. Lee goes all-in with an A-10 flush draw and knocks out another sucker when his flush comes on the turn. I'm next to go when my Q-J fails to pair up against Lee's pocket fours. He then risks his all on another flush draw but this time draws a blank. Once Lee's gone, we all lose interest.

Cindy has already registered for another, in which she comes second, when her all-in pair of queens is called by 5-6 on the button and the flop comes 5-5-6. Welcome to the world of the new poker. At least she's now ahead financially. Just one more, we agree, and no one seems to mind when this apparent couple draw seats next to each other. With half the table gone, I look down to see a juicy pair of tens – and am not sure whether to be pleased or dismayed when the Moll, on my right, goes all-in in front of me.

I have to call, don't I? Everyone is looking at me impatiently as I hesitate, while my poker psyche hosts a brief skirmish between Mars and Venus. Mars wins and I call. Cindy turns over pocket eights. The rest is (or had better be) silence.

The evening of Day Four, our last here, will see the final table of the EPT tournament. Meanwhile the punters are obsessed with sit-and-gos, some as high as €10,000, even €20,000 per head entry. The Moll and I decide to rise above such frivolity by heading into town.

Unlike me, Cindy has never before been to Monte Carlo; and unlike most women, as she is the first to admit, she is today less interested in checking out the shops than its celebrated casino. Twenty-five years ago, just before I met her, this was the scene of a rare blackjack triumph on my part when I won a chunk of money while being photographed and interviewed for a Sunday colour magazine article about gambling. I remember being irritated that the photographer wanted me in James Bond-ish white tux and black tie, not my natural attire. But that's when you want to win – when the entire event is being recorded for posterity. As I regale the Moll with all this, she reminds me that the tournament down the road is also being recorded for posterity. In which case, how come I'm not still in it?

There's no answer to that. Better, instead, to take her across the road to the Hotel de Paris and show her the bronze horse in the lobby whose fetlock you're supposed to stroke for luck before heading out to the casino – as testified by a shiny patch on its leg, buffed by countless punters over the years. Then comes the one bright idea even Vegas hasn't yet come up with. This is a casino where *you have to pay to get in*. Ten euros a head is what it will cost you to hand over more of your money, once you've got past its grand entrance into the huge marbled halls that smack more of a mausoleum than a sink of gaming iniquity. A few smartly dressed, elderly people are wagering hefty amounts at roulette and blackjack in silence worthy of an ancient library; otherwise the place has become as much a tourist attraction as a casino – and feels more like a museum.

The Moll and I wonder whether to take the same thrilling risk we once braved when we first got together – impulsively stake £1000 on red at roulette (we won) – and decide, given our bankrolls, against. Just as well, as the next four spins all come up black.

That feels like a win as we wander out past the next-door opera house, the Salle Garnier, where the unmistakable strains of Puccini's *Tosca* are drifting out of the rehearsal room, reminding the music critic that this is yet another week off earning an honest half-living. This must be the Italian soprano Carla Maria Izzo, billed to play the role there the following week. Sad that he'll be gone by then, the critic makes a mental note that he might one day be able to bring the poker player back here to Monte Carlo, given the right opera at the right time.

That evening we watch from the bleachers as further evidence unfolds of the remarkable rise of the student generation in the world of the new poker. The EPT final table is dominated throughout by a teenage American university freshman, who goes on to win the first prize of €900,000 ($1.1 million) after refusing his opponents' pleas for a deal.

In his native United States nineteen-year-old Jeff Williams, a first-year political philosophy major at the University of Michigan, wouldn't even be allowed into a casino yet. Still won't be for the best part of two years. Here in Europe the legal age for entering a casino is eighteen.

Jeff's parents have flown in overnight from Atlanta and are beside us in the bleachers as their son wins his way to dollar-millionaire status. The Moll and I are especially impressed by his self-confidence when the table is down to four people and play stops as the other three suggest a carve-up.

This may not be allowed on the WPT but the EPT seems to have no problem with it – even though John Duthie has told me that at the final table of the Poker Million he wound up winning, he was escorted by armed heavies during breaks (even into the men's room) to ensure that he was not secretly cooking up an off-camera deal with the other players. Here Thomas Kremser himself comes over to supervise the negotiations, ready to enforce any settlement. Young Jeff just sits there impassively behind his shades and his giant stack of chips, shaking his head and saying no – he intends to win this thing. He is offered a guaranteed 800,000 (rather than 900,000) euros, with a proportionate split for the others – and play for the title plus a chunk of change. No, insists Jeff, let's play on.

Which they do till he duly triumphs. As a father, I felt for his own in the bleachers during those negotiations; young Jeff never even looked towards his parents for support in this moment of high drama. I think I'd have been straight down there myself, welcome or not, making sure these shysters didn't rip off my brilliant but less than worldly teenage son.

Once your offspring are embarked on their twenties, nineteen does seem very young. You remember all the crazy, irresponsible, irritating things they got up to at that age. Together the Moll and I brought up five children over some fifteen years. If one of them, I ask her, had said at nineteen, during their first term at university, that they were off to another continent to play in a poker tournament, would we have let them go? Probably, we agree – if, like Jeff, they had won the entry fee and expenses in an online tournament. Still, wouldn't one of us have gone with them? For sure – but, she adds sagely, for all the wrong reasons.

These are the moments that bring out the best in Lee Jones, one of the true heroes of the online poker scene. He's got a routine that he takes round American universities, which he now wheels on for the benefit of Jeff Williams and his parents. Finish university, he tells the nineteen-year-old millionaire (who seems very cool about it all; maybe he's still in shock). Don't lose all this money playing poker. Set a chunk of it aside for poker, say $50,000 tops, and invest the rest, maybe buy some condominiums. Above all, remember this: poker isn't going anywhere. It'll still be there when you leave university. And I, Lee H. Jones, offer you my personal guarantee that the first hand you play will never have been played before.

This last, gnomic remark is the cause of some debate as I pass it around the travelling poker community. The rest of Jones' gentle lecture is manna from heaven to Jeff's parents. Thanks *so* much, they tell him, that's exactly what we would have said – but we're his parents so he wouldn't have taken the slightest notice. Coming from you, however . . .

Jeff's mother was especially pleased with the bit about condominiums. Turns out she's in real estate.

At Nice Côte d'Azur Airport the next morning I gallantly escort the Moll into the VIP lounge – only to get an odd look from a slight, flame-haired woman who turns out to be someone I have known for thirty years. 'I thought you two weren't together any more?' says television's favourite dominatrix, *The Weakest Link*'s Anne Robinson – getting straight to the point, as is her wont. Annie and I were both reporters in the *Sunday Times* newsroom in the mid-1970s.

'We're not,' I reply enigmatically, 'but we're still, er, close.' Annie, I can tell, is on the point of asking about the sleeping arrangements when around the corner comes her travelling companion, another woman I have known for thirty years. It's the 'Queen of the Jungle' to British TV viewers – Carol Thatcher, daughter of you-know-who, always delightfully full of the joys of spring.

Doubly so today, because it transpires that these two have been on a weekend yachting expedition, courtesy of a glossy magazine, along with other media names who have failed to make it into the VIP lounge. With some relish Annie points down below, and through the lounge's glass walls I can see the TV newscasters Anna Ford and Peter Sissons, plus another long-standing friend of mine (from the magazine) and her husband. This is all getting beyond the bounds of coincidence. As we meet up in the queue to board the flight, we are all suitably astonished to see each other – and everyone is as impressed as ever at the macho reasons for my trip to Monte Carlo. Such are the little satisfactions of masquerading as an itinerant poker pro.

The day after my return to Blighty and the Job, I receive an email from my blogger friend Madeline 'Mad' Harper of PokerStars. 'I just have to tell you about my last night in Monte . . . I ended up in a ten-euro sit-and-go with the film crew. At 4 a.m. we were joined by Jeff Williams, who'd been having a quiet drink with his parents at a nearby table. Needless to say, I outlasted him (in fact, did a deal for first place). So I am now forty-five euros up (from a starting point of zero) and Jeff Williams is now ten euros down (from a starting point of 900,000). Hasta la vista! Mad x'

Little did Mad know how fitting her Spanish sayonara would soon prove. How could either of us know that before too long I would be seeing her again in her adopted home town of Barcelona, in circumstances against which I would have laid heavy odds?

8

My Moneymaker Effect

What is the supposedly umbilical link between writers and poker? Is there one? Or is it merely an urban-myth hangover from the days of Damon Runyon and the *New Yorker* round table at the Algonquin?

Back in 1990 *GQ* magazine tried to find out by paying five writers to play poker together, then come up with their own individual accounts of the same game. In a food- and liquor-fuelled private room at Morton's Club in London's Berkeley Square (where no nightingales could be heard singing that night), the five were paid £500 each for their trouble – in poker chips, with which they had to play. If they lost it and wanted to keep playing, they would have to dig into their own pockets for more. Over six hours at the table the £2500 in play eventually rose to £4000.

The writers were the playwright, screenwriter and director David Mamet, the novelist Martin Amis, the poet and critic Al Alvarez, a GQ editor named John Graham – and myself. In fact the event was *GQ*'s gratifying way of giving some promotional oxygen to my newly published book, *Big Deal*.

Alvarez and I had broached the subject of writers and poker over many a meal together in Vegas but either got distracted or could never remember the conclusions we had reached. In a book of tributes to him I co-edited in 1999 for his seventieth birthday, I wrote of Al's penchant for risk: 'On one such occasion [in the Binion's poker buffet], we actually managed to define the umbilical link between poker and poetry. The moment can never be recreated, but it was again something to do with risk. Not for him Camus' dictum (of Nietzsche) that a man can lead a life of wild adventure without ever leaving his desk. "For five or six days a week," as Al has put it, "I sit at my desk and try to get the sentences right. If I make a mistake, I can rewrite it the next day, or catch it in proof. And if I fail to do so, who cares? Who even notices? If I make a mistake climbing, or playing poker, the consequences are immediate, embarrassing, and probably painful."'

True, all too true, but where's that umbilical link? If you ask me, writing is such a tricky, solitary business that writers play poker to avoid writing. Forget the notion that writers are good at reading, i.e., other players' cards as well as other writers' books; it's a neat idea but entirely devoid of substance. The only thing the two occupations have in common, for sure, is their financial fragility.

Which is maybe why, as the *GQ* team packed up to leave us to it, they seemed a tad concerned as to how involved we had already become in the game, not least because the results were going to be *published*. Would we remember to write our pieces? 'I'd just like to remind you', said the departing executive, struggling to get our attention, 'that you're all supposed to *write* about this. We need your copy by Monday lunchtime.' There were startled looks of semi-panic all round, even some groping for notepads. Everyone was so intent on winning that we had indeed forgotten this was also a writing assignment. No one wanted to lose, as much for reasons of street-cred as the dough – not to mention the volatility of the writer's ego.

As Alvarez wrote in his account of the evening, 'Ego is a writer's disease. Publishers' advances, sales and position on the literary ladder tend to figure large in their preoccupations when they get together. I planned my strategy for the game accordingly. I knew I would be the oldest person at the table, so I thought I might as well play the part: sit, wait, look benign and let those with something to prove destroy each other.'

Of me, he said: 'Holden is an aggressive player who knows how to play tight and is dangerous when the cards run in his favour.' From Mamet's writings on poker he assumed he would be 'patient, dour and dedicated to winning'. He knew that Amis played chess, Graham bridge and backgammon. 'If the game had been just us four Englishmen, I suppose there might have been a lot of showing off, backchat, and flashy play. As it was, Mamet set the tone for the evening. He is a burly, bearded man, very sympathetic and subtle to talk to away from the table, but an unsmiling, no-nonsense player, unwilling to be drawn into London literary twitter and, I suspect, wary of being set up. He watched the dealer like a hawk.'

All this was even truer than Al knew. None of us had met Mamet before, though we were all ardent admirers of his work. Before the game, over a sociable drink or two, he was both courteous and charming, throwing me for a loop by managing to mention Trollope and Lake Tahoe in the same sentence. Once we sat down, however, he was all concentration, edged with a distinct wariness, not saying a word even when spoken to. And when he and I happened to meet in the men's room, he told me of his dark suspicions that he was somehow being set up. Was the dealer straight? Were we all out to get him?

Maybe, I can only guess, that's what Chicago does to a guy?

As for Al, it was not to be his night. 'We started at 7.30 p.m. and played for six hours, and in all that time I was dealt only two unequivocally decent hands: an A-K of clubs and a pair of nines. On both occasions I raised before the flop, got no callers and merely won the antes. I stole a few pots by using position if it was checked around to me when I was last to act. I bet – not because I had good cards, but because I was sure no one could call me. The rest of the time I sat folding unplayable cards.

'Two and a half hours into the game I called on Q-8 of hearts. The flop was 9♥-10♠-J♠, giving me a straight. Holden bet. He was playing very tight, so I assumed he had a straight like me, possibly to the king. I called warily. A 4♥ fell on fourth street, giving me a four-flush to go with my straight. He bet again. Now I was certain of his hand, but I called, hoping to fill my flush. A second nine fell on fifth street. Tony checked. I could have tried to bluff a full house, but I didn't think he'd wear it. We turned over and, yes, he had the straight to the king and I was down to £250.'

Fifteen minutes later a 'stupid mistake' against Mamet, calling rather than raising with a paired ace and a post-flop flush draw, cost Al the rest of his £250. He had to dig in his pocket for another £500. He then lost £120 of that – a total of £620. 'This is the first and only time', he concluded, 'I have paid to write a magazine article.'

Amis was foxier, if equally generous to me, whom he confessed to having known for twenty years. 'It was Anthony Holden who seemed to me to possess the most dangerous mixture of froth and flair. Tony is toney; he has his Vegas mannerisms: the exaggerated slouch, the languidly scornful flickaway of the dead cards. When the pot gets high, the hour late, and you need to see what he has in the hole, then the lounge lizard melds into a loan shark. Holden writes whole books about Hold 'em. He is the Imam of Hold 'em. He is practically *called* Hold 'em.'

I also seemed to be getting to John Graham: 'The worst [beat] was when I got dealt the only full house I got all night. I held 4-3 and the flop came 9-3-3. I got them all out except

Holden, and when the fourth card was a four I bet the lot. Holden called, and called again after the fifth card. He had been dealt 9-9, an almost unbeatable hand after the flop, but he never raised me. He just wiped me out.'

Tony Holden, Mamet reported, was sitting on his left: 'I didn't see him do anything extraordinary throughout the evening. He played quietly, unremarkably and patiently. When I left he was winning all the money. Ahah!'

It is true; somehow I emerged the big winner. Looking back over those pieces, I do seem to have pulled some cards that night. The five articles duly appeared – and then, as is the way of such things, disappeared. Apart, of course, from Martin's, which resurfaced between hard covers in his 1993 collection *Visiting Mrs Nabokov and Other Excursions*. On page 181, at its end, he adds in a footnote:

'Anthony Holden was the big winner (well over a thousand pounds); David Mamet doubled his money; Al Alvarez lost, and John Graham lost heavily, as they say; I came out with £200 of the magazine's money. But then I had to write the piece. Holden, in effect, was paid £2 a word for his contribution; I was paid 25p.'

In fact, Mart, £1835 (and so £2.30 a word). Generous of you to add that footnote on hardback publication; but what beyond fond memories of a handsome win would have moved me to dig so deep in the archives?

No conclusions at all were reached about this supposed link between writers and poker. Maybe I'd find one at the first-ever Poker Writers' Tournament, to be staged in Atlantic City?

Between the Caribbean cruise and Monte Carlo, I had received an invitation from the American poker writer Sheree Bykofsky to play in the inaugural Poker Writers' Tournament at the Trump Taj Mahal in Atlantic City in March. As it happened, I had never been to Atlantic City. Although universally told I hadn't missed anything – the place was a hell-hole – I had always wanted to check it out for myself.

Also, I was overdue another visit to New York. Simon Russell Beale had now taken over from Tim Curry as King Arthur in *Spamalot*. Other friends, not least Charlie Simmons and the Yonkers crew, had also been promised another visit. I decided to head west again.

The fact that anyone could even think of organising a Poker Writers' Tournament is another crazy index of the new poker boom. In 1990, when I made my debut as a poker author after my year on the professional circuit, a convention of poker writers would scarcely have filled the cloakroom of Binion's. There was Brunson, David Sklansky, Mason Malmuth, 'Mad' Mike Caro, Tom McEvoy, Alvarez, Spanier and me. These days, it seems, a new manual appears every week, dealing with online play as much as the real thing, while the poker memoir – or the poker 'narrative' – almost keeps pace with the profusion of autobiographies by star players. I've even heard of plans for a Bloggers' Tournament at the start of the next World Series.

Even though the first list of potential attendees included such exalted names in the thin ranks of poker literature as James McManus, Andy Bellin, Michael Craig, Nolan Dalla and Peter Alson, I couldn't persuade Alvarez to come with me. His gammy leg pretty much rules out long-haul flights these days. By the time I had emailed my acceptance and booked my own air ticket, none of the above was coming. But the dozen who did turn up were an interesting – and assorted – group.

I have long known Lou Krieger, co-author with Bykofsky of a new tome called *Secrets the Pros Won't Tell You About Winning Hold 'Em Poker* – the book which, I suspect, the event was really set up to plug. The same goes for Richard Sparks, as in *Diary of a Mad Poker Player*, with whom I used to play in London before he decamped to California. I was pleased to meet two writers whose work I knew and admired: David Apostolico, as in

Tournament Poker and the Art of War and *Machiavellian Poker Strategy*, and Matt Lessinger, *The Book of Bluffs*. Also on hand were Mike Cappelletti (*How to Win at Omaha High-Low Poker*), Gary Carson (*The Complete Book of Hold 'em Poker* and *The Complete Book of Casino Poker*), Neil D. Myers (*Quick and Easy Texas Hold 'Em*), Henry Stephenson (*Real Poker Night*) and J. Phillip Vogel (*Internet Gambling*). Finally, too, I got to meet Greg Dinkin, literary agent as well as co-author of the invaluable *The Poker MBA* and more recently *Amarillo Slim in a World Full of Fat People* (in which Slim seems to think I was chasing him round the world during *Big Deal*). A literary agent who can make a living from representing poker players – that's a striking new development, as well.

The night I arrived, hours before the tournament, I took a stroll along the boardwalk and immediately saw what people meant about Atlantic City. It was like Vegas twenty years ago: architecture of faded grandiloquence peopled by crazy, degenerate gamblers and groups of drunken pals (of both genders, but rarely mixed) out for some noisy fun. It was good to be beside the seaside; having grown up there, in north-west England, I have an elemental need for that – and a soft spot for piers. But forty-eight hours here would be quite enough.

This being a publishing occasion, the following morning saw the arrival from New York of my editor, Amanda Murray of Simon & Schuster – along with five girlfriends, all in publishing, who made up their very own poker school. They had recently been to Vegas together for a wild weekend, but in vain did I try to persuade them to enter the tournament. The buy-in was only $120 – and each author was to be a 'target', i.e., there was a bonus for knocking him or her out, if only a signed copy of the relevant book. No, they would be my cheerleaders – as indeed they became after a raucous lunch at the Hard Rock Café.

What a table-image I acquired as this bevy of beauties lined up beside the table when the tournament began, linking arms for a cheerleaders' dance with cries of 'Tony Hol-den! Tony Hol-den!' The other players were completely fazed. For the first hour or two, I ran over the table effortlessly.

It was after the first break that things began to go wrong. There was no sign of the girls, who seemed to have lost interest and gone out on the town. And no reply from Amanda's mobile phone, either; they must be deep within some other urban pile. My chips began to diminish. By the fourth level I was somehow down to just three big blinds. Suddenly Q-10 seemed a good enough hand to justify an all-in on my part. It was called by A-K. The flop came Q-A-5 and rags. End of story.

Still no sign of my support group, so I wound up having dinner with Greg Dinkin and Time Warner's Colin Fox before Colin and I decided to do battle in the cash games downstairs. We found seats together at the $2–$5 No Limit Hold 'em table and tried to take on the rest of the players rather than each other.

Sometimes, however, such well-laid plans just don't work out. On the small blind Colin called with what turned out to be 10-9; on the button I raised with K-Q suited. He immediately called. The flop was an astonishing A-A-A. Colin checked; I bet out again, figuring my king was good. Out of optimism or sheer stubbornness – well, we had had a few drinks – he called, only to be gifted (little did I know) a ten on the turn. Now he bet and it was my turn to exhibit some weird combination of optimism or disbelief – or maybe just stubbornness – by calling. The river came a king. We both checked, out of friendship, only to discover I had rivered him out of a hefty pot.

The night went on that way. I could do no wrong. These Atlantic City players are, like the town they inhabit, just *awful*. Even when the jet lag kicked in and I began to fall asleep during hands, I kept on playing – until one careless loss persuaded me to retire for some rest between 3 and 4 a.m., $1500 to the good.

Come 8 a.m., however, I was awake again – and straight

back down to the night before's table, where most of the same inept poker junkies (apart from Colin) were still beating each other up. I scored another grand in a couple of hours before hitching a ride to Newark with a cheery Richard Sparks, full of stories about his coaching from 1983 world champion Tom McEvoy for his forthcoming book, *Getting Lucky*.

Writers are competitive people. As, of course, are poker players. This had been a convention of people competing at cards, who write about competing at cards, while competing about the books in which they write about competing at cards. The very thought is exhausting. I don't think I'll be back next year. And I still haven't found that supposed link between writers and poker.

Flying back from New York a few days later, I missed out on 2006's British Open poker tournament, a TV event staged by the Poker Channel at London's new mecca of televised poker, the Riverside Studios in Hammersmith. According to the invitation, it would provide 'an unparalleled opportunity to meet celebrity and professional players in fun and informal surroundings'. Is this what poker has come to these days? Meeting celebrity players? What about playing?

'What's more, one lucky guest will win a seat worth £3000 in that afternoon's PKR.com Super Series 2006, one of the British Poker Open heats.' Ahah. So this would have been my chance 'to play for one of Europe's most prestigious poker titles and a first prize of £50,000'.

Ah, well. I've got to concentrate on the Job for a while; another week off in the US was raising editorial eyebrows. Besides, I've got a better invitation – to an event boasting three world champions and the chance to win the $10,000 entry for this year's main event at the World Series.

Ten days later, after a whistle-stop flight to Glasgow and back for an indifferent version of my favourite opera, Mozart's *Don*

Giovanni, I head to a Soho nightclub appropriately called the Play Room for the chance to win that trip to Vegas. Twenty-four poker journalists are to take on the last three world champions – Joe Hachem, Greg Raymer and Chris Moneymaker – in a generous freeroll laid on by PokerStars. The second prize is a box of chips. First prize: the $10,000 entry fee into the 2006 WSOP world title event, plus a return flight from London and a hotel for the duration.

This is a prize worth winning. I'm going to have to make this expensive trip anyway, to round off my year's adventure; if I can do it for free, I'll be way in profit before I even arrive in Vegas. When I reach the Play Room, the presence of the three world champs has drawn quite a crowd; there are a couple of hundred journos drinking PokerStars dry, including several of my acquaintance who are *furious* at not being invited to play. Why have I made the cut? I, too, wonder in all modesty. But I'm not going to complain, let alone offer my seat to someone else.

After a few drinks before play starts I discover that this is one of those rare occasions when smoking will also be permitted at the table. Hmmm, this could be my kind of game. With a world champ at each of three tables, I look around and size up the opposition. There are some pretty good players here – not least my journalistic poker nemesis, Matt Born – but none that I don't think I can beat. Hachem and Raymer then confirm my suspicions – that they're not supposed to win – by going out in the first quarter of an hour.

Yet I have drawn Moneymaker's table and am sitting on his right. We chat amiably but it soon becomes clear that the 2003 world champ has no intention of making merely a token appearance here. He is playing in earnest, for real – and playing well, reading the other players like, not books, because Chris doesn't read books (including, I can only hope, his own less than overwhelming autobiography), but like the lesser players they were. Including me.

Gradually I form the impression that Moneymaker still resents the abiding view that his 2003 world title win was a fluke. His eights beating Humberto Brenes' aces when the turn brought him a set. That gutshot straight against Phil Ivey's trip queens. And that bluff in the heads-up with the experienced pro Sam Farha, who had already refused his offer to split the prize money and play for the bracelet.

As Moneymaker (with $4.62 million in chips) prepared to make a small raise to $100,000 with K♠-7♥, Farha ($3.7 million) jocularly drawled, 'Don't do it!' So Chris did, moving Farha to call with Q♠-9♥, before a flop of 9♠-2♦-6♠. With top pair, Farha trap-checked, only for Moneymaker to check behind him. The turn, the 8♠, brought straight and flush possibilities. So Farha tried to drive Moneymaker out of the hand with a huge bet of $300,000 into a pot of $210,000. But Moneymaker stunned him with a tournament-swing raise of $800,000.

'We said it was going to be over soon,' smiled Farha as he called. The river came the 3♥. Again Farha trap-checked, planning to call Moneymaker when he bluffed all-in – as indeed he did with only a king-high against Farha's pair of nines. Then, fatally, Farha hesitated. 'Must've missed your flush, eh?' he mused, accurately. Facing a make-or-break call, Farha had another shot at eliciting information. 'I could make a crazy call on you,' he said. 'Mine could be the best hand.' Moneymaker sat there like a basilisk, giving nothing away; he later revealed that he was thinking about his trip home and how much his quality of life would be improved by the second-place prize money. In the end Farha thought himself all the way out of his place in poker history by picking up his cards and throwing them into the muck. Moneymaker had made 'the bluff of the century', according to ESPN's Norman Chad. 'He didn't play it well,' said Farha later. 'I played it badly.'

Folks tended to side with Farha, who had just made the worst play of his poker life, and for nearly three years Moneymaker

had been called the living incarnation of one of poker's oldest
expressions: 'I'd rather be lucky than good.' So give him a
barrelful of journalists, and these are precisely the people he
wants to shoot down, to show that he can play, that his world
title win was no one-off wonder.

'Hey, Greg,' I plead as Raymer wanders by. 'Can you please
tell Chris here that he's not supposed to win this thing?' There
is uneasy laughter. Everyone within earshot knows it is true but
Moneymaker is all over the table, uncannily reading his opponents' hands whether they called, raised or folded. This guy,
take it from me, does know what he's doing.

An accountant on $40,000 a year when he won that $2.5 million first prize in 2003, soon doubled by sponsorship deals,
Moneymaker played bridge with his grandmother as a child,
then blackjack with his father and grew up to find gambling
indissolubly in his blood. He secured an accounting degree from
the University of Tennessee, despite spending most of his time
there gambling, and soon settled into suburban marriage and
number-crunching. Gambling was now beyond his means – just
a fantasy world until he saw the movie *Rounders*, which drew him
and his pals towards Texas Hold 'em. Before long he was beating them up in small-stakes games and looking for bigger action;
but his home town was four hours' drive from the nearest legal
casino. He took to playing poker online, drifting between several
sites until he discovered the multi-table tournaments on
PokerStars.

It seemed that Chris had a gift for this kind of play; good
results were soon turning into cashes, even a few wins. Then he
entered a thirty-nine-dollar, eighteen-player satellite and won it.
Now he was in a bigger satellite, with sixty players competing for
a $10,000-dollar seat in the main event of the 2003 World
Series of Poker. When he got $8000 ahead, he pleaded with
someone to buy him out; he needed the money more than the

trip to Vegas. No dice. Then, to his own surprise as much as anyone else's, he won that tournament, too.

When Moneymaker arrived at Binion's for the World Series, it was like nothing he'd ever seen before. There was Johnny Chan – star of, among other things, *Rounders*! Chris was 'too ignorant', he now thinks, to be intimidated. He just loved the fact that he had got there at all. With no casino experience, all he could do was try to hide any tells – did he have any? He had no idea – by donning a baseball cap and wraparound shades. And get down to work.

With 839 starters, Moneymaker's first goal – like anyone else's – was to survive Day One. He did better than that; he survived Day One with more than $60,000 in chips. Now, he decided, he could aim to get in the money. But his chip lead at the end of Day Two meant, to his dismay, that Day Three saw him seated on the TV table – right next to his hero Chan, with other big-name players such as Howard Lederer and Paul Darden.

In one hand subsequently made famous by television, Chris was brutally reminded of his amateur status among these top pros. Chan raised the pot and Lederer reraised. Moneymaker sat back and studied Chan, wondering why he was taking so long over his decision. Then Chan spoke – not to the dealer or to Lederer, but to him. 'You know it's on you, right?' Moneymaker looked down to see two cards sitting in front of him. He had not just forgotten to fold; he had no idea he was still in the hand.

It was such a traumatic moment – revealed as a stumblebum on global TV – that now he became intent on showing them otherwise, on showing them just what he could do. He became determined to win. And so he did, to the tune of $2.5 million, beating Sam Farha in that celebrated heads-up while still dazed to have made it to the final table.

*

Chris seems to be in much the same vein tonight. Now that he's a global ambassador for the game, however, he has also learnt how to be generous. 'Nicely done,' he says when I craftily sucker a pair of fives belonging to one of the 'celebrity' players – World Cup-winning rugby star Mike Tindall, boyfriend of the Queen's granddaughter Zara Phillips – to go all-in against my pair of tens. The flop comes A-2-3, the turn an eight, the river . . . PLEASE, no four or five! . . . Another trey.

Then my A-K – oh Anna, oh my beloved Anna, please look after me tonight – for once stands up and knocks out *The Times*' poker correspondent Howard Swains.

Over at Hachem's table I see Elkan Allan bobbing and weaving with all the aggression and ingenuity he had recently acquired at a Vegas boot camp. Then I remember it cannot be Hachem's table; he's already been knocked out. What this turns out to be is a consolation event for those journalists not invited to play in the main tournament; it's an honorary sit-and-go, with Elkan, Des Wilson and others, including the comedian Richard Herring, who claims the world title for himself by knocking out Hachem.

Looking behind me, at what was once Raymer's table, I see that we're down to fourteen players. We're approaching the final table. I'd better start taking this thing more seriously than I have thus far. Thanks to my success in the cash games at the Bellagio and Atlantic City, my UK dollar account already boasts the $10,000 required in an emergency to enter the main event without winning a satellite when I get to Vegas. But that's what I'm worried about: getting to Vegas and staying there for three weeks. This is the time of year when bills beyond a writer's budget pour in: income tax, motor insurance, renewal of four Arsenal season tickets. My sterling overdraft is already beginning to hurt. If I can get to Vegas for free, including all of a month in a hotel, and use my $10,000 to ease the financial pain back home, then winning this would almost be like winning the world title.

So I decide to show the others I mean business by knocking out Chris Moneymaker. As, before too long, I do. Don't ask me how. I'm taking this so seriously now that I've stopped taking notes. Which is probably why I'm playing better.

Another hour or so and we're down to the last nine players. I've made it to the final table. During the brief break before it begins, Elkan Allan comes over to say goodnight and good luck. It's past midnight and he's going home to north London.

'I hope you're not on your bloody motorbike, Elkan,' say I, concerned that a man in his eighties, however sprightly, should choose such a hazardous method of getting around town.

'Of course I am!' he grins and dashes off into the night.

How could I (or he) know that this would be the last night Elkan would ever go out? That within two months I would be attending the funeral of a man so full of life? It was the very next morning, his widow Angie later told me, that Elkan woke up feeling unwell. Septicaemia set in; then he suffered a series of small strokes. But Elkan remained absurdly cheerful in hospital while receiving a constant stream of visitors. He died six weeks later, leaving his wife and three children with the memorable words: 'Don't be too sad. I've had a long, marvellous and happy life, and know I'm loved as well as loving.'

Eighteen months back, Elkan wrote a profile of me for *Inside Edge* magazine, calling me the 'Mephistopheles' who had introduced this penny-ante player to the world of high-stakes poker. He recalled one evening in the early 1990s when he was living and working in Hollywood and I had taken him along to the Bicycle Club in Bell Gardens – where we were apparently 'treated like royalty' because I had enthused about the place in *Big Deal*. I'd forgotten that; but I won't forget Elkan or his tireless passion for the game.

*

As the final table begins, the 'betting correspondent' of Rupert Murdoch's *News of the World*, Lee McCreery, is the huge chip leader; yet there's a general sense at the table that he doesn't really know what he's doing. He gets damaged by Nic Szeremeta, editor-in-chief of *Poker Europa*, and Will Buckley, a sports writer for the *Observer*, a pal of mine as well as a colleague. The *Observer*'s editor Roger Alton, it occurs to me, would be proud to know he has two representatives at the final table. Also playing well is the *Sportsman*'s Geoff Marsh.

Beside me in Seat Two is the *Guardian*'s Barry Glendenning, who misquoted *Big Deal* in his report on the EPT finals in Monte Carlo. Right at the top of his piece he cited Holden as his text for the day: 'Whether he likes it or not, a man's character is stripped at the poker table; if the other players read him better than he does, then he has only himself to blame. Unless he is both able and prepared to see himself as others do, flaws and all, he'll be a loser in cards as in life.' Well, quite, but even after fifteen years I remember that the first sentence should read 'stripped *bare* at the poker table'. A fine point, perhaps, but mine own. I remonstrate briefly then get back to the game. Barry, though, keeps wanting to spin out the conversation. 'Look,' I tell him gently, 'I don't know about you, but I *really* want to win this thing. It means a lot to me. Let's concentrate.'

'So I'm sitting at a poker table being read like *The Da Vinci Code*', his *Guardian* piece continued, 'and my character is being stripped bare and served up in bite-sized chunks speared on cocktail sticks. My six remaining opponents are devouring it hungrily and I have only myself to blame. I am a loser in cards as in life.' That was Monte Carlo in March; but I fear it proves true again in Soho in May. Barry is next out.

Then goes Buckley and we're down to the last four: Marsh, McCreery, Szeremeta and Holden. Now I'm really beginning to think I can win. But I'm seeing no cards at all, not even strong enough for four-handed play; and, besides, people keep trying to talk to me. Buckley has been summoned to see the *Observer*'s managing editor tomorrow; now he sits down next to me to start moaning about all the managing editors on all the newspapers in all the world. Sorry, Will, I tell him, I've got other things on my mind right now.

Next out is Marsh, then McCreery, and it's down to Holden versus Szeremeta. After snagging most of McCreery's chips – largely, I suspect, through canny bluffing – Nic enters the heads-up with a three-to-one chip advantage. The thought of leaving with just a box of chips is intolerable. We both plead with PokerStars' communications director, Conrad Brunner, to make it two trips – or the buy-in for one of us, the flight etc., for the other. Conrad musters a sympathetic smile but walks away; he's having no deals. Nic and I agree that it's going to be a crapshoot, like any head-to-head, and so the winner will give 5 per cent of any Vegas winnings to the loser. We shake hands and get down to business.

It takes a while, and some lucky breaks, but gradually I get back into contention and begin to wear him down.

By sometime between midnight and 1 a.m., I am ahead.

Then, Y-E-E-E-E-E-S! Reader, I won it.

At 2 a.m.-ish, after buying drinks for the dealers, I emerged from the Play Room punching the sky as if I had won the world title. This moment deserved to be savoured. I wandered down the narrow street towards Piccadilly Circus – and its celebrated statue of Eros, with whom I thought I'd have a chat while smoking a celebratory cigarette.

As I was doing just that, running over a few hands with Cupid, and few people around to call the men in white coats, an attractive young woman came up and asked me for a cigarette. Normally I am notoriously mean in these situations, telling these surrogate smokers to go buy their own. But she'd chosen the right moment. In much the same balmy mood as the moonlight,

I was only too happy to help her out. While I fumbled in my pocket for the pack, she began rubbing herself up against my front. Ahah, I thought, with a conspiratorial look at Eros, what have we here? As I then proceeded to reach for my lighter, and lit her cigarette, she moved her hands to my backside and pushed my loins hard against her own.

Now I knew what we had here. I tried to be polite – 'Look, you're very attractive, but I'm not in the mood for sex right now, thanks' – yet still she wouldn't give up. Anyone chancing down Piccadilly towards 3 a.m. that morning would then have seen me yelling at her to go away – 'I DO NOT WANT SEX!' – and quoting a favourite line of Alvarez: 'Sex is good, but poker lasts longer.'

I felt so good about winning that I wanted to tell someone – anyone – but it was two o'clock in the morning. So I went home with my secret safe until others began to write about it. In a vivid report in the *Sportsman* that weekend, Geoff Marsh wrote with pride of how he had knocked out England rugby player Mike Tindall, the significant other of Princess Anne's daughter. Hang on, I thought it was me who had knocked out Tindall? Then maybe that had been England's other rugby star, Andy Goode. Having hated the game at school, I'm not much of a rugger bugger, infinitely preferring the version with the round ball.

Despite lasting longer than three world champions, Marsh went on, 'I was undone by Anthony Holden, author of the legendary poker book *Big Deal*. Should I have gone all in with 8♠-9♠ against a player as experienced as Holden? Probably not, but I was flying short-stacked and above all, I guess, I thought he was bluffing.'

Bluffing? Moi? 'I guess', concluded Marsh, 'I'll read the sequel more carefully.'

Meanwhile in my own paper, the *Observer*, a sports writer

named Geoffrey Mortlake gave an account of Will Buckley's evening:

'To the still bright lights of London's West End for a high-octane poker tournament. I have been playing the game since Ian Fleming introduced me to the delights of it, and other adult pleasures, during a fondly remembered summer holiday from another age. It is now, apparently, deeply fashionable, which I find wearisome, but not quite so debilitating that I don't occasionally attempt to keep my hand in.

'Thankfully, it was an old-fashioned crew who gathered at the tables deep in Piccadilly. Arrayed against me were Anthony 'Hold-Em' Holden, a three-quarter line of England rugger internationals (Tindall, Simpson-Daniel et al.) and [then England football manager] Sven-Göran Eriksson. The action as you would expect was fluid and intelligent and surprising. The last ingredient being provided by the Swede who is renowned for being as tight as 2004 World Series of Poker bracelet-holder Greg "Fossilman" Raymer, but on Tuesday night played with a Mortlakesque flamboyance.'

I didn't see Sven there. This guy's making it up.

But not this bit: 'Anthony Holden won.'

Am I too nice a guy to be a world-beating poker player? As elated as I was the next day, I also felt a surge of sympathy for Nic Szeremeta, last seen slinking off into the night with just that box of chips to show for his pains. I decided to send him an email:

'I'm so sorry, Nic. I won't pretend I'm not happy things went my way, but you must be feeling pretty sick about last night. I know I would be if it had turned out the other way around. A crapshoot, as you said when we started. I hope you can take consolation in the fact that you will be an even more major star in the forthcoming tome than was already scheduled. A privilege to play against you, and one for the old-timers! Thanks for taking it so well, and all v best, Tony.'

Before long, Nic replied: 'No problem, Tony. I long ago learned what can happen, so I take it all quite philosophically. If I do win I look back and recognise that I had a bit of luck to get where I was anyway. This is the key . . . too many people imagine that they are so skilful (etc.) that bad luck is cruel to them . . . it affects their game in a detrimental way. You hung on in there to get a bit of luck so I really do feel "Well done, Tony". Cheers and keep in touch, Nic.'

My alter ego, the music critic, should have spent that evening in black tie at an upscale dinner at the Dorchester in Park Lane for the UK's most prestigious classical music awards, handed out each year by the Royal Philharmonic Society. Thank God the poker player prevailed. Now they had both won their way to Vegas – and the $10,000 entry fee, all expenses paid, for the World Series of Poker's main event!

A week or two later, just as I began to wonder if I had dreamed the whole thing, an email arrived from Lee Jones:

Dear Anthony,

Congratulations on winning a WSOP qualifier! You're now poised to follow in Chris Moneymaker's, Greg Raymer's, and Joe Hachem's footsteps to become a member of Team PokerStars wearing the WSOP bracelet. If you agree to wear our logo gear the whole time you're in the tournament, we will provide you with accommodation at a large hotel/casino property in Las Vegas. On the day you sign your Terms & Conditions in our Hospitality Suite, you'll get a nice travel bag filled with PokerStars clothing and other goodies. Furthermore, if you make it to the final table, we'll have some more goodies for you:
   * $100,000 if you make the final table
   * $250,000 if you make it to third or second place
   *$1,000,000 if you win the event

Again, congratulations on this win and perhaps we'll be taking pictures of you with Joe Hachem, Greg Raymer and Chris Moneymaker as this year's new world champion!

Perhaps? Line up those lenses. After beating those three, I must surely be a shoo-in.

9

'The Cards Don't Know'

I would like to think it was for my sake that the Royal Opera House, Covent Garden, chose to mount the opening night of its first-ever production of Franco Alfano's opera *Cyrano de Bergerac* on a Monday evening. I rather doubt it, to be honest, but I have to say that it suited me just fine. The music of this justly neglected work by the Italian composer better known for finishing Puccini's *Turandot* is nothing to write home about, even to the *Observer*. Still, the presence in the title role of the great Spanish tenor Placido Domingo – his twenty-fifth new part in more than two hundred appearances at the Royal Opera over thirty-five years and perhaps his last – made this one of the musical events of the year.

So I could justify that rare self-indulgence, a one-item column, and knock it off on Tuesday in time to head for Heathrow the following evening, dump the car and catch a few hours' sleep before flying to Vienna early Thursday morning – thus avoiding another week off work but making it by taxi to the nearby spa town of Baden in time for that evening's start to the Howard Lederer–Annie Duke 'fantasy' poker camp.

I had planned the trip as intensive training for the World
Series, now barely a month away. After a less than distinguished
year so far at the green baize, I thought I should send myself
back to school if I were going to have any kind of shot at the
world crown. Needless to say, my London triumph had rather
skewed that. News of my victory over three world champions
and my freeroll into the World Series had preceded me to
Austria. When I greeted my host, Howard 'the Professor'
Lederer, he said with a grave smile: 'Maybe you should join the
faculty?' No, no, I replied modestly, that was a freak one-off.
'I'm here to learn.'

Poker camps are a recent development, designed less to make
their hosts yet more money than to attract more players to the
websites via which they make millions. The first such camp to
be held in Europe, this was the fifth hosted by the Professor
and his feisty sister, who together have pioneered a format since
followed by the likes of Phil Hellmuth, the WPT, Doyle's Room
and others. Lectures and seminars in the mornings, tournaments in the afternoons, sit-and-gos with the pros in the
evenings – hole cards turned over and hands analysed: this was
what a hundred players from twenty-six countries, including
many all the way from the US, thought well worth the $3000
attendance fee. According to the brochure, after all, 'Many
camp participants actually win back the price of their admission.'

Or as one of the visiting Americans put it to me, 'They get
four or five hundred people signing up for these things in Vegas.
You can't get near the pros. Here I reckon I'll be able to get up
close and really talk to them about my game.' He was right.
With the popular Dutch professional Marcel Luske and
German online whiz Thomas Bihl also on hand, we all lived,
ate, drank and played poker together – finding interesting new
dimensions even to bad beat stories – for three and a half days.
A suave Lederer dictum was adopted as the camp motto: 'Luck

determines who has the best hands. Skill determines who has the most chips.'

Card-playing is in the Lederer blood. Growing up in a New Hampshire family of five, Howard and Annie were learning all sorts of games, including poker, from childhood. Howard credits his academic father, Dr Richard Lederer (whose many books on the English language have between them sold more than a million copies), with instilling into him his potent will to win. He still remembers the thrill of the first few times he beat Dad – who never, he believes, lost to him deliberately.

Now a multi-millionaire professional and the driving force (with Chris Ferguson and others) behind the Full Tilt website, Howard has one regret in life: that he never finished college – unlike his egghead sister. At eighteen he put off his education for a year to move to New York and pursue his love of chess. In the back room of his favourite chess club, however, there was a poker game, which soon had him hooked. Forgetting about college, he played obsessively for a couple of years, as many as eighty hours a week, and would go home broke six nights out of seven. Howard was discovering the hard way that poker, unlike chess, is a game of imperfect information. Sometimes sleeping rough, he would earn his stake money running errands for the other players. It was not until he slowed down this frenzied routine and began to build the game into a healthier lifestyle that Howard's poker improved.

Then his expertise improved immeasurably when he started to play at New York's legendary Mayfair Club. Howard was there when Texas Hold 'em arrived in Manhattan in the mid-1980s, one of a tight circle of players who have since gone on to become big poker names: Erik Seidel, Dan Harrington, Steve Zolotow, Jay Heimowitz and Mickey Appleman. They would play from 4 p.m. till 2 a.m., then retire to a bar for detailed post-mortems – precursors, perhaps, of the analytical sit-and-gos we'll be playing here in Baden.

Soon Howard was working on her game with his sister Annie, who would ply him with questions all evening after playing all day. Gradually, he says, those questions became more difficult to answer. Annie clearly had what it takes. So he encouraged her to travel with him to Vegas and play in some tournaments, including the World Series. At first tutored and bankrolled by Howard, Annie has now won more cash than any other woman in WSOP history. In 1994 she and Howard also made poker history by becoming the first brother and sister to reach the same final table at the World Series. She knocked him out, as she has at all four final tables they have both reached since.

Lederer has lived in Vegas since 1993, more of a cash player until TV's World Poker Tour revolutionised the tournament scene. His wife Susan helped launch the poker room at the Bellagio, considered by most top players to be the best in town. A large, imposing man – though half his previous weight since, like Doyle Brunson and others in this sedentary pursuit, going in for a gastric bypass operation – Lederer is by nature more pensive and soft-spoken than most poker pros, not least his feisty sister. But he also has a distinctive sense of humour; a strict vegetarian, Howard once went through the agony of eating a cheeseburger for a $10,000 bet. And he was so intrigued by Doyle Brunson's card protector, with its 'Caspar the Ghost' motif, that he bought it for $3500; their agreement is that Doyle can keep it for life but has left it to Howard in his will.

Annie could not be more of a contrast to her reserved, ruminative brother. A brash, bright-eyed party animal, she struggled in childhood to fit in, as the product of a liberal family, to the privileged conservatism of her private prep school. Pretty, smart and popular, she went on to major in English and psychology at Columbia University, New York, intending to follow her parents into teaching. Instead she enrolled as a graduate student in cognitive psychology at the University of Pennsylvania. Then in 1991, midway through her doctorate research, she suffered a 'panic attack' and impulsively proposed marriage to an old friend named Ben Duke, whom she had never even dated. They moved to Montana and started having babies. Living in romantic poverty, Annie drove fifty miles to the nearest card room to play poker for the rent on their 'love shack'.

In 1994, at her brother's suggestion, Annie tried her luck at the World Series, placing thirteenth in the first tournament she entered, eliminating Howard in the process. After winning $70,000 in her first month of competition, she and her husband decided to move to Vegas so she could play professionally. There is a celebrated TV image of Annie squirming uncomfortably in her seat during the 2000 World Series, in which she played during the final month of her third pregnancy.

By then she was an established poker star who would go on to win her first WSOP bracelet in 2004, beating a field of 234 in the $2000 Omaha High-Low Split event. That same summer she knocked out eight of the game's biggest names – including, again, her brother – to win the $2 million first prize in the invitation-only WSOP Tournament of Champions, a winner-takes-all No Limit Hold 'em tourney staged by Harrah's for ESPN. Annie wept onscreen after the flop made her pocket sixes a set to beat Howard's all-in sevens, then went on to surprise a confident Phil Hellmuth (and delight all the other participants) by whupping him in the heads-up. After his defeat the TV cameras cruelly followed Hellmuth into the shadows, where he raged as only he can about the cruel injustices of poker: 'If luck weren't involved, I guess I'd win all the time.'

Annie is now a consultant to, and sponsored by, the online poker site UltimateBet.com. She has also become a sought-after teacher, coaching the likes of Ben Affleck and Matt Damon on their game. In June 2004 Annie's pupil Affleck won the $356,000 first prize in the California State Poker Championships, beating some of the world's best players in the process. Typically she has now published a candid, outspoken volume of autobiography, subtitled 'How I Raised, Folded, Bluffed, Flirted, Cursed and Won Millions at the World Series of Poker', in which she pays due tribute to Howard's early role in her success, while chronicling in vivid detail the unusual problems of juggling the life of an itinerant poker pro with that of a (now) single mother of four children. 'Not a day goes by,' she says, 'when I play poker and don't learn from it, when I don't add something new to my game, when I don't see people differently.'

Howard and Annie have done pretty well for themselves, it seems to me, given their chaotic if comfortable New England upbringing with an alcoholic mother who left their father to become an actress in New York, only to wind up keeping the books for Howard's illegal betting operation in Las Vegas. The dysfunctional Family Lederer has been vividly described by the third sibling, their younger sister Katy, in a family memoir entitled *Poker Face*. Now a poet, Katy describes the young Annie as 'the toughest of us all – confident and blunt'. Nor does Katy shrink from her memories of the days when Howard was either broke or getting arrested (on both American coasts) for bookmaking.

I devoured Katy's elegant book en route here to Baden, where I check into a pleasant room in the Hotel Herzoghof, right across the road from the stately Monte Carlo-style casino, with a couple of hours to spare before the show begins. Beneath my balcony in the park outside the casino, men are wandering around in wigs and period costumes dressed as Mozart, whose anniversary year this is. It was to the spa here at Baden, I remember, that Mozart's wife Costanze used to come for thermal treatment for her fragile health; while visiting her here in 1791, in what turned out to be the last summer of his thirty-five-year life, Mozart wrote his exquisite '*Ave verum corpus*' for the local choir.

This vague sense of proximity to one of my major non-poker

heroes makes me feel curiously at home. It also sets me to wondering whether I am a better (or even worse) music critic than poker player. Maybe this week will tell. One thing, at this particular moment, I do know: I'd rather be here than at the opera, even one by Mozart. Does that mean I should give up the Job and turn poker pro?

No, of course not. I'd love to but I'm not (yet) a good enough player. The only reason I stand a chance in any tournament is that I broadly know what I'm doing and can hope to take advantage of those who don't, along with the odd slice of luck. As I muse I remember from the first time around what it is I *really* love about the pursuit of poker: the outsider-dom, beholden to no boss; risking going broke to earn a crust ('a tough way', in the old phrase, 'to make an easy living'); the romance of the road; the communal sense of delight in sharing a particular skill which leaves the outside world baffled; and treating money with the contempt it deserves. All this creates an unlikely sense of community among people openly out to rob, even bankrupt each other.

The reading of other people's minds. The thrilling sense of triumph when you sense something that turns out to be right; the disproportionate despair when you're wrong or the poker gods rule against you. These are the kind of highs and lows sensible people avoid. But who wants to be sensible when you can get all the kicks needed by any, okay, addictive personality?

Yes, these days I'm somewhat older and maybe a tad wiser than I was first time around, when these heady notions first struck home. To get pompous about it, this phoney sense of superiority to non-poker players emerges from an entirely self-absorbed, indeed selfish activity, which contributes nothing at all to the state of the nation, the good of mankind, the future of anything or anyone except oneself. It's an escape at which some people are good enough to make a living – many of them, like Howard and Annie, with plenty to escape from.

Poker is also a fruitful field for self-analysis. So what I am escaping? Is my everyday life that humdrum, even unhappy? Not, as far as I am aware, at the moment. I have work in which I take pride, a family I love, plenty of friends to cherish, enough female companionship to keep any single man warm. But maybe of late it's all got just a bit samey? Yes, maybe so.

I need no shrink to tell me that these are dark and dangerous thoughts, which I had better keep to myself. Especially here among all these players who, with a few notable exceptions, are better at reading other people's minds than their own.

Over at the casino that evening there is a welcome dinner, at which I sit with Howard and Annie discussing among other things the complex politics of the current poker scene. Neither is playing on the WPT circuit at present, being unwilling to sign the release allowing Steve Lipscomb's enterprise to use their names and images in WPT promotional material 'in perpetuity, throughout the universe'.

'We just can't do that,' says Howard – who does, after all, run a rival website and naturally enough wants to keep his name and image exclusively for his own commercial use. 'But it's a bummer. We want to play in those tournaments. We're both professional players.'

Getting Full Tilt up and running has been pretty much a full-time job for Lederer for the last couple of years. 'I wasn't born to be a businessman, which is all I've really been doing for two years. I've seriously missed playing poker. I can't wait to get back to it – and I intend to.'

In the meantime the Professor and his business partner, Rick Bierman of All In Enterprises, can't agree on whether this is a 'fantasy' camp (Rick) or a 'reality' camp (Howard). Soon Lederer rises to make a speech of welcome to his newly assembled 'class' – intermediate players like me, on the whole, looking to improve their game. 'You're not going to be a great poker player by Sunday,' he warns us, 'but we'll give you plenty of hints and point out all the pitfalls.' We head to the casino's very grand, gold-leafed card room, where I pay all of twenty euros to play a sit-and-go with nine others – including Howard.

On the first hand I am dealt J-J, bet 200 and get one caller. The flop brings an ace, so I check and he bets 500 at me. I stare him down, think for too long, then fold. We flip over the cards, to find my opponent was holding A-K and Howard tells me: 'You played it perfectly. What can you do?' After another such setback my suited A-J is beaten by K-Q, knocking me out. I've played three hands 'faultlessly', according to Professor Lederer. I'm a 'solid' player. 'It's just that you're not allowed to win any hands tonight.'

These post-hand debriefings are fascinating. In his calm, considered way, Lederer imparts the wisdom of a master. Some of it we know already; it's just that we don't always put it into practice. 'Never limp in,' he commands. 'If you're good enough to call, you're good enough to raise.' How many times have I heard *that* one? 'If not, wait for a better spot.' Some of it is more subtle, namely: 'Faster intervals means playing more marginal hands.' Some is so original that I'm not going to pass it on.

We go straight into another twenty-euro single-table tournament, which winds up with Lederer going all-in against me. I'm holding – guess what – A-K again. I think for a while – well, this *is* Howard Lederer – then call and beat him. 'You thought too long,' he tells me. 'Always call with A-K.' I tell him the statutory Kournikova joke. He laughs but says he likes 'Big Slick' more than I seem to. Well, it's beaten him into third place, leaving me to lose the heads-up to an American and win fifty euros for second place.

The following evening I play sit-and-gos with Annie, which is a whole different ball game. While playing with her *sotto voce* brother last night we could hear her barking orders from the other end of the vast room. Now I'm on the receiving end of a pretty intimidating tirade or three. I remember her parents – their parents – were teachers, too. But each of their offspring has a very different coaching style.

On the first hand I limp in with suited connectors, 6♣-7♣. 'Never limp,' says Annie, too. 'Always raise. That way, you eliminate other players and improve your odds.' Then she gets *really* animated . . .

'And you shouldn't have been playing that hand anyway. Do you know the percentage on suited connectors?' I don't understand the question, let alone know the answer. 'Do you? DO YOU? It's 3 per cent. Those cards being suited adds a maximum 3 per cent to their value – 2 per cent for A-K, 3 per cent for most other hands. Your chances of flopping a flush are one in eight. So suited connectors are only good for getting you off the fence. Would you have played 6-7 off-suit in that spot?' I shake my head meekly. 'No, of course you wouldn't. So you shouldn't have played 6-7 suited.'

Then she commands: 'Give me those cards. GIVE THEM TO ME!' I hand them over. 'See here,' she says, holding them up together. 'They're pretty, ain't they? Well, take 'em home and frame 'em and hang 'em on the wall. They're more use for that than they are for playing poker. Especially in bad position.'

This fusillade goes on so long that the dealer gives me a knowing look and stops the tournament clock. Otherwise we'd scarcely get through one hand per level. But Annie is giving us her all – real value for money. She's so passionate in her views that I don't think any of us are going to be playing suited connectors, let alone *limping in* with suited connectors, for quite a while.

More of Annie's tips: 'Take the lead on the pot. If you're ever willing to call a raise, you should be making the raise yourself. So if you're first to act, and this is true, then raise. At this stage you have 10 per cent information – i.e., you know two cards out of twenty dealt to ten players. Raising increases that percentage.'

The hand most likely to win before the flop is? Yes, a pair. 'Look at the hand and think about the possibilities. Your chances of flopping a set are one in 7.5. Think through the negative implied odds: if I hit this hand and don't win, what do I stand to lose?'

'Raising is a way of finding out more information as well as thinning out the opposition . . . The guy who merely doubles the big blind obliges the big blind to call . . . Bet the least amount for what you want to accomplish. But when you're short-stacked, bet ten to twenty times the big blind because you want to bet enough for it to be significant. To cause damage.'

This is all strong, sound poker thinking, most of which I knew already. I've just got to remember it not simply when I'm theorising about the game, but while I'm playing it.

That morning the first of the seminars had been given by Thomas 'Buzzer' Bihl. Thirty-one years old, from Frankfurt, Germany, Buzzer was a stock trader before turning professional poker player only a couple of years ago. He reckons he's played more than a million hands during those two years and has won several big online tournaments. This year he's added some final tables in European ranking events. So Howard and Annie are not alone in tipping him for stardom. Bihl has won six-figure sums in online play, which is his specialist subject this morning.

With the help of slides and charts projected from his laptop, he goes patiently through sound advice about the choice of levels, the changing values of hands as a tournament progresses, when the blinds really become worth attacking, etc., all the way to heads-up play. I am feverishly taking notes, as if back at school, and so are many of the packed classroom. As Bihl's hour-long talk progresses, however, it begins to go way over my head. Some of his calculations of odds are mind-blowing. I look around the room and see others, especially older players like myself, with equally furrowed brows. 'A-K versus 7-2 is 66-33 with only two players in the pot. A-6 versus Q-10 is 56-44 . . .' There are websites, he reminds us, to do such calculations for you. But not, of course, while you're at the table in a hand. How the hell are you supposed to keep these figures in your head?

When the time comes for questions, Bihl gets cutesy. How much, for instance, does he use the chat-box? 'Chat? If you're playing six to eight tables at once, as I do, there's no time to chat!'

I suspect that other, more frequent online players than me have got more out of this session. No doubt they'll be putting it all into practice on their laptops in their time off from the camp schedule. Not me; I rarely if ever play while on the road. Unlike most poker players, I'm vaguely interested in my surroundings. Here I'm planning to check out the Mozarthof, formerly the 'Haus zum Blumenstock', at number four Renngasse. Maybe, come to think of it, that's part of my problem. Luckily there's not enough time to explore that thought further. Next up is the wit and wisdom of Marcel Luske.

Based in Amsterdam, Luske is known as 'the Flying Dutchman', not least because he claims to log more air miles than any other poker pro. After turning professional in 1999, he made his name five years later when he finished second in the 2004 World Series of Poker stud event and tenth – one off the final table – in the main event. Renowned as one of the snappiest poker dressers, seldom seen in anything other than a stylish suit and tie, Marcel also enjoys singing at the table from time to time – to entertain (so he says) or psyche (so they say) his opponents. His other trademark is his eccentric pair of sunglasses, which he wears upside-down – because, he says (though few believe him), of the overhead lights.

Unlike Bihl, Luske has no laptop up there with him on the podium projecting graphs or pie charts. His easy charm is in itself enough to carry his audience along for an hour. And he has a beguiling way with words, even though English is not his native tongue. My personal favourite is his catchphrase, 'The cards don't know' – an elegant way of reminding us that our fate at the poker table is entirely in our own hands. We should not take whatever may happen personally and should not feel fated or victimised by the poker gods. Whatever role luck, or chance, may play in any hand, any session, any tournament, it's the same for everyone over the long haul. The guy who gets lucky today will get unlucky tomorrow. If that guy happens to be you, so be it. That, as they say, is poker.

'Don't try to play like me,' says Luske, quoting T. J. Cloutier. 'Take bits of my game and build them into yours. Play your own game.' He also believes that the way people play poker reflects their characters – another self-evident truth well worth spelling out and examining. People play, as he puts it, 'like they are'. If they are polite, well-mannered types, for instance, they'll behave that way at the table. And play that way. Which presumably means they're ripe for the picking.

Luske is one of the few poker pros ever to have told me that 'you need to be fit to play well'. In these days of marathon, multi-hour tournaments, I have often thought that, but rarely heard it said. Many of the tracksuited younger pros work out, jog, eat healthily, don't drink much, if at all. This is not just, as it may appear, a fashionable lifestyle choice; it is part of the route to success in the world of the new poker. 'You need to be relaxed at the table,' says the ever-relaxed Luske. 'You need to feel comfortable or you're going to lose.' In cash games, in other words, exercise a careful choice over who you play with, where and for how much. 'Work out your own comfort levels and stick to them.'

Set yourself personal targets, however modest – in a cash game, for instance, perhaps to double your buy-in. If you fail, it is important to sit down afterwards and work out why. 'I have won but felt unhappy because I didn't play well,' confesses Luske, 'and lost but felt happy because I knew I had played right.'

These are 'quiet, internal, self-management techniques' as logical as looking at a roadmap before setting out on an unfamiliar car journey – something many male motorists are notoriously too stubborn to do. 'Show the other players your hand sometimes, to get information about theirs . . . Recreational players tend to be loose because they want to play . . . You knew you did the right thing, but you lost, even though you were a 4-1 favourite to win. Well, remember that means the other guy's *entitled* to win once in five hands. Of course you were right to call. But don't complain when you lose. You're going to win the other four times.'

With simple, homegrown truths like these, no matter how hard-won, Luske beguiles us all for an hour. Of the table bully, for instance: 'I don't like this guy. So let's give him more money' (i.e., by being bullied into making a bad call). Men, he believes, don't like being bullied; women don't mind – they've got their intuition. 'You want to play as long as possible, so you play solidly. You want to win, so you take more risks.' Coming from him, these seemingly simple statements sound like deep poker truths.

Listening to Luske, I'm coming to the conclusion that there can be no hard and fast rules about anything in poker. Likewise there are many questions with no single answer.

Someone asks him if you should wait till it's your turn to look at your hole cards. Luske is big on looking at your hole cards one by one. 'The first is a three. Who cares what the other one is? The first is a king – ah, that makes the other more interesting.' Don't let the other players watch you while you're looking at your hole cards. It's more important to watch them looking at theirs. Waiting to look at yours also denies them information while they're making their own decisions. 'You go into the bank. They smile and say "Hi, how are you doing?" – because they know they're going to charge you money, whatever you do. The same is true of poker. Don't let them see you looking at your cards before they have to make their own decisions. You're giving them free information.'

There are tells, too, in how you place, handle and protect your cards and chips. Many players leave a good hand in a 'neat, pretty pattern'. It's important that you treat your cards the same way on every hand, to give nothing away. By the same measure, as I learnt years ago in the Tuesday Night Game, neat piles of chips denote a tight player.

After his lecture Luske happens to come over and sit next to me at lunch. 'I've got a question for you,' I tell him and the whole table leans in. 'I just won this tournament in London – but I don't know how I did it!'

It was meant, of course, as a joke; Marcel has already answered his fair share of questions for that morning. Yet he takes it quite seriously and gives a ten-minute answer – along the lines of, 'I expect you played tight to begin with, loosened up a bit in the middle phase and got lucky at the end.' Of course. I knew that, really. Didn't I?

I'd like a glass of wine but daren't ask for one. It would look unprofessional to drink before this afternoon's tournament. Besides, there appears to be none on offer – one way, presumably, of keeping camp costs down.

Apart from the hosts' expertise, the tournaments at this camp are a generous part of the package. Today there is an €11,750 prize pool for a freeroll. Those who get knocked out can go and play more sit-and-gos with the waiting pros, at entry fees from €10 to €100.

We've not been playing long when there's a roar over in the far corner and news of a truly bad beat spreads rapidly around the room. Player A bet 500 with 10♣-J♣ and was raised by Player B with Q♠-Q♥. Player A calls and sees the flop come 8♣-9♣-Q♣. A bets 1000, B goes all-in. A calls. The turn is the 8♦, the river the Q♦. Player B's full house on fourth street has become quads on fifth, only to be drawing dead all along to A's flopped straight flush.

What a ridiculous game poker can be. Me, I'm knocked out in mid-tourney in much more mundane style when my A-Q is beaten by K-K. Already there are lines for the sit-and-gos; so I join a cash game against some high-spirited Oregonians – and get up a few hours later after playing in my tightest, old-fashioned style almost €1000 to the good.

Who needs this new poker?

Nine o'clock in the morning seems a horribly early starting time for anything to do with poker. All-night sessions, sure, but most other poker players are asleep at this time of day. The best I can do to cheer myself up is remember Andy Beal demanding 7 a.m. starts against 'The Corporation'; it helps me drag my heavy feet across the road to the casino for the first of two lectures which have all campers in a high state of expectancy – Annie Duke on the rarefied art of reading other players.

Except that it isn't. Annie has brought the wrong slides. She's very apologetic about it but the talk she's now going to give is rather more advanced – about the finer points of post-flop Hold 'em play, before and after the turn and the river.

I can't wait to tell my buddy Alvarez. 'Look, Al,' I'm already saying to him in my head. 'You go off to all these literary conferences in Scandinavia and I know you enjoy the saunas and the birch-twigs and all that, but you always come back complaining that it was so *boring*, that some dreary academic banged on for two hours about "John Berryman: The Blue (or 'Blues') Period". What if it were Annie Duke, with blackboard and slides, on the finer nuances of late position moves after the flop?' I can already see Al's face lighting up.

Annie may not need a microphone but she's got a tough audience this morning. With a first full night of drinking in Baden behind them, many paying punters have failed as yet to put in an appearance; a few are still drowsily trickling in and the room is hardly two-thirds full. Some of the class are looking pretty dozy. Not our enthusiastic instructor, however; she's off and running as if her life depended on it. 'If you're going to bet, in general bet half to all of the pot. More means laying a mathematical price to your opponents. Your objects are: One, to get the most money in the pot with the best hand. Two, to gain information. Three, to control the mathematics of the situation for yourself and your opponents. Or maybe, four, to bluff. With a good hand, the bet should be designed to get as much money as possible in the pot and gain information about your opponent's hand. With a bluff, risk the minimum to accomplish your goal while still being believable.'

I'm not going to give away all of Annie's wisdom – she and I would rather you paid for it yourselves – but she moves on to stack size ('Your stack size is the same as your opponent's, whichever is the smaller'), position and the 'texture' of the board. Then she starts to get really detailed about certain hands in certain positions – which to play, which not. I'm taking it all in, writing it all down, but I know it's going to be tough to keep it all lodged in my crowded cranium. Next up, when to invite an opponent into the pot and when to make a bet that stops the action; how to bet so your opponent makes bad decisions. If you have 13.5 ways to win, you're getting even money. 'Betting zero – i.e., slow-playing – is asking for something really bad to happen to you, for your opponent to suck out on you. *Never* do that!'

The more detailed she gets – 'A check-raise often stops the action and gives away your hand. Always know who raised before the flop – or in position terms where from, e.g., before or behind you' – the more my weary brain seizes up. These are things I know, I tell myself, things I've been doing for years (or if not, knowing I should). It does help, in a curious way, to hear them systematised like this. But should one adopt a systematic style of play?

Then I finally realise the blindingly obvious: Annie is teaching us aggression. It is not billed as such. But that's what's going on here and it's exactly what my game lacks. I take feverish notes as she goes into complex detail about different plays in the different positions and adjusting to weak or strong opponents. Later I can't even understand some of my jottings. Still, I feel like I've got a recipe for success here and can't wait for the chance to put it into practice.

As I slip outside during the break between lectures, I meet Howard Lederer coming in. The Professor is next up. 'Take it easy on us, Howard,' I implore him. 'Your sister's just fried my brain.'

Annie's brother smiles knowingly.

Howard's talk is entitled, 'The Road to Poker Mastery'. Again, I'm not going to pass on too much of the advice others pay him thousands for. But it's no secret that Lederer is into eastern religions – one of the keys to his success, he firmly believes, at poker. And, once more, they help to codify things.

Under the heading of 'The Beginner', for instance, he quotes the Zen master of the Soto school, Shunryu Suzuki, one of the pioneers in bringing Buddhism to America: 'In the beginner's mind there are many [questions], in the expert's there are few.' I ponder the (dubious?) profundity of this remark, which remains on the screen as Howard does scant service to his sister's talk – though, to be fair, no one had told him she'd switched subjects – by insisting that post-flop play is 'much less important' than pre-flop. 'There are many good players who are very strong pre-flop but much weaker post-flop.' Or in the words of Eugen Herrigel's *Zen in the Art of Archery* about Howard's next category, the Student: 'He is forced to admit that he is at the mercy of everyone who is stronger, more nimble and more practised than him.' I'll second that.

Howard advises beginners to create their own unique style, which may take five to ten years. It did him. His knowledge of chess heightened his appreciation that poker is a game of less than perfect information and how to handle the consequences. 'You will sometimes win or lose in a session without knowing why. Maybe you make a good lay-down, but you don't actually *know* it was a good lay-down.' It is very hard, he remembers with a grimace, 'to get bad plays out of your game'.

The Expert is introduced with a Japanese proverb: 'He who has a hundred miles to walk should reckon ninety as half the journey.' Now that's more like it as far as I'm concerned. The advice under this heading comes apparently at random: 'Have a *reason* to win . . . Just about every great player has gone broke numerous times . . . You want to turn pro? Only when you get to the point where you think it's costing you money to go to work – over the course of at least a year.'

So the tournament starts at noon. Lederer will stay up till 3 a.m. the night before and get up at 11 a.m. 'It's a disservice to yourself to do otherwise. By the end of the day, when the stakes (and blinds) are at their highest, my opponents will be tired and I'll be at my peak.' Likewise he does not believe in staying on the premises where the tournament is taking place. 'If you don't stay at the tournament hotel, you're making a positive choice to go play that day.'

Then he says some things that strike nearer home. 'Some players don't like themselves enough to win. They think, I don't deserve it, or, I should give it all back, because they have other issues in their life.' People in married or stable relationships, he believes, i.e., people with responsibilities, perform better than singles. 'If you aren't hurting anyone but yourself by going broke, then it's easier to do.'

And I still savour his chess-player's analysis of poker reality: 'If your aces beat tens, you got lucky. You didn't deserve all the pot. You deserved 82 per cent of it. But that's what poker is about.'

For Howard's final category, the Master, it's back to Suzuki:

'If one really wishes to become a master of an art, technical knowledge of it is not enough. One has to transcend technique so that the art becomes an "artless art".'

'I'm still working on this,' smiles Lederer. Everyone has an A-game, a B-game, a C-game. His advice as to playing your A-game is to 'stay in the moment'. This is Zen thinking: 'Forget the past. Don't think about the future. Relax. Allow the game to come to you.' Under this heading, I muse, I should be allowed to smoke at the table – as in the tournament I just won. This heretical thought is dispelled by two closing, contrasting anecdotes from Lederer.

'In 1995 I was playing in the $300–$600 game at the Mirage when my sister Kate comes in to visit. She's playing $3–$6, and strikes up a conversation, makes a buddy, with whom we wind up having dinner. This guy says that he played the perfect session, won $400 and is going to turn pro. "You've gotta be kidding," I tell him. "I don't think I've played a perfect fifteen minutes in my life." The guy disappeared.

'Contrast that with a couple of years ago. In the summer of 2004 I was commentating on the American Poker Championships in upstate New York. Phil Ivey, one of the best players in the world, won it against a very tough field. Eighty of the one hundred and twenty starters were pros. When Ivey was presented with the half-million-dollar cheque for first place and the cameramen crowded round, the organisers told him: "You *could* smile." So Ivey cracked a smile. Later I took him aside at the post-event party and Phil said to me: "I couldn't stop thinking how poorly I had played".'

I head off for lunch wishing that, just once in a while, I could play as poorly as Phil Ivey.

In the second tournament, that afternoon, I played much better – and went out tenth of 180, one off the final table. This was worth €150, which I took straight over to Marcel Luske's

€100 sit-and-go, where I learnt one last lesson. Having looked like the table rock, after an hour of unplayable cards, I was down to 1000 of my original 2000 when I was dealt 8-9. On the button I went all-in, only to be called by the big blind's K-Q. The flop, of course, promptly came K-Q-x. So I'm a goner. But Marcel cheers me up by saying: 'You chose the right moment. It's much better, as the short stack, to go all-in with a medium hand with chances than risking it all on a high card with a weak kicker.'

Did I know that? I *think* so, but now I do for sure.

And so to the farewell dinner, a gala affair in the courtyard of the upscale Schloss Hotel, where the pros have been staying. I find myself sitting next to an American mathematician called Lawrence who is currently based in Dublin, advising the Irish government on macro-economic policy.

'So what have you learnt this week?' he asks me.

I say what's on my mind. 'I've learnt what my weaknesses are. Primarily, doing the maths.'

'Me, too,' says Lawrence, provoking me to a squawk of surprise.

'But you're a mathematician advising the Irish government.'

'Ah,' he says inscrutably, 'the thing no one realises about mathematicians is that they're often lousy at mental arithmetic.'

On my other side is my new buddy from Oregon, Stan Turel, a lawyer much my own age who has lived an unusually eventful, at times tragic life. But he's far from being a tragic man. Forceful and courteous, he thinks it's bad form that most of the professionals are sitting together at the same table, where Annie is parodying her brother's cheeseburger bet by offering her boyfriend $2500 to eat a whole bowlful of especially disgusting rice.

'You're right, Stan,' say I, 'they should be mixing and mingling. What's more, they don't show any sign of making speeches. We need some farewell speeches!'

For a while I turn back to Lawrence, in pursuit of the higher

maths, only to be interrupted by some tapping on a microphone – and there's Stan up on the stage, giving a speech of
thanks on behalf of the punters. Now that's my kind of guy.
Naturally he moved Lederer and others to reply.

Then it's back to the casino for some wild cash games, the
demob-happy Americans unilaterally abolishing the card room's
no-smoking rule, while out on the casino floor a tap-dancing
duo entertain Baden's demure, dressed-up Saturday-night-out
crowd. It's a weird phantom from my past, spookily reminiscent
of my petit bourgeois Northern childhood. How far my life has
travelled from that well-behaved world where golf took precedence over opera or poker. In which room do I really belong?
The ever more anarchic card room, where the liquor is increasingly taking its toll on the behaviour of young Americans
abroad? Or out here in the casino, where the smartly dressed
couples moving around arm-in-arm, greeting each other cour-
teously before indulging in a little flutter, remind me so vividly of
my parents? I know but I'm not telling.

The two worlds collide in a celebrated golf anecdote that
echoes many poker stories. In a major tournament Gary
Player's only way of winning is to chip in from the sand-trap at
the eighteenth. He does so to tumultuous applause. As he walks
to the green to pick his ball out of the hole, someone in the
crowd yells out as he goes by: 'You lucky bastard!'

Player turns and fixes him in the eye. 'You know,' he says
thoughtfully, 'the more I practise, the luckier I seem to get.'

There's an inescapable poker truth in that tale, reflected in a
Lederer quote from his friend and Full Tilt colleague John
Juanda: 'People say I'm lucky. That must mean I'm winning.'
The element of luck lurks beneath my favourite remarks from
these four intensely enjoyable days, distilled in Marcel's 'The
cards don't know' and Howard's 'Let the cards come to you.'
There comes another in Sunday morning's farewell question-
and-answer session, when someone asks Lederer (under the

general heading of 'gut play') about the virtues of 'playing a rush'.

Don't do it, says Howard sternly. 'Never. *The cards don't have a memory*. Playing a rush is one of the fastest ways to stop the rush. Poker is not magic.'

Poker would not be as popular as it is, he concludes, were it not for the element of luck. 'The better players love that.' Because they're the best at ruling luck out of the equation.

On the flight back to London I wonder if I should have gone to camp at the beginning of my adventure rather than now, towards the end. Phil Hellmuth had offered me a place on his own poker camp right after last year's World Series; but the Job had prevented me returning to Vegas so soon. No, I persuade myself, this has been the perfect timing to tune you up for this year's World Series next month.

Back home I discover that's not all I've been tuning up for. On my machine is a message from Conrad Brunner of PokerStars asking whether I could take another week out pretty soon – the week after next, in fact – to go (all expenses paid, of course) to Barcelona.

'I'd like to think so,' I tell Conrad. 'What for?'

'You've been selected to play for England in the World Cup of Poker.'

10

Kournikova's Revenge

One of London's most chic, see-and-be-seen-at restaurants, the Ivy is as much a haunt of itinerant Hollywood stars as a pit-stop for the London glitterati. While the likes of Julia Roberts and Steven Spielberg dine down in the main restaurant, my previous visits to its private room upstairs have been for upscale literary dinners with the likes of Harold Pinter, Salman Rushdie and Melvyn Bragg.

In February I was back there for a Ladbrokes lunch to launch 2006's instalment of its televised tournament, the Poker Million, in the company of promoter Barry Hearn and handpicked others. It's a measure of how seriously the new poker takes itself, and the sheer amount of money that is sloshing around.

Four months later Hearn invites me to a poker weekend to be held in the board room of Leyton Orient Football Club, of which he is chairman – and whose underground car park plays host to PartyPoker's televised game in the *Poker Den*, where players are frisked as they enter the brick-walled room and play with wodges of £50 notes rather than chips – an ironic, almost *noir* homage to the pseudo-gangster-land atmosphere of the old poker.

There will be £100 satellites on the Saturday for £1000 satellites on the Sunday to win two of the £35,000 seats in the heats for the final of the Poker Million – which, as its name suggests, guarantees the winner a cool million. This fifth year in the event's history will be its biggest, with a record £4.12 million in prize money making it the richest tournament in European poker history. For once, however, I cannot contemplate entering, let alone winning, as I would not be able to play in next week's heats; I have to be in Barcelona for the World Cup of Poker. I'm leaving, in fact, tomorrow. So, determined (for once) to lose, I opt for the £100 option – a cheap enough price for a fun day out with my old pal Alvarez.

I arrive, as is my wont, rather early and find myself parking at the same time as the club's esteemed chairman. Barry Hearn is one of British poker's most engaging figures. A former accountant who moved into sport in the early 1980s as the manager of snooker champion (now turned expert poker player) Steve Davis, he soon signed up a lucrative stable of snooker and pool players before moving into boxing, darts and golf. When all of these became huge on British television, Hearn managed to get even less likely sports such as fishing and ten-pin bowling, even the martial arts, on to TV – all under the umbrella of his management and production company, Matchroom, which these days has its own poker website as a 'skin' of Ladbrokes, with whom he runs the Poker Million.

An Essex man oozing East End charm and mischief, Hearn was a latecomer to poker. Already a multi-millionaire through his other sporting interests, he went to Atlantic City for the first time in 1998, to promote a fight with Don King. On the flight over he read an article in the in-flight magazine by Donald Trump about the sudden growth of poker. Next day, as he wandered past Trump's Taj Mahal Hotel and Casino, Hearn saw a line of two hundred people queuing for something, stretching right out of the casino and round the block. Many were clutching wads of hundred-dollar bills. Intrigued, he went over to ask what they were standing in line for. A poker tournament, he was told. And the dough? That was the entry fee.

'A light bulb flashed on over my head, Tone,' Barry tells me. 'Wow, here's a sport where the players pay the prize money! Well, I just had to get into that.' And so he did. Within five years Matchroom was producing four hundred hours a year of TV poker programming – 10 per cent of its four thousand annual hours of sports programming – including the Poker Million, for which Hearn got the idea from the global success of TV's *Who Wants To Be A Millionaire?*. It is Hearn's proud boast that Poker Million gave out its first £1 million prize (to its first winner, John Duthie) before *Millionaire* did (to a cousin of Camilla Parker Bowles, now the Duchess of Cornwall). Hearn himself, meanwhile, swiftly became a respected player, regularly seen at final tables.

Barry loves to tell his story about Dave 'the Devilfish' Ulliott, who rang him demanding a fee to play in the Poker Million, boasting: 'It ain't nothing without the Fish.' Hearn agreed to meet him for a drink in a hotel in Barry's home town of Brentwood, Essex. 'Who *are* you?' Barry asks the Devilfish. 'No one knows who you are.' Now Dave gets 'stroppy'. So Barry points at a guy in the lobby and he says: 'See that guy over there? I bet you five hundred pounds he doesn't know who you are.' While the Devilfish is thinking, Hearn adds: 'And I'll bet you another five hundred he *does* know who I am.' Barry explains: 'Well, it helps that I've lived in Brentwood for thirty years . . . But the Devilfish declined the bet and that was the end of that.'

Also typical of Barry were his dealings with Henry Orenstein after the Poker Million was first shown on Fox in the US. 'I get this phone calling saying, "We've got a problem." Turns out there's this guy in New Jersey who says he's got the patent rights to under-the-table cameras. I can't believe it. But even if he does, I think, I'll do what I normally do: I'll ride a bulldozer over him. So I call him and he says, "Come and see me", and I say, okay. Before I go, he sends me a copy of his memoirs. When I read it and discover that this guy's survived five concentration camps, his parents and his siblings killed, and all his other sufferings, I think, My God, I'll pay him whatever he wants.' Barry, of course, winds up becoming friends with Orenstein, though he declines an invitation to play in his Friday night game. 'I said I was still learning. He said: "Oh, don't worry, nobody loses more than a quarter million."'

Upstairs in the Leyton Orient boardroom, which naturally commands a spectacular view of the ground, the joint is soon hopping. While the first satellite is being won by the British pro Jac Arama, I find myself drawn for the second in Seat Four, next to Hearn in Seat Three, at the same table as Alvarez (Seat Ten). In Seat Eight is Mel Judah's sister Esther Nye, supported by her husband Peter and Mel himself, who won last night's televised Poker Million heat. On the very first hand, Hearn goes all-in with A-Q, after a flop of Q-9-3, only to find himself called by Q-9. The turn and the river bring rags, so Barry's out straight away; now he can go and schmooze with his guests, secure in the knowledge that he's already bought himself a $1000 seat for tomorrow, anyway.

All I want is to avoid a confrontation with Alvarez – until the heads-up, at least. Soon he goes all-in, under the gun, with K-K, as we discover when he's called by 4-4. The kings hold up and Al doubles up.

I then fold 8-4 and accidentally flip them over en route to the muck. Well, it happens sometimes. But the board does not usually proceed to reveal itself as 8-4-2-8-A. There is much laughter at my expense, especially when the guy on my left says he folded 8-2.

All too soon A-J loses me four of my ten thou. With no interest in winning, I'm using this session as an experiment, implementing some of the lessons I've learned in Baden: vary-ing my play, changing gears, attempting to play aggressively and run stylish bluffs from time to time. Even so, A-J is the best hand I've seen all day; and the blinds, now £200–£400, are going up fast – every fifteen minutes.

Next hand I'm dealt K-8 suited and my pre-flop raise of £1000 gets one caller. The flop comes K-3-2 and all-in I go. My opponent calls before rolling over a pre-flop pair of threes that have now morphed into a set. The turn and the river both bring fours, so I'm third to be knocked out – by, as it turns out, a pleas-ant guy called Steve. Hey, this losing business is e-a-s-y.

As I root for Al, and Mel Judah for his sister, I settle down for a chat with the only man ever to have been thrown out of the Tuesday Night Game for being just too good. It's a compliment Mel remembers fondly, although he says with some feeling that the game still owes him money. Judah was a hairdresser with Vidal Sassoon in London when we used to play together in the late 1970s and early 1980s; now he's a respected professional, with several million in tournament earnings to his name and the pro tour nickname of 'Silver Fox'.

Esther's been playing only two months, Mel tells me, mostly on the internet, and doing pretty well. We watch her bluff her way to a pot, raising with 5-6 to get rid of K-K. 'I'm proud of that,' says Mel, 'the way she's bluffing sometimes.' Sure, I reply, but delicately remind him of another of poker's brother–sister relationships: Howard Lederer taught Annie Duke how to play and bankrolled her early career, but she has since knocked him out of all five of the five final tables they have reached together. Mel seems unfazed.

After luncheon is served – Essex-style kebabs washed down with Leyton Orient FC white wine – I settle down to support Al, notebook in hand.

'Boswell to your Johnson,' I laugh.

'Yeah,' he replies, 'Al Johnson.'

After two hours of play, Esther is finally knocked out, leaving Al among the last three players. There is brief uproar at the next-door table when Mad Marty Wilson's quad sixes are beaten by quad sevens. But Al, with the blinds now up to £300–£600, has the satisfaction of seeing his opponents beating each other up. Another Barry (not Hearn) eliminates one James, giving him a 5-1 chip lead against Al as the head-to-head begins.

Alvarez plays like a master, getting to only 2-1 down when his A-J beats Barry's A-3. With the blinds now £400–£800, Al goes all-in three times in a row and wins all three, easing into the lead. Then comes the decisive hand, when all the chips again go in before the flop. Al is holding 2-2, Barry K-3. The flop comes 5-5-4; Al's two pairs are still ahead. The turn is a three, giving Barry two better pairs. Then the river brings a six, giving Al a straight – and victory. He is suitably chuffed.

We have a celebratory sandwich outside in the directors' box, looking down on the out-of-season ground, bereft without its goalposts, in blazing June sunshine. I tell Al that I had a call from the Moll this morning to say that she dreamed he won £3 million in a poker game. Clearly she brought him luck. So we get her on my mobile, so he can tell Cindy her dream came 0.3 per cent true.

The following day Al is back at the Orient ground again, one of seventy starters in the £1000 satellite from which two will emerge as winners of the £35,000 seats in the Poker Million heats. Again he is in masterly form and reaches the final table. Third place is a consolatory grand – but he just misses even that, dammit (a politer version of his own language), when A-Q beats his all-in A-8 to knock him out in fifth place.

Me, at the time I'm en route to Gatwick, to fly to Barcelona early the next morning – to play for England in the World Cup.

There is apparently another World Cup going on elsewhere – something to do with football in Germany. In Barcelona, meanwhile, forty players from eight nations (out of forty-eight starters) are arriving to contest the third annual World Cup of Poker for a handsome trophy and $200,000 in prize money. The previous two titles have been won by Costa Rica, who have not made it to this year's finals; so this week will see a new country crowned world champions. The very existence of the tournament, invented for television, is yet another sign of the worldwide reach of the twenty-first-century poker boom. And maybe, just maybe, that poker actually has become a sport.

We're all missing the Ladbrokes Poker Million, as well as the 'Grosvenor World Masters' tournament at the Vic. Tonight the music critic should be at *The Marriage of Figaro* at Covent Garden, with a new cast under a new conductor, Sir Colin Davis. Instead he's at a cocktail party in Barcelona's Gran Casino, to meet the teams and introduce their fifth members, the so-called 'celebrity' players. These are former world champion Tom McEvoy for the USA, WPT title-holder Isabelle Mercier for Canada, online professionals for Brazil, Iceland, Ireland, Israel and Portugal – and, er, me for England. Sponsored by PokerStars, the event is hosted by EPT boss John Duthie, whose production company will be making this into six ninety-minute TV shows.

My England teammates, who have all qualified online, are thirty-seven-year-old Derek Morris, a bookies' assistant from Wigan; twenty-year-old Rob Fairs from Chesterfield, a politics student at Lincoln University; John Loftus, a twenty-three-year-old maths teacher from Hull; and our captain, Andy Booker, thirty-seven, a plasterer from Garstang. None of them has met each other before in the flesh, only in poker cyberspace. Derek ('Purrofaces') is an online hero to Rob ('Carnivex'); Rob has played with him, or watched him play, 'for hours'. Andy ('Andy134') is our captain because he leads this year's PokerStars tournament rankings. During a strategy session over (many) free drinks before tonight's 'friendly' freeroll, Andy says he wants me to go first, i.e., play in the first of the five heats to decide which four teams make it to the final. The first heat takes place tomorrow.

Is this wise? I wonder aloud, trying to conceal my horror at the responsibility he is placing on my shoulders. Andy is going for 'experience', he says. I'm not just the team's veteran but the only one to have played on television before. I tell them that my online play is looser, more experimental than my b&m play, which seems to confirm Andy in his decision to play me up front – and laid-back Derek last, when we'll know where we are and how many points we need. The 'strongest' players, I hear Andy say, should go first and last. This is scary, not least because I'm sure all the other teams are making the same decision. Before I can protest further, Andy hands his team selections to Duthie.

The 'fun' freeroll is ruined for me by the prospect of being first up for England the next day. Spain, the country in which the groans around the room remind me I am, have meanwhile gone 0-1 down to Tunisia in the other World Cup on the TV screens above our heads as we play. By the time I am knocked out – A-K again, beaten by A-10 with a flop of K-3-J-7-Q – Spain are winning 3-1. I console myself by telling the Anna Kournikova joke – ever the good loser, even I'm now getting sick of it – then withdraw gracefully and go back to my hotel room to brood while the others stay to sink a few beers.

I take my pill and get a few hours' sleep, even if they are stalked by dire dreams. Breakfasting alone in the hotel dining room next morning, I am greeted cheerily by skipper Andy. I tell him I'm having an early lunch so as not to play on a full stomach. He nods approvingly.

Only now do I realise just how unusually nervous I am about this event. The unfamiliar dimension of playing for a team, rather than just myself, imposes an uncomfortable burden of corporate responsibility. Also, playing on the TV table will of course mean that people will later see your hole cards and pass judgement (ditto the commentators) on any weak or wacky plays you make or indeed don't make – on the team's behalf, rather than your own. At ninety minutes, each episode will contain an unusual amount of detail for poker on TV – maybe, I am advised, as many as one hand in three. In the hotel lift, a friendly Irishman tells me they've fielded their best player first. He thinks most teams have. Oh shit.

In Vegas this thing would start at noon, giving less time for brooding before the off. Here the casino doesn't even open till 3 p.m., which leaves me five hours to fret. Alone. That seems a huge amount of time. How I wish I had a companion with me, especially a moll, that moll, the Moll, *any* moll – preferably one that worships me, admires my remarkable versatility and understands poker inadequately enough to think it's incredibly impressive that I've been drafted into England's World Cup set-up. I try to calm myself by going for a swim in the rooftop pool. Then, back in the tense privacy of my room, I shower and shave as per Edward G. Robinson's Lancey in *The Cincinnati Kid* before his heads-up with Steve McQueen. But I cannot put on an elegant suit and tie like Edward G or even the Devilfish. The England shirts with which we have been issued are compulsory wear for the entire tournament, even after you've been knocked out.

Normally I feel a strong aversion to the cross of St George; its sudden appearance on taxis and white vans all over England during the football World Cup rings less to me of patriotism than ugly, right-wing nationalism. But now I've got one on, with my name stitched into the polo-shirt beneath it – the first of six issued last night by the organisers. And England are playing in the other World Cup later today. Their match against Sweden kicks off at 9 p.m., local time, after five hours (or ten intervals) of the tournament. Will I be out of the poker in time to watch it? This is a matter of supreme indifference to me because I'm much more a club than country supporter. So, in fact, I doubly hope not.

I try to persuade myself that in truth it's a relief to be going first, to be getting it out of the way, so as to enjoy the rest of the week. Unless I'm the first to be knocked out, letting the team down and feeling totally humiliated, which will ruin the ensuing five days.

I wonder about wearing a nicotine patch but decide it might do terminal damage to my bio-rhythms. Should I wear my shades – if only for the TV lights? For a while I weigh up trying the Greg Raymer technique – putting them on only when in a hand. The trouble is: mine are prescription specs, and my short-sightedness means that I can't see my hole cards with them on and sometimes can't see the flop with them off. Some people think it's a tell if I put my specs on – which is useful because it isn't. (If you look back at your hole cards, so conventional wisdom has it, it means you've got a strong hand.) In the end, on balance, I decide to take them with me. But I'm obliged to wear short sleeves, which at a poker table makes my elbows sore . . . Oh, come on, Holden, stop fretting like this, stop looking for things to worry about, get yourself into a positive frame of mind.

Okay, as Gary Gilmour put it, let's do this thing.

As soon as I get downstairs it feels a whole lot better to be in company. Yet the coach ride to the casino then feels like the wagon to the guillotine. On arrival I confess to my relaxed, happy teammates that I'm feeling more apprehensive than usual, not wanting to let them down. They are, of course, reassuring, urging me to play my own natural game.

Interviewed by the PokerStars blogger Jo Haslam – girlfriend, as it turns out, of Gutshot blogger Steve Bartley, he of Monte Carlo and Vivaldi fame – captain Andy says that he has gone for 'experience' in Player A. This, I tell her, is a euphemism for age. I've been playing poker since before some of my teammates were born. Unlike them, I am more of a felt than an online player. But all you can do, I hear them telling me, is your best.

And there's more than national pride at stake here. There's money, potentially serious money. After five heats, one per player, the top four of the eight teams will make it to Saturday's final – and into the money, with $100,000 (or $20,000 per player) for the winners, $50,000 ($10,000 per player) for second, $30,000 ($6000 per player) for third, and $20,000 ($4000 per player) for fourth. The points system for each heat is that the winner will get 15 points, second 12, third 9, fourth 7, fifth 5, sixth 3, seventh 2 and eighth 1.

Before the 4 p.m. start there's the ordeal of the TV interview, made less so by the charm of the lovely Sam Mann, our onscreen hostess for the week. I confess candidly about my nerves, the responsibility of going first, the potential embarrassment of being the first to be eliminated. As I emerge my Irish counterpart is waiting outside. He's next up. 'It's like the dentist's waiting room, isn't it?' he jokes. At least someone else is feeling the same way as me.

At last the time comes and we draw for seats. The TV cameras roll and John Duthie announces the names of those chosen as Player A. In Seat One, for Iceland, is Gustaf Bjornsson (the team's 'celebrity' member, a top internet player); in Seat Two, for the USA, its captain, Joe Harwell; in Seat Three, for England, Anthony Holden, its 'celebrity' player; in Seat Four, for Israel, Klemi Hagag; in Seat Five, the Brazilian captain, Christian Kruel; in Seat Six, the Polish captain, Marcin Doliwa; in Seat Seven, the Canadian captain, Aaron Haw; and in Seat Eight, the Irish captain, Daniel Bolton.

Five of my seven opponents are team captains. This is going to be even tougher than I thought. We start with $5000 in chips and the blinds at $50–$100 for thirty minutes, then $70–$140, then $100–$200 and up fast, at half-hour intervals. They want to get this over today, in four or five hours. My strategy, as agreed last night with Andy and Derek, is to stay super-conservative during the first two, maybe three levels, playing only monster hands and trying occasional positional raises, in the hope that online players with less b&m or TV experience will err on the side of caution or maybe knock each other out.

After ten minutes or so I make my first play, betting $500 in early position with 5-5 against Ireland's big blind. Ireland folds and I win the blinds, to a huge cheer from my teammates in the gallery. I'm $150 up – which, as captain Andy has agreed, might even be a satisfactory result for the first session, just hanging along with the blinds. I look round and wave to my fellow England players, absurdly chuffed by so small an advance.

During the second session, with the blinds at $70–$140, Ireland bets $500 into me. I think about reraising with 9-9, which I certainly would if I were playing for myself; but I remember Andy's instructions and reluctantly fold. The flop comes K-2-10 and Ireland bets again, so maybe I did the right thing. I won't know until I see it on TV. Unfortunately I soon lose the $500 I won in the first round by raising $500 with 8-8, getting called and seeing a flop of paints. When America bets into me, I have to fold. Now I'm back where I started, which at least is the chip average with all eight players still standing and everyone playing very tight.

Early in the third session I get J-J on the big blind. The small blind (US skipper Joe Harwell) raises $500 into me. I reraise him $1000. He thinks long and hard, then folds, showing me 7-7. I show him my J-J – well, I figure, why not? – to more heart-warming cheers from the England contingent behind me, to which I respond rather self-consciously because of the cameras.

At this early stage of the proceedings, especially when playing for a team rather than oneself, all you need to survive is one such hand per session. It seems a modest goal, but I've got my instructions. There's no doubt that the TV pocket-cam is affecting my play; I feel I can fold an ace with a weak kicker, several of which I see, even a middling pair if the pot has been raised before it reaches me. But monster hands – well, alas, I'm not seeing any, so the dilemma has yet to arise. TV, I know from experience, edits out most hands; with a programme this long, however, plays that I'd rather people didn't see will probably survive.

At the end of the second session I am lying in third place for England, with $4160, behind Israel with $13,060 and Poland with $8600. Ireland has $3450, Canada $3250, the USA $2730, Iceland $2610 and Brazil $2230. The others have not been that much more antsy than me; these disparities are down to just a few biggish hands.

During the fifteen-minute break before session three, Andy buys me a drink – yes, I'm allowed a glass of red wine – and we discuss tactics. The skipper cheers me up by saying he thinks I'm right to be biding my time. I should keep playing super-safe in the hope that the others begin to start knocking each other out. That has to start happening soon. Then, we agree, I should go for broke if I catch a premium hand.

During level three, with the blinds now up to $100–$200, the American captain Joe Harwell, on my right, has a great session. I know from the blog that he has run his own real estate business since leaving college and been playing poker only four years, but has plenty of live tournament experience, including three events at last year's WSOP. Joe is one of the top US players in the online rankings, rated the fourth-best US player for 2005 and the sixth best in the world. And now he is lucky enough to see pocket rockets; he plays them beautifully, extracting the maximum from unlucky Poland after flopping a full house.

On the very next hand he raises $500 into me and I reraise another thousand with another J-J; Joe smiles knowingly and folds. Things are beginning to loosen up around here. I know

Joe is playing from strength; but I have long had the problem that the biggest stack at the table, Israel, is sitting to my left. Still, I end the third session in fourth place, with $4260. So far, so good-ish. Israel, the USA and Brazil are ahead of me, with $12,420, $8760 and $5160 respectively. Behind me are Iceland with $2710, Poland with $2270, Canada with $2250 and Ireland with $2160.

We've been playing ninety minutes and something surely has to give soon. As the fourth level begins, with the blinds at $150–$200, the USA's Joe Harwell asks me where the UK captain is, what he looks like; he's played with him online and would like to meet him. I look around to find that Andy is not in the bleachers behind me. Where is he? I mouth to my teammates and they make glass-to-mouth gestures. So I look over to the bar, to see him deep in conversation there with Derek, oblivious to the poker. I take it as a sign, I tell America's Joe with some satisfaction, that my skipper has confidence in me.

Soon Ireland doubles up, largely at the expense of Canada, who then goes all-in himself and wins it all back. We can't seem to get rid of anybody at this table and I'm still aching not to be the first out, to the point of cravenly folding tens on the button. Then the Canadian captain sets himself all-in. An Edmonton-based internet pro, who goes by the screen-name of 'HooBangin', Aaron Haw has claimed to the blogger that he has 'no particular tactic' for the game; he's going to 'wing it'. Well, he's wung in the wrong direction on this hand, which sees him eliminated – first out, in eighth place, winning his country just one point. Aaron 'HooBangin' looks crushed, as I would in his place.

Then Iceland's celebrity player, Gustaf Bjornsson ('Gusti.is'), also bites the dust when Ireland calls and beats his all-in. An online pro for the last year, Gustaf chose this profession, he says, because 'the pay is good'. He's out in seventh place, earning his country two points.

Now I'm on the button and I see dear old A-K again. As I hope, American Joe to my right lobs in his usual raise from the cut-off seat, this time $1300, and I don't have to think too long before going all-in, to the tune of $4500. The small blind, Israel, folds; but I am surprised and alarmed to find myself called by Brazil in the big blind. Surely the big blind can't have pulled a monster hand? America duly folds and I roll over my Anna K. Brazil's captain, the aptly named Christian Kruel, shows me a pair of kings. Only the three aces left in the deck can get me out of this; I'm a three-outs dog.

All year I've seen people go all-in with A-K and an ace has obligingly landed on the flop. Not this time, of course. Don't ask me what cards came; I can't remember, except that none of them was an ace. England is out in sixth place with three points. I go to shake the Brazilian's hand, to look sporting for the cameras, but he's too busy stacking my chips to notice. So I wish good luck to America's Joe Harwell ('AppSt2004'), whose company I've enjoyed and whose play I've admired, before retiring gracefully from the fray.

I feel dreadful, of course, as if I've let down both team and country. I'd love to have won them more than three points; but my teammates are wonderfully reassuring. 'Who could expect the big blind to be holding K-K?' asks skipper Andy. 'You played that hand perfectly.' Derek also tells blogger Jo that the hand 'pretty much played itself'. I was more or less equal short stack with Poland; I had to do what I did, which it's nice to hear them all agreeing. They all say they wouldn't like to have gone first and that they had learnt a lot from my patient, accurate play over nearly three hours. I haven't, they tell me, made a single wrong move. I wonder how they know. But the general consensus is that it's a decent enough start and the others now know what they have to do.

Just as Team England is escorting me to the bar, I'm grabbed from behind and taken off for the post-exit interview with the lovely Sam, who has now turned into the casino *tricoteuse*. I must be feeling gutted, she says, and she's right, of course. All I can think of doing is to tell her the Kournikova joke yet again. I'm beginning to loathe it now; but Sam hasn't heard it before and laughs gratifyingly, exonerating me from all charges of sexism. 'There's only one woman in the world who wouldn't,' I say boldly, 'and I doubt she's watching.' Sam promises on air to buy me a drink and I tell the watching world that I'll hold her to it. For now, though, that's Team England's job.

After this the pressure of the World Series will seem a doddle. As my teammates console me at the bar, Ireland is next out, winning five points, then Israel comes fourth for seven. Third, equal with me when I went all-in, comes Poland, for nine points. In the heads-up, the USA's Joe receives a crippling blow when his 9-9 is called by Brazil's A-J and the flop immediately brings an ace. Now why couldn't that have happened to me and my A-K? Joe had been down below two grand at one point and had played a gutsy game to get back into contention. He winds up coming second, with twelve points for the USA, to my nemesis, Brazil's Captain Kruel, who notches fifteen.

So the first round is over before the dinner break. After a few more glasses of wine, I hear myself joking that I went out early so that my teammates could watch the England–Sweden game on the giant screens scattered around the casino. Both are already through to the next round so it's only about who wins the group and winds up with the weaker opposition in the last sixteen. England haven't beaten Sweden at football for thirty-eight years, since 1968, just after beating Germany in the 1966 World Cup Final. And still they don't. Sweden are 1-0 down at half-time but they equalise and the match ends 2-2. So England get what they want, first place in the group, but even with a Swedish manager they still can't manage to beat the Swedes.

Who cares? Not me. Conrad Brunner of PokerStars does,

though, because this means that England's next game will be on Sunday, as we all travel home, rather than on Saturday during the World Cup of Poker finals. As the others go off to play in sit-and-gos, for which I'm feeling too tired, I have a last drink with an equally weary Conrad and share a taxi with him back to the hotel.

On the evening of Day Two, I should be at a gala dinner in London for the London Philharmonic Orchestra. Instead, of course, I'm back at Barcelona's Gran Casino, rooting for England's Player B, young Rob Fairs.

Round two gets off to a very slow start. People say, gratifyingly, that today's table is even tighter than yesterday's, which was also 'rougher'. But yesterday's players seem to have set a trend; Rob plays super-carefully for the first three sessions, as do all seven of his opponents. Captain Andy has told Rob it doesn't matter if he doesn't play a single hand during the first three sessions; I can see why he's saying that but am not sure I agree. Still, there's virtually no action at all during these rounds. Rob plays one hand in the first session and wins the blinds. During the second session, with the blinds at $70–$140, he raises to $340 and Poland goes all-in. Rob folds 10-10. Ireland and Brazil are now the most active players. At the start of the third level, Rob wins his own big blind unchallenged.

During tonight's break one of England's travelling supporters, Derek's friend Sue Lawrence, gives Rob a massage. While he lies prone on the front bench of the bleachers, the TV cameras love it and I protest that she didn't offer me one yesterday. But it does nothing to alter the fact that he begins level four ($150–$300) as the low stack. And Rob plays not one hand during the level, which he ends down to $2600. Finally he goes for it under the gun – a good position because he could have tripled up – with J-J, which is called by the USA with 7-7. The board comes 5-8-9-A . . . 6, giving the USA a 10-1 chance gutshot straight. Today, England is the first team out. The winners turn out to be Israel.

After two days of play, the USA is leading the field with 27 points, Israel is second with 21, Brazil third with 17, Poland fourth with 16, Iceland fifth with 9, Ireland sixth with 8, Canada seventh with 6 and England last with just 4. Heat three is Andy's turn and we're going to need a captain's innings.

Especially when we see who he's up against: Tom McEvoy for the USA and Isabelle Mercier for Canada, two of the world's top professionals – one a veteran of the old poker, the other a star of the new.

Fired from an accounting job in his thirties, Tom McEvoy grew up playing penny-ante poker with his grandmother, from whom he says he took 'quite a beating'. But he's gone on to write some of the most admired poker manuals available, while winning the 1983 world championship and three more WSOP bracelets. He's also a very nice guy, if a little tired and dishevelled today; a few years older than me, he is still suffering, he tells me, from his long journey at the weekend from Vegas via Newark to Barcelona.

Isabelle Mercier took a law degree in Canada before morphing from a lawyer to a blackjack dealer to a poker dealer and eventually poker room manager of the Aviation Club de France in Paris. Since moving to the other side of the table and turning pro, she has become a poker columnist and TV commentator while winning more than $250,000 in tournaments, including the WPT's 'Ladies Night Out' event – during which Mike Sexton gave this diminutive woman the fearsome nickname that has proved her passport to poker fame: Isabelle 'No Mercy' Mercier.

The third heat starts after dinner on Day Two, around 10.30 p.m. These poor players have been waiting around all day. McEvoy may be looking weary but his play soon suggests otherwise; and he seems to have his beady poker eye on Mercier above all the other players. There are rumours around the room that between them, for some reason, it's 'personal'. I manage to get this information to Andy, who may be able to take advantage of it.

The play at this table is faster, as expected, than its two predecessors. Ireland's Paul Redmon and Israel's Boaz Lavie are both out, each to the USA's McEvoy, before play is called off for the day at 1 a.m., after three sessions – to the evident annoyance of Mercier, who wants to carry on through the night. She must be feeling in the groove. Andy Booker has been folding with a more calculated reluctance than I or Rob could manage; there is a calmness, a due consideration about his play which I find impressive, and hope his opponents do.

At noon the following day, the six countries left are led by the USA's McEvoy, with the best part of $10,000, to the $9430 of Poland's Jacek Ladny, Mercier's $6170 for Canada and Booker's $3930 for England, with Brazil's Hugo de Carvalho and Iceland's Thorkell Thordarson bringing up the rear in the lower three thousands.

On the very first hand of the day Brazil's all-in 4-4 is called by Mercier's A-K for Canada and the flop comes 2-A-2. Immediately she's got the ace you need, and I never see, when you hold Kournikova. With a nine on the turn and an eight on the river, Brazil is first out. Then Mercier lives up to her nickname by mercilessly stealing blinds. Her eyes dart everywhere when she's involved in a hand and when she's not. She stares fixedly at any player contemplating calling her bet or raise; when she does this to Andy, he has promised us he will blow her a kiss. This is a moment to which Team England is looking forward.

But Mercier is on a roll and soon she cripples Poland. After a flop of 9-10-J Ladny bets $1000 and she immediately raises him all-in. He has a chip advantage over her so he calls, revealing J-Q. Isabelle turns over A-J. The turn brings a four, the river a seven, so she doubles up – just as we reach level five, with blinds of $200–$400.

With Poland down to barely $3000, he raises $1500 – half his stack – into Andy, who has even fewer chips and promptly goes all-in. Poland's Ladny shows Q-K and Andy a pair of fours, before the flop comes 6-4-A. Trip fours! At last some luck for England; this is the first flop in our favour in the entire tournament, in two and a half heats adding up to more than twelve hours of play. The turn brings a six, the river a five, and England's skipper doubles up. Now we're in business.

The play is getting feistier. Poland goes all-in with A-Q suited against Iceland's A-J and doubles up on a board of rags. England's Andy goes all-in again but gets no callers, showing an ace as he scoops up the blinds. Iceland goes all-in with A-Q, called by Canada's Mercier with a suited A-7, and they split the pot when the board comes 2-5-K-5-K. The same soon happens again, intriguingly, with both players on A-J. But Iceland is dangerously low-stacked.

Tom McEvoy has been pretty quiet during this session, carefully watching Mercier's antics from beneath the brim of his trademark Stetson. By the beginning of level six, the blinds now $300–$600, she is leading the field with all of $19,900 as opposed to his $7500, England's $5200, Poland's $4600 and Ireland's $2800. Now it's Andy's turn to play Mercier at her own game.

England raises all-in on the button and wins the blinds. On the big blind, after Mercier has called on the small, Andy raises her all-in to the tune of $6100 – and after a long hard stare (during which, to our disappointment, he does *not* blow her that kiss) she folds. Then he goes all-in with A-9 against her pair of sixes on the big blind. This time she tries every trick in the book, staring him down as she riffles her chips and eliciting nothing beyond an inscrutable smile when she asks our skipper 'D'you want me to call?' She's obviously read today's blog because she muses, 'So you've unleashed your secret weapon' – which is what I am quoted as calling Andy last night. Eventually, after an eternity, she calls and a flop of 9-10-K gives Andy a pair of nines. With an eight on the turn and another king on the river – no repeat, at least, of yesterday's gutshot straight draw against England – Andy wins a pot of $15000.

Can things at last be turning our way? The thought is interrupted as Tom McEvoy goes all-in for the USA with A-Q, and is called by Mercier with 5-5. The board brings 8-2-3-Q-10 so McEvoy doubles up at her expense just as we reach the next break. After ninety minutes' play today, three hours in all, and the blinds now up to $400–$800, Canada's Mercier has been reduced to $3900, the same as Poland, with only Iceland behind them on $2300. America's McEvoy is up to $11,400 but the chip leader is now England's Andy Booker with $18,500.

Mercier begins a new assault by taking the blinds four times in a row, which at this stage adds up to a not insignificant $4800, putting her right back into contention. Then, with A♠-10♠, she calls Iceland's all-in 5♦-6♦; the flop comes 10♣-9♠-Q♠, giving Mercier middle pair, then the turn is the 8♠, giving her an unbeatable nut flush. Iceland goes out in fifth place.

Now the team in danger, Poland, goes all-in with A-3 suited, to be called by McEvoy with 10-K. The flop of K-4-6 gives Tom middle pair and the turn brings an apparently irrelevant five. Poland has no flush draw; only a two on the river can save him from extinction. But the miracle duly happens; Polish supporters go berserk when the dealer defies the odds of 10-1 by rolling a deuce and Ladny lives to fight on.

Then comes the ultimate confrontation between McEvoy and Mercier. Wounded by the Polish miracle, McEvoy goes all-in for $4700 with Q-10 and is called by Canada's Mercier with K-J. The flop comes 6-Q-J, giving McEvoy top pair. Then the turn card is a king, giving Mercier top pair. The river is a four, eliminating the USA's Tom McEvoy in fourth place.

At 6.05 p.m., some five hours into this thing, England and Poland split a pot when Ladny's A-7 is called by Andy's A-3, and the board brings 9-10-J-6-J. Tense stuff. Then Andy has another run-in with Mercier when she bets $2000 after a flop of 2-Q-J; Andy thinks a long time before folding. Five minutes later he goes all-in with A♠-7♠ and is called by Poland with 10♦-9♦. The board brings 4♣-5-♠-6♠-4♠-K♦, giving England a flush and showing Poland the exit. It's now down to England's heroic captain Andy Booker and Canada's Isabelle 'No Mercy' Mercier.

As the heads-up begins at 6.15 p.m. (yes, all this is happening rather fast), with the blinds at $600–$1200, Mercier has $11,300 to Booker's $38,700. Before long the Canadian goes all in with A-J and Booker calls with a pair of nines. The flop comes 5-7-K. So far, so good. The turn brings a five, putting England within one card of victory and maximum points. And the river is . . . an ace, another 10-1 shot against us – and typical of England's luck all week.

Isabelle has 'sucked out' on Andy. Now Mercier has $22,600 to Booker's $17,400. After ten minutes of jousting, she raises his big blind and he calls. The flop comes 6-2-9, with two spades, and Andy bets $5200. She raises and Andy throws in his hand. For quite a while it goes back and forth in this way, with England's Andy getting ahead of Canada's Isabelle again – by two to one, then three to one – before falling back behind. Then, at last, comes the decisive hand. After a flop of 4-9-10, Andy checks and Isabelle bets $2000. Andy goes all-in and she calls. Our man turns over 9-4, giving him two pairs, while Isabelle reveals a ten, giving her just the top pair. The turn is an irrelevant deuce and fifth street . . . a devastating ten, giving Isabelle trips and victory. Again, at 20-1 against, she has rivered him.

One card from winning just twenty minutes ago, England wind up getting 12 points for second place. Andy Booker was very unlucky not to prevail; but he has played that captain's innings we needed and got us back into the tournament. Suddenly Derek's determination to play last looks like a good decision; we were worried that we'd be out of it before he sat down. 'Well,' I say to him, 'there's no pressure on you then!' Derek plans to go off to bed well before midnight, without waiting to see the outcome of heat four, about to get under way.

After three rounds the USA is leading the tournament with 34 points, Poland is second on 25, Israel third on 23, Canada fourth on 21, Brazil fifth on 20, England sixth on 16, Iceland seventh on 14 and Ireland is eighth on 9. Will that six-point swing between Mercier and Booker prove crucial to England's fate? For now it's in the hands of our pensive maths teacher John Loftus ('Monge Toot').

During the first session, before much has had a chance to happen, Team England startles its player by calling a 'time-out'. Each team is allowed one per three sessions. In the secretive time-out chamber, just outside the tournament arena, we pass on some intelligence to John, as well as some straightforward observations. Ireland's Dawn Marshall, in Seat Two, is going for broke; she will play 'shit or bust', as it's her team's only chance of getting to the finals. Brazil's Jose Arenstein, to John's left in Seat Six, is clearly playing to the cameras; there's nothing at stake for the USA's Michael Elbert, to his right in Seat Four, so he should watch out for some wayward betting. And Poland's Marcin Meinardi, opposite him in Seat Two, is so tight he plays only the nuts; Derek knows this after playing at his table in the first night's 'friendly' tournament.

Okay, we could have told him most, if not all of this before it started. But we thought it might be fun to cause a diversion by calling a time-out – the first to be called during the first session in the entire tournament. And it works. As I watch from the casino, the Israeli captain 'Sugar' Teddy Tuil wanders over to ask me what it was all about. Under no obligation to answer, let alone tell the truth, I tell him we had reads on all the other players at the table. 'Oh yes?' says he with an amused grin. 'And what was your read on ours?'

'She's betting too big,' I tell him. 'She's already risked half her stack during the first session.'

Teddy suddenly looks anxious. 'You're right,' he says and goes off to call a time-out of his own. I ask the PokerStars team if the time-out room is bugged; no, they tell me, adding (as England supporters all) that it's beneath the stairs, so you can hear what they're saying if you send someone up there to listen. But we don't bother. We're English, after all, with an ingrained sense of fair play.

Back at the table, sure enough, the USA soon self-destructs – which is great, as it brings the leaders back within reach. Israel's Aliza Broude then disobeys orders by setting Canada all-in with K-J versus K-Q after the flop has brought a K. Israel goes down to $1500 and now it's Canada who calls a time-out.

By the end of the second session, England's John Loftus lies in sixth place with $4660; Brazil is chip leader with $9160 and Israel bottom with $2840. As the tension mounts, I am becoming increasingly relieved I went first. For the only time all week, I leave the casino for a while to have a terrific fish dinner at the harbour-side with Conrad Brunner and his boss Tamar Yaniv, PokerStars' marketing director. By the time I get back, Iceland has gone out and England is all-in. It's John's A-6 against the, guess what, A-K of Brazil's Arenstein, a professional player who is his team's qualifier via frequent player points. 'A six killed me yesterday,' mutters Rob as the flop comes Q-6-5. The turn brings another queen, the river a four, so England doubles up.

Forced all-in again soon after, Brazil goes out when Arenstein's pair of eights is beaten by a diamond flush for Ireland on the river. With the blinds $600–$1200, England's John again goes all-in to the tune of $3200 with a $2000 raise.

Everyone else runs for cover and we cheer wildly from the stands. Then Canada's Trevor Diks doubles up at the expense of Ireland when his A-J beats Dawn's J-4 (on her big blind) with a board of 2-2-5-9-5. Disaster follows for England, all-in for $5000 with A-Q and called by Canada with a pair of tens, when the first card in the flop is a ten. Poor John, who has hung in there heroically, is now all but dead.

After Ireland wins an all-in pot, England's maths teacher again commits all his chips – blind this time, only to discover he has a pair of aces, called by Ireland with a pair of nines. The flop comes 8-J-Q, but the turn is a third ace and the river is not a ten (phew!), so England doubles up again. Now it's John's big blind but with only $1600 he's again got to go all-in whatever cards he is dealt. And so he does, to be called by Canada. England's A-8 looks okay against Canada's Q-10, as the flop brings an eight, but then a queen, sending John out in fifth place.

Poland exits in fourth place while Team England settles in at the bar, trying to work out what Derek (known to his friends as 'Des') has to do tomorrow to get us to the final. By the time Israel goes out in third place, Des has already retired to bed, mindful of the task ahead. The A-Q of Canada's Diks, playing only the second live game of his life, beats Ireland's J-9 in the conclusive heads-up hand, so Canada has won two in a row. Little does the sleeping (we hope) Derek know that he needs to WIN tomorrow to get us into the money.

Or does he? The maths is bewildering. Two wins today for Canada have pushed them to top of the table with 36 points, one ahead of the USA, with Poland and Israel equal third on 32, Brazil on 23, England and Ireland equal sixth on 21 and Iceland out of it on 16. A second-place finish might get us to the final if Poland, Israel and Brazil all fare badly.

Back in the real world, the USA have gone out of the other World Cup, complaining about a penalty awarded by the

German referee in their 2-1 defeat by Ghana. It was a 'tough one to deal with,' said US coach Bruce Arena, as his team packed their bags to head home.

Well, Poker Team England knows just how he feels about bad beats, suck-outs and the like. *International Herald Tribune* columnist Roger Cohen picks up the theme in a column from Nuremberg, quoting a World Bank report that countries winning the World Cup add 'about 0.7 per cent' to their economic growth. As if economics weren't enough, muses Cohen, 'it's when football and philosophy get entangled that things get deep'. Still complaining about that penalty – now an 'astonishing' call by the referee – he quotes an email from John Morgan in Los Angeles: 'To me, this is why soccer's particular drama is so compelling. It's a mirror to life, and all its inequities, its rare brilliance, and, yes, its boredom.'

Hang on, I thought that was poker – which, like life, is at least spared the seemingly arbitrary whims of a referee. Back to the *real* World Cup in Barcelona, where today promises a tense climax to the preliminary rounds as no fewer than five teams have a chance of three of the four places left in the final. England and Ireland must win to get through. Even then we need Israel and Poland to go out early. It is even possible that the leaders, Canada, could fail to qualify if they go first. To the organisers' delight, this thing is still wide open.

All the teams have saved their best player till last. Our Derek (or 'Des') Morris is up against tough opposition – and he manages to get off to a truly disastrous start. On the very first hand, with the blinds at a mere $50–$100, Poland raises under the gun and Des calls from the big blind. The flop brings 2-3-9 rainbow. Derek bets $400 and Poland calls. The turn is a two. Derek bets $1100 and Poland calls again. The river brings an eight. Derek checks, Poland bets $1600 and Derek calls. Poland shows Q-Q – and Derek mucks his hand. It turns out afterwards that he had 9-10. England has lost $3400 – two-thirds of his stack – on the first hand.

Ireland doesn't fare any better, going out first when Niall McNamara's A-9, which becomes two top pairs on the flop, is beaten by a flush on the river for Canada's Christopher Comely. Since Ireland's exit, Canada has been assured of a place in the final, so Comely can play as freely as he wants. The same is not true of England's Des, who goes all-in for $1230 on his big blind of $140, to be called by Brazil under the gun. England has A-K against Brazil's A-10, and the board brings Q-5-J-4-10. So Des makes a Broadway and doubles up to $2460. For once England has rivered someone else.

There are several more such dramas before it happens again, half an hour later, when England's K-J finds a king on the river against Iceland's all-in pair of nines. Des is back up to around $6000, in third place to Iceland and Poland when the blinds go up to $100–$200. He continues to bob and weave, duck and dive, playing with guts and imagination until disaster strikes in a hand against Canada. After a flop of 2-Q-10, with two hearts, England's all-in with Q-K is called by Canada with 10-8, both hearts. The turn is the nine of hearts, giving Canada a flush. A jack on the river gives Des a straight but he was drawing dead. He's lost $2360 and is just hanging in. 'England haven't had much luck in this tournament,' says commentator John Duthie. He can say that again.

Des takes some mints from his pocket and offers them round the table. 'Have one,' cry the England supporters. 'They're drugged!' Then he goes all-in yet again with a pair of nines, to the tune of $3500, and is called by chip leader Iceland with 3-4 off-suit. The flop is a horrible 5-6-8, the turn another six, the river a beautiful seven. Maybe England's luck is changing? Des doubles up to $7000. By the next break, he's still lying third, with $6460 to Iceland's $10,120 and Canada's $7720. Brazil, Israel and Poland are on $4000-plus and the USA is on $3280.

Now the blinds are up to $150–$300. It's been two hours

since anyone was knocked out and the tension is mounting. Another half-hour goes by and the blinds increase to $200–$400. When the USA goes all-in with A-6, Des calls with a pair of kings. It's a pot of $5400 but yet again England gets stuffed when the flop brings an ace, then another on the turn. Twenty minutes later, short-stacked Israel goes all-in with $1500, holding the dread A-K against two callers, Canada's 5-6 and England's pair of sevens. The flop brings K-3-5, the turn a ten, the river . . . a six. England has been sucked out again, rivered by Canada's two pairs. But Israel is out, in seventh place.

Des is down to $1600, just four big blinds. Five minutes later he goes all in ($1200) with Q-6 and gets called by Poland's 2-6. 8-4-5 is the flop, the turn an eight and the river a three – the only card that could win it for Poland. Again we've been beaten by a 10-1 shot on the river. Eliminated in sixth place, we have a total of 24 points from five heats. We are not going to make it to the final.

Tricoteuse Sam descends yet again and we English are our practised national selves in taking sporting defeat graciously. A magnanimous Des says on camera that I've been a 'great' part of the team – 'a father-figure to us all', to which I protest that I'd rather be seen as an older brother. While all this is happening, Iceland goes out in fifth place and the USA in fourth. There are cries of 'Polska, Polska!' as Poland's Philip Hilm eliminates America's Phil Myers. Israel is now praying that Brazil will be next out; it's between the two of them for the fourth spot in tomorrow's final. Israel's agony goes on right through the ninety-minute dinner break.

Tonight is the San Juan Festival in Barcelona, so the menu is an exotic 'San Juan Special', which the England team attacks in cheerful, only slightly subdued style. When play resumes, Brazil's celebrity player, a pro named Raul Oliveira, plays as if his country's future depends on it. Which, in poker terms, it does. Canada, Poland and America are definitely through to the final; England (24 points), Ireland (22) and Iceland (21) are out.

Israel will go through on 34 and Brazil will go out on 32 if Canada and Poland can see off Brazil.

Raul doubles up once, to the Israelis' dismay, before going all-in with A-9. Canada calls with A-J and the flop brings Q-10-2. When the turn comes a six, there is the chance of a split pot. When the river brings another six, Canada's jack comes into play and Brazil's Raul is knocked out in fourth place. The Israelis go berserk. They are through to the final – and the money – by just one point.

On the next hand, with nothing to play for, Canada sets Poland all-in with 10-9 to 10-8. The flop comes 4-2-10, then a three, then a queen, and Canada's Christopher Comely has won his country's third successive heat. Canada leads the league table with 51 points to Poland's 44, the USA's 42 and Israel's 34. The rest of us can but stay on to watch.

At least we losers can go partying tonight, as Barcelona goes San Juan-crazy. Team England reconvenes at lunchtime the next day with sore heads and heavy hearts. Today, I don't tell them, the world is missing my Old Adam in a production of *As You Like It* at the Stevenage home of the novelist Ken Follett, a friend since we were trainee journalists together in Cardiff in 1970. Bardolaters like myself, Ken and his MP wife Barbara lay on a production for family and friends every year. For months I'd been cast in one of only two roles we know the actor Shakespeare played himself. At the last minute, alas, the World Cup has taken precedence – as it also has tonight over the umpteenth performance in Mozart's 250th anniversary year of his early opera, *Il Re Pastore*, which I confess I am somewhat less dismayed to miss.

The World Cup final is a short-handed match of just four players in which the captain is obliged to make occasional substitutions – a 'tag match', in poker parlance. As it gets going, I read a copy of *The Times* found in the hotel lobby, to see poker parlance infecting coverage of the other World Cup. 'Carrick to Hold the Aces for Gambler Eriksson' is the headline on the back-page piece about team selection for tomorrow's knock-out match against Ecuador. While perpetuating the contentious view that poker is a form of gambling, it reminds us how poker-rich the English language is, with such phrases as 'the buck stops here', 'poker face', 'an ace up the sleeve', etc., in everyday use. But even *The Times*, which once prided itself on its reputation as 'the newspaper of record', inexplicably fails to mention that England has come sixth in the World Cup of Poker in Barcelona.

As Germany play Sweden in football's World Cup, the democracy of poker sees two men and two women lining up in the other: for the USA (David Smith), Poland (Philip Hilm), Israel (Aliza Broude) and Canada (Isabelle Mercier). Each starts with $25,000. This is going to take some time.

At $50–$100, Mercier is in virtually every hand; by the time she goes all-in during the second level ($100–$200), the Canadian captain looks a nervous wreck. But she's got them into second place, with $25,650, behind Poland's $39,200. Israel is on $21,800 and the USA is down to $13,350. Canadian captain Aaron Haw – the player first out of my own heat – has the courage to substitute himself for Mercier after the break, while the USA retains Smith and Israel inserts Sugar Teddy and Poland Andrzej Skawinski, a student pharmacist who is second in his country's online rankings.

On the last hand before dinner, Israel makes a lousy call and is knocked out by Poland. After dinner I am interviewed yet again by the lovely Sam, with whom I enjoy an onscreen kiss as I tell her that Team England is rooting for Poland – they have been the most enterprising players all week. The USA has now inserted Tom McEvoy, who can but watch as Poland's substitute Jacek knocks out Canada, then takes a big pot off McEvoy. The American is playing with a sign propped up in front of him reading: 'Think before you act' and other such self-instructions.

America's captain, my new friend Joe Harwell, bravely puts himself in to play the endgame – which, at 2-1 down in chips, is not looking good. The coup de grace comes at 11 p.m., when Poland's A-6 calls a surprising bluff from the USA: all-in with an unsuited 6-3. The flop comes 5-Q-4-9-4 and Poland are poker's new world champions. As the champagne flows and they pose for joyous team photographs, each of the five team-members is $20,000 richer. 'We're going to play poker,' they joke, 'to decide who takes home the trophy.'

The next day, Sunday, when I fly back to London, is the first of this year's World Series of Poker. Today sees the beginning of satellites and live action, tomorrow the first of forty-five events over seven weeks, of which no fewer than thirty-four are some form of Hold 'em. There is much muttering about this from players of Omaha, stud, razz and other poker variants, and above all about the giant HORSE event for an entry fee of a whopping $50,000. 'Why not just ge 'em out and measure 'em?' as Annie Duke put it in Baden.

I myself will be obliged to miss, alas, playing in the seniors event – which would have meant going all that way twice or staying for all of two months. Even for me, that's just too long in Vegas. Given the Job, I am able to go for only three weeks – which will count as my summer vacation. But I don't even leave for another month. The day I could have been playing in the seniors, I'm a world away at Covent Garden for a revival of Donizetti's *Don Pasquale*. Where would I rather be? I think you know.

Another night that week I was chuffed to defy the experts by discovering another reference to poker in opera – in John Adams' *Nixon in China*, revived by the English National Opera in Peter Sellars' justly celebrated production, during which Air Force One dramatically lands onstage. In the last act, as his historic trip to China flounders in cross-cultural misunderstandings, Nixon reminisces gloomily with his wife Pat about his wartime service in the South Pacific. As her husband tells her things she has never heard from him before, Pat tries to console him with the words: 'But you won at poker?'

'I sure did,' replies Nixon. 'Five-card stud taught me a lot about mankind.' He goes on: 'I had a system. "Speak softly and don't show your hand" became my motto.'

In this context, of course, Alice Goodman's words are a metaphor for politics, the futility of which is the composer's subtext for freezing a moment of recent history as the most unlikely (but thrilling) piece of music-theatre. Towards the end, the dying Chou En-lai says: 'How much of what we did was good? Everything seemed to move beyond our remedy.'

With Israel and Hezbollah now at each other's throats, and troops and civilians dying every day in Afghanistan and Iraq, Chou seems to have a timeless point here. There are moments when the poker life, which tends to proceed within its own obsessive shell, cocooned from the outside world, can seem not just irrelevant but grotesque. I make a vow to keep in touch with world events, however incongruously, while in Vegas.

As I pack for three weeks there, I receive an email from the World Series of Poker telling me that I have been drawn to play in the fourth 'flight', on Day 1-D. Because of the size of the field this year, with at least eight thousand starters expected, there will be four Day Ones – each flight starting with more than two thousand players and continuing into the wee small hours until only eight hundred are left each day.

Is it good or bad, I wonder, to have been drawn to play on the fourth and last? Well, look at it this way: a third of the field will have been knocked out before I sit down to play. This must be my year.

11

The New Poker

In the olden days, as long as ten years ago, a stretch limo would have been awaiting my arrival at Las Vegas' McCarran Airport, courtesy of Binion's Horseshoe, with a uniformed (and armed) heavy to carry my bags and see me safely downtown after a fourteen-hour journey from London via LA or San Fran. Today, after a ten-hour direct flight from Gatwick on Virgin – business class, courtesy of PokerStars – I stand in line for a twenty-dollar cab ride to the Monte Carlo Resort and Hotel Casino.

I've been to Vegas so many times now that I no longer get the same kick out of the sight and sound of the slot machines at the airport – that foretaste of the mayhem to come before you've even picked up your bag. Today I find them mildly depressing. If it's possible to feel a tad jaded about the whole Vegas she-bang, that's the mode in which I arrive for the 2006 World Series of Poker. The truth, about which I'm in denial, is that I'm in mourning for a one-of-a-kind moll who has slipped through my fingers; but I'm determined not to let the moll that got away affect my stay – or, more importantly, my play. (Yes, I used to write her sonnets.) So I clutch at self-deluding straws like a fond memory from her that a previously untried hotel is 'always a treat'. Hmmm – let's see if that works. The Monte Carlo is a new one on me, its sleek if monumental exterior apparently designed to reflect its European namesake's reputation for effortlessly elegant opulence.

The Monte's stately façade boasts none of the look-at-me gimmicks that make most of the garish Strip hotel-casinos distinctive – until, that is, you go into them. Behind the skyscraping Manhattan landmarks atop New York, New York, amid the Grand-ish Canal snaking round the Venetian (gondoliers and all), beneath the Pyramid of Luxor or the Eiffel Tower atop Paris, these surreal fun palaces are all exactly the same inside: the incessant babble and gurgling of the electronic slots, the deranged yells and groans of crap shooters, the amorphous mass of degenerate humanity seething across your path in search of new excitement, new thrills, new ways to lose money.

This is the Jerry Springer, obese trailer-trash side of Vegas. And it makes a lot of noise. The card rooms at the heart of all these places – some large and sleek, most (like the Monte Carlo's) more modest, tucked away in casino corners – seem, by contrast, welcome oases of calm, their players sitting in reflective mode, often comparative silence, winning and losing money to each other rather than the house. This is where I shall rigidly keep my focus over the three long weeks ahead. This time around, no 'leaks' like craps or blackjack for me.

Yet another of Steve Wynn's European-style fantasy resorts, now part of the MGM Mirage Group's nine-property chain stretching from the Mandalay Bay to Treasure Island, the Monte Carlo is one of three hotels on the Strip where PokerStars is housing its 1623 online qualifiers for this year's world title event (an increase of almost 50 per cent on last year's 1116). The Vegas version of the Empire State Building is right outside my window – which is weirdly déjà vu, as the real thing was right outside my window when I lived on the forty-eighth floor of a sleek new apartment block on East 29th Street, just off Fifth Avenue, at the turn of the twenty-first century. In the siege mentality of the weeks after 9/11 my personal brand of the paranoia then gripping Manhattan was genuine surprise as I awoke each morning not to see a tail fin sticking out of it.

Vegas' version of paranoia this week has been to cancel an international gaming conference – not for fear of terrorists but of online gambling executives getting arrested as soon as they set foot on American soil. As Congress debated the legality of internet betting – which theoretically contravenes Bobby Kennedy's 1961 Wire Act forbidding the use of 'wire communication facilities' for betting purposes – the first such arrest had been made only a few days before. On touching down at Dallas-Fort Worth Airport to change planes on his way from the UK to the company's headquarters in Costa Rica, the British boss of the online betting group BetonSports was detained by the FBI after a federal grand jury in the Eastern District of Missouri returned a twenty-two-count indictment charging him, ten other individuals and four corporations on charges of racketeering, conspiracy and fraud. As forty-eight-year-old David Carruthers languished in Fort Worth jail, BetonSports shares were immediately suspended, sparking a plunge in the values of other such companies' shares. And Vegas lost its nerve.

Guests at an annual online gaming conference in Sin City were to have included a roster of top honchos from the multi-billion-dollar online gaming industry. The basketball star Magic Johnson had been booked as a keynote speaker. But the event's organiser, Calvin Ayre of Bodog.com, got cold feet and called it all off at the last minute because of 'a high level of concern over the uncertainty surrounding the US government's recent actions against one of the companies in our industry'. Many of his peers, said Ayre from his base in Costa Rica, feared setting foot in America – and the same seemed to go for himself, even though he had recently been featured on the cover of *Forbes* magazine's 'Billionaires' issue. 'This will cause all executives of any substance trading in our space to change their travel plans until some certainty comes into play,' he said. 'I would be surprised if there's any executive who isn't sitting down with their lawyers trying to work out the implications.'

Shares dived again amid fears that the FBI could be about to broaden its crackdown on America's online gaming industry. Meanwhile there was growing unease among online gambling operators listed on the London Stock Market about what was called the 'loose language' emanating from the US Department of Justice about the legality of poker and casino websites taking bets from American punters. Online gaming firms that do not take sports bets were insisting their operations are legitimate. And British firms like Ladbrokes and William Hill were thanking their prophylactic stars they did not take sports bets from American customers.

But what of PartyGaming, which had announced it was planning a move into sports betting on top of all its other gambling activities, only one of which was poker? And which would, before the WSOP was done, almost brazenly buy up the Bulgarian-based but Antigua-registered sports betting website Gamebookers for €102m (£69m), urgently stressing that none of its customers were from the US? All this despite taking bets on American football, basketball and ice hockey, while rejecting the US Department of Justice's claims that internet poker and casino games were outlawed by the Wire Act, if not three different sections of Title 18 of the United States Code.

The facts at the time were these. The House of Representatives had just voted 317–93 in favour of H. R. 4411, or the 'Unlawful Internet Gambling Enforcement Act', other-wise known as Goodlatte-Leach. Introduced by Representative Jim Leach, Republican of Iowa, this was a watered-down version of the more draconian H. R. 4777, or 'Internet Gambling Prohibition Act' proposed by Bob Goodlatte, Republican of Virginia. The net effect of H. R. 4411 was to prohibit US credit card companies and financial institutions from sending payments to gaming sites. Before it could become law, however, the bill also had to pass through the US Senate. Many Republicans on Capitol Hill were anxious to push it through before November's mid-term elections, in which they feared (rightly, as it transpired) that they could lose control of Congress; but the Senate appeared at the time to have other priorities.

The state of Washington, meanwhile, had set an ugly precedent by unilaterally declaring online poker illegal – a law as unenforceable as absurd in a state where poker in casinos remained within the law. What were they going to do? Raid people's homes and send them to jail for five years for going all-in with pocket jacks? It was like closing down Amazon.com, as one observer put it, while leaving high-street book chains such as Borders free to ply their trade. 'Poker is part of America's heritage', read a T-shirt seen all over Vegas, 'Keep it legal'.

Nonetheless there was something in the air, which had savants muttering that Harrah's was busy maximising its profits from the World Series while the going was still good. The Nevada Gaming Board was sniffing around the transfer of money by all these dot-com websites sponsoring players; presumably it had arrived in cash, rather than by wire transfer?

In fact, of course, it had come from the dot-net side of the internet business, the 'educational' side where people learn to play poker, or polish their skills, without risking real money. And there was no direct link between the dot-net sites, where people play poker for 'fun' money, and the dot-com side, where they play for real money. Oh no, of course there wasn't. Shirts and caps with dot-com logos had the 'com' covered up by masking tape in the Rio's card room, for fear that it might appear on American television (where all the adverts for online poker are strictly dot-net). Dot-net shirts were fine on TV – as indeed were the PartyPoker.net logos in the middle of every World Series table.

So that's all okay, then. Poker-only sites like PokerStars, Full Tilt and countless others felt safe enough for now, as the authorities seemed to be targeting sports betting more than poker. But their long-term unease was evident in the striking fact that Chris Ferguson and Howard Lederer, founders of Full Tilt, had recently led a delegation to Washington, DC, with PokerStars' Greg Raymer, to lobby senators to lay off online poker. The issue was very like that in a long-running dispute between London's Gutshot Club and Her Majesty's legal eagles: that poker is more a game of skill than of luck, and that poker-exclusive clubs and websites were looking after their players far better than the casinos or sports betting sites. But would the Gutshot win? Would Capitol Hill listen?

There's a movie in all this, I kept thinking – *Jesus Goes to Washington* – as it proved an edgy backdrop to the three weeks ahead, which would otherwise constitute the richest sporting event in history.

With the field half as big again as last year, could conditions in the Rio be any worse? A dental health conference had replaced last year's shrinks and mini-boppers along Convention Way but even insiders were apprehensive. A month before it started, under the headline, 'The 2006 World Series of Poker: It'll be Hell – Just Don't Miss It', PokerStars' own Conrad Brunner began his column for the European edition of *Card Player*: 'Let me beat the rush and be among the first to complain about the 2006 WSOP.' The World Series had become 'an over-populated and absurdly long poker festival that has clearly travelled too far, too quickly, expanding to become a bloated victim of its own success and vaunted over-ambition . . . The true spirit of the event has disappeared with the tumbleweeds across the Nevada desert, only to be replaced by a global poker marketing conference. As Sam Goldwyn would say, "Include me out".'

But here he is, Conrad in person – including himself in, after all, even if he does arrive a few days after everyone else. So I'm able to tell him that a few changes have been made since last year in a bid to defuse criticisms like his own. Most, however, will only refuel it.

For a start, product placement has run amok. The World Series of Poker is now 'presented' (which presumably means sponsored) by Milwaukee's Best Light (which presumably means beer). Also aboard the poker-boom bandwagon is the Swiss luxury watchmaker Corum, now 'the official timepiece of the World Series of Poker', who will be handing out new wristwear to all nine players who reach the final table of the main event, with a 'unique' one for this year's new champion.

Damn – this reminded me that I had forgotten to bring the Watch, that uniquely vulgar timepiece with the queen of diamonds set in a sea of fake gold given me by the Moll last time around as a good-luck charm. But it hadn't won me the world title then, so why should it now? Maybe it was better off back in Blighty.

These sponsorship deals are among the first initiatives of the WSOP's new Commissioner, Jeffrey N. Pollack. Yes, like baseball, poker now has its very own Commissioner, hired by Harrah's from NASCAR for 'his creativity and entrepreneurial insights'. Pollack's track record also includes the foundation in 1994 of the *Sports Business Daily* – must reading, apparently, for 'top decision-makers in the sports, entertainment and television industries'. His brief from Harrah's is 'to further establish the World Series of Poker as the number-one brand and nothing less than the "Wimbledon of Poker".'

To which end, Pollack has proudly announced a five-year 'pact' (have they smoked a pipe of peace?) with ESPN, which will now broadcast the final table live (on pay-per-view), as well as a beefed-up version of its usual extensive coverage. The poker games on AOL are now World Series of Poker-'certified'. This summer marks the launch of the WSOP's first-ever mobile game, 'soon to be available on cellphones everywhere'. The WSOP's second action video game, 'World Series of Poker Champions', will also be hitting the stores before long and the WSOP website has been 'refurbished by the talented team at IGM Media'. In a $1.6 million deal, *Card Player* magazine has also bought exclusive rights to live online coverage and other media privileges. And *Bluff* magazine has secured the live radio rights for its Sirius Channel 125.

Harrah's has clearly learnt from the WPT, whose majority shareholder Lyle Berman expressed its aspirations with complete candour: 'Our whole goal was to create a brand around poker and monetize it.'

Pollack is less explicit. The WSOP's partnership with Milwaukee's Best Light 'reflects', he says, 'our own sense of fun, creativity, excitement and authenticity'. The deal with Corum watches reflects mutual 'boldness, distinction and excellence'. Even the famous WSOP bracelet has been redesigned 'to a higher level of sophistication, elegance and richness' by Triton, a division of Frederick Goldman, Inc. of New York – crafted from fourteen-karat gold, enhanced with sixty-six full-cut white diamonds. The new world champion will receive a fourteen-karat gold bracelet studded with one hundred and seventy 'hand-picked, full-cut' diamonds, with the words 'World Series of Poker' raised in yellow gold in the centre and fifty-three diamonds embedded into the word 'poker'; the four suits will be picked out in black sapphire, black diamonds and rubies.

And this year's Gaming Lifestyle Expo will also be, guess what, even 'bigger and better'.

As well as making the WSOP brand name yet more lucrative for Harrah's, Pollack has, to be fair, also been spending some time trying to improve conditions for us mere players – the thousands whose entry fees make this event so phenomenally lucrative. After feedback from last year's competitors, the commissioner established a player advisory council featuring such big poker names as Lederer, Ferguson, T. J. Cloutier, Jennifer Harman, Daniel Negreanu, Scotty Nguyen and Robert Williamson III. A questionnaire answered by 1400 of last year's participants apparently praised the tournament dealers, staff, venue and 'overall experience' but bemoaned the inadequate restroom facilities, the cost and quality of the food available, and the fog of cigarette smoke in the corridors around the card room.

Now there are extra restrooms adjacent to the tournament area and staggered break times to reduce congestion. Smokers have been thrown out of the corridors next to the tournament area – out of the building altogether, in fact, to 'an outside smoking facility under cooling canopies' (which I never found during countless cigarette breaks in the 110-degree heat). And as the price of poker goes up the price of pizza is coming down, at a specially built Food Court behind the tournament area. This turns out to be a tent full of nutritious burgers, hot dogs, pizzas and potato chips, etc. A few unappetising salads are on offer but there's not a stick of fruit in sight. Next door are a couple of Portakabin restrooms for men only, with a queue already snaking back out into the torrid Vegas temperatures.

The first thing I saw when I arrived back at the Rio was a line of top-heavy, scantily clad damsels urging me to try out the new Food Court, as well as sundry other infernal poker temptations. Before the day was out, however, I was bombarded with more evidence of Harrah's seeking to maximise their profits on the event. The rakes (or percentage of the buy-ins they cream off the top) went as high as 9 per cent for most tournaments; for the main event it was six, which alone amounted to a cool $5 million – or six hundred dollars per player. For this we got cheap plastic playing cards (rather than the usual casino Kems, so tough you can clean them in a dishwasher); damaged cards, moreover, were replaced individually rather than by new decks. The tables were so smothered in sponsorship logos that the cards occasionally got lost in the Technicolor haze; and the dealers were in open revolt at their rates of pay – more than halved, they said, since last year.

So dissenters were delighted by one unforeseen occurrence, arising from another innovation insisted upon by the Players Advisory Council (especially, apparently, Negreanu): a new item on the tournament agenda to sort the top pros from the masses, something expensive and versatile, where the winner would likely be a name the poker world already knew. Let's get rid, they were saying, of the ridiculously high luck factor in the mass-entry No Limit Hold 'em world title tournament.

'I heard them loud and clear,' says Pollack. 'We needed to create an event that was different.' The result was a 'HORSE' tournament – HORSE being an acronym for forty-minute rounds of Hold 'em (both limit and no limit), high-low Omaha eight-or-better, razz, stud and high-low stud eight-or-better, with each segment costing the same $10,000 buy-in as the main event, adding up to a staggering entry fee of $50,000.

A test of all-round poker skill, in fact, played for the highest entry fee in the history of poker. How many starters would they get? The answer (after a few satellites) was 143, making a total prize pool of $6,864,000, with a first prize of $1,784,640. The event lasted a gruelling four days, or a total of forty-three hours. As expected the final table was entirely made up of big poker names, with twenty-seven World Series bracelets between them: Doyle Brunson, Chip Reese, Andy Bloch, Phil Ivey, Jim Bechtel, T.J. Cloutier, David Singer, Dewey Tomko and newcomer Patrik

Antonius (the short stack, who was the first out). For the benefit of television, and to the indignation of all true HORSE aficionados, the final table was restricted to, you guessed it, No Limit Hold 'em.

After a marathon, all-night heads-up against Bloch, the $1.7m first prize eventually went to the veteran David 'Chip' Reese, his first WSOP victory in twenty-four years. Unwittingly, the sheer length of the heads-up was some sort of revenge on the Harrah's bigwigs, including Pollack, who all showed up at midnight to present the prizes and were then kept up all night. It began just after 1 a.m. on the fourth day and ended – after more than three hundred hands, many more than it had taken to eliminate the previous seven final-table players – more than eight hours later at 9.10 a.m, with surviving spectators asleep all over the arena.

The winner, Chip Reese, has for years been regarded by general consent as the best all-round poker player alive. Now he had proved it.

How would Chip fare against Pamela Anderson, the enhanced, then de-enhanced, then re-enhanced *Baywatch* babe who took to the stage of the Doyle's Room hospitality suite with the great Texas Dolly himself, to herald the launch of her very own new website PamelaPoker.com in conjunction with the Doyle Brunson Poker Network?

My money would be on Reese, as Pamela confessed that she hasn't actually played much poker yet. She will 'guest-play' on her site after she's had a few lessons from Brunson, a friend of her father, who is an 'avid Brunson fan' (says Doyle himself). Pamela is dressed in full bridal veil, above a skimpy, figure-hugging outfit because she's getting married this weekend – 'twice, to the same man' – once, it transpires, on each coast. In the front row, Robin Leach of *Lifestyles of the Rich and Famous*, now writing a Vegas blog for AOL, peppers her with questions about the ceremony. And I thought we were here to talk about poker? So did the menacing master of ceremonies, who curtly announces: 'No more questions about the wedding.' Intriguingly, he adds: 'And no questions at all about Mr David Carruthers of BetonSports'.

As Pamela babbles on, herself defying his instructions, seventy-two-year-old Doyle grins inanely beside her, looking pretty bushed and anxious to be somewhere else, anywhere else. Why does he keep up this helter-skelter pace? Why subject himself to such indignities, scooting around in his motorised wheelchair on behalf of Doyle's Room? I find the all too candid answer in a recent interview in *Card Player*: 'I think the ultimate goal is to sell it because it's just too much work for me at my age. They keep me going all of the time and I would kind of like to relax.'

This rampant vulgarisation of poker continues at the second Gaming Lifestyle Expo, where the first thing I see – at the stand of Calvin Ayre's Bodog.com – is a queue of men stretching up a flight of stairs to have their pictures taken in a pillow-fight on a king-size bed with two well-endowed, barely clad cuties. Bodog has brought the bed in especially for this stunt, available to any red-blooded male who might just want to sign on to their website. Although the bed is upstairs (natch), the proceedings are cheerily broadcast to passers-by on a giant TV screen below. It's the first thing visitors see on entering the exhibition.

Cleavage seems as important an exhibit at the expo as cards, chips or dealer buttons. There are large-breasted sirens everywhere, ready to have their picture taken with any poor sap who signs on to pretty much anything. As passionately as I'm in favour of cleavage, as indeed of cards and chips, I find this debasement of the game I have so long loved even more dispiriting than last year. So many people making so much money. Beyond its descent into corporate capitalism, poker is now in danger of becoming just another branch of showbiz.

Worst of all is a chilling glimpse of the future. Here are two tables occupied by ten players each, with no dealers, no cards, no chips. The surface is merely a giant green screen, making *Star Wars*-style swooshing noises as two cards are electronically dealt face-down to each player. Put your hands over them, as you would for real, and they flip over to reveal themselves. Remove your hands and they go face-down again. Then you press buttons in your control panel: check, raise, fold, followed by a 'confirm' button. Around the table you can see in numbers how many chips each player has got and the size of the pot, just as you can on the web. There follows the flop – check, raise, fold, etc. More swooshing noises. Someone wins . . . Start again . . . but there are no cards to handle, no chips to riffle, no dealer to abuse. Or tip, winks the promotional material for the manufacturers, PokerPro. Or pay, I reflect, on behalf of the casinos already installing these dire devices.

'Fastest and most accurate dealer on the planet,' yells the handout. 'No mistakes, ever. Keeps the game moving. Lets you see more hands. Bottom line: more pots, no tips, more money.'

'I love it,' exclaims one player, leaping up and dancing around like Phil 'the Unabomber' Laak, so called because of the hood behind which he hides his poker face. Hey, behind the hood hiding his face I see that it *is* Phil 'the Unabomber' Laak. 'You *love* it?' I ask him incredulously. 'Yeah, it's great, man! Give it a whirl!' He offers me his seat. Which I decline, as I realise he is obviously being paid to say all this.

PokerPro tables are already installed in casinos from Florida via Oklahoma to the Hollywood Park near the Los Angeles airport, LAX. They are coming soon to poker cruises and no doubt to a casino near you. This, I can only suppose, is the long-term future of the World Series of Poker. A cavernous room without that trademark clatter of chips, like two thousand cicadas at sunset. Instead the yells of players blaming the computer for their bad beats, maybe even a Matusow or a Hellmuth shoving his chair through the giant screen.

No wonder the chairs are cocktail stools anchored firmly to the floor. I have seen the future, and it sucks.

A monkey, name of 'Mikey', has been entered for this year's main event. It's a publicity stunt by a website called PokerShare, based on the tricksily punning slogan that 'any chump' can win the thing. Harrah's insists that the chimp cannot play as it would be 'unhygienic'; the website responds that the animal will be wearing a diaper. Eventually, after a long search through its extensive rulebook (full of regulations about rabbit-hunting, etc.), Harrah's sees off PokerShare's determined representatives with the definitive ruling that the chimp cannot play because it is . . . under twenty-one.

The veteran professionals T. J. Cloutier and Billy Baxter are this year's new members of the Poker Hall of Fame – which on the sacred wall down at Binion's, as no one apart from me seems to have noticed, is still stuck at 2003's Bobby Baldwin. Not even the face of last year's inductee Jack Binion has yet appeared in the gallery at the casino which bears his name. But someone, I am told, is soon going to buy it and turn it into a new Vegas attraction built around poker. Of course they are.

At the ceremony in the Rio's showroom, neither Cloutier nor Baxter quite musters the eloquence of last year's Addington quoting Thoreau; the usually gracious Cloutier's speech, indeed, consists largely of complaints that this hasn't happened to him sooner. But each deserves better than second billing to a Hollywood-scale plug for Curtis Hanson's new poker movie *Lucky You*, which features a mock-up of the Bellagio card room and real poker pros from Doyle Brunson to Jennifer Harman. We are shown the trailer, then clips, then granted an audience with Hanson and the film's star, Drew Barrymore. Even Brunson turns up again on his branded wheelchair, tireless in his promotional zeal.

During the question-and-answer session some savvy poker

journalist asks Commissioner Pollack how come Harrah's is not juicing up any of the World Series events – ploughing back some of its vast profits from players' entry fees, in other words, into the poker economy? But we are, replies Pollack, citing the $2 million prize money 'given away' for this year's WSOP Tournament of Champions – an invitation-only event in which the $1 million first prize was won by none other than the WPT's Mike Sexton. The other million was shared between such other poker paupers as Daniel Negreanu ($325,000), Mike 'the Mouth' Matusow ($250,000), Chris Reslock ($150,000), Andy Black ($100,000), Darrell Dicken ($75,000), Chris Ferguson ($50,000), Daniel Bergsdorf ($25,000) and Thang Pham ($25,000). Of twenty-seven starters the unlucky players who missed out on the freeroll prizes included Doyle Brunson, Phil Hellmuth, Gus Hansen and reigning world champ Joe Hachem. Yeah, sure. Giving yet more money to those least in need of it is Harrah's idea of poker philanthropy.

For me, the highlight of the occasion is my reunion with Tamar Yaniv, marketing director of PokerStars, whom I had last seen at the opera in London; my two current worlds collided when Tamar escorted me to an open-air production of Verdi's *Rigoletto* in Holland Park. It was my last assignment before heading for Vegas and the last music I would hear for a whole month – apart, it turned out, from high-decibel Wagner (*Tannhäuser*, no less), courtesy of one aberrant Vegas cab driver.

Tamar and her American colleagues have just announced a host of new members of Team PokerStars, from Barry 'Robin Hood' Greenstein and the popular Costa Rican pro Humberto Brenes to the former pro golfer Paul Azinger. The first professional athlete to become a sponsored poker player, Azinger would (according to the press release) 'meet and hone his skills with mentorship from Team PokerStars: Joe Hachem, Greg Raymer, Chris Moneymaker, John Duthie, Wil Wheaton, Steve Paul-Ambrose, Vanessa Rousso, Lee Nelson, Luca Pagano,

Isabelle Mercier, Victor Ramdin, Tom McEvoy, Bertrand "ElkY" Grospellier . . .'

. . . and (for a while, at least) me! As I settle into the Monte Carlo, I reread with disbelief the email from Lee Jones that arrived after that memorable night in Soho. The previous month, a few weeks after my own win, Mike Craig emailed me that he too had won a seat, via Full Tilt, with whose leading lights he is now writing a tournament poker manual. 'Well, 155 of us put up $200 and we played for two WSOP packages, which include the $10,000 buy-in and $2000 cash. I finished first. The second seat went to Full Tilt pro Keith Sexton. I'm starting to think the advice the pros are giving me for the book might be pretty valuable.'

'At the end of July,' I replied, 'you'll be in one of those Full Tilt football shirts (with your own name, I hope – not Matusow's – on the back) and I'll be in a sleek black PokerStars shirt (or maybe a less sleek T-shirt). Either way, it's you versus me in the $10m heads-up . . . shall we do the deal now and just play for the bracelet???'

Back came the message: 'Full Tilt will pay me a $10 million bonus if I win the main event after getting my seat on their site. So the deal might be, instead of some kind of equitable split, encouraging each other to "take a dive". But it's good we work this out in advance.'

Yes, Full Tilt was guaranteeing $10 million – or $1 million a year for ten years – to any of its qualifiers who managed to win the main event. Which made Craig's reply, I thought, a tad miserly. More positive thinking came from Vicky Coren in an exchange of emails about something else, when she sweetly replied to my polite enquiry: 'Yes, of course. You can take the money and I'll have the bracelet.'

On the flight over I had reread volume one of Harrington. With volume three, *The Workbook*, just published, Dan

Harrington's trilogy of manuals on Tournament No Limit Hold 'em is becoming the bible of poker for the new generation. The 1995 world champion, Harrington came third to Chris Moneymaker and Sam Farha in 2003 and made the final table again the following year, finishing fourth to Greg Raymer. With fields in their thousands, this must be the most remarkable achievement in the history of the World Series. And, yes, this is the same Dan Harrington who came second to Minh Ly in the WPT's Doyle Brunson Championship at the Bellagio last October. With remarkable consistency, Harrington has cashed in numerous tournaments in between, accumulating lifetime winnings of $4.4m.

Ironically nicknamed 'Action Dan', because of his way of waiting patiently for the best hands, Harrington is my kind of pro. A former state chess champion in his native Massachusetts and a winner of backgammon's World Cup, he is also a few years older than me – which may just prove it ain't over yet for us wrinklies, suggesting that poker experience and a lot of living can still rise to vanquish youth and recklessness. A bankruptcy attorney before turning poker pro, Harrington is another graduate of New York's Mayfair Club, along with Lederer, Seidel et al. He reached the final table of the WSOP main event at his first attempt in 1987, finishing sixth after winning his way there via a satellite. His 1995 world title victory run started the day after winning his first bracelet in the $2500 No Limit event.

Interestingly, and most unusually, Harrington then returned to the world of business, working the stock market and loan industries for eight years before the arrival of the World Poker Tour re-fired his competitive juices. His first year back on the scene proved the first of those two back-to-back final tables. Now he is a revered poker figure in his Boston Red Sox hat, green to reflect his Irish ancestry.

Dan is, in fact, a cousin of Padraig Harrington, the Irish pro golfer, who notched up a tour victory the same weekend that

Dan won poker's world title. When Dan told his mother of his triumph, she was much less impressed by his achievement than by cousin Padraig's.

In his books, now ranked up there with Brunson's *Super/System* as the best available guides to no limit tournament play, Harrington details the way to wait patiently for those good hands to come along, and maximise their value, while milking his image as a 'rock' to his advantage, occasionally forcing his opponents out of pots when holding complete rags. This is the style of play I propose to adopt myself in this year's main event: get a table rep for playing tight, then sock it to 'em every so often with a sly semi-bluff. It's an upscale version of the style I have always used, to limited effect; but Harrington has turned it into an art form.

When I go down to the Monte Carlo's pool for the first of my daily swims – yes, as Marcel Luske reminded me in Baden, even poker players have to think about fresh air and fitness – pretty much everyone around the pool is reading Harrington.

Maybe I'll have to rethink my strategy.

Other World Series news, as we all limber up for the main event: Phil Hellmuth has finally snagged his tenth bracelet, putting him up there with Chan and Brunson. ('Yeah,' says an unimpressed Cloutier, 'and they're all at No Limit Hold 'em.') This is Hellmuth's forty-ninth finish in the WSOP money, equalling the record of Men 'the Master' Nguyen. As he swaggers around the Amazon Room, the Poker Brat's ambition to break both records next year is so palpable you can just about reach out and touch it.

Reigning champion Joe Hachem and his predecessor Greg Raymer have both signalled that their victories were no one-offs by cashing away consistently this year. Hachem added another $250,000 to his bank balance by coming fourth in a pot limit event while Raymer became the first player ever to get into the money in all five tournaments boasting more than two thousand players.

At fifty-three, Britain's John Gale defied the new poker ageists by winning his first WSOP bracelet, not to mention $375,000, in the $2500 pot limit Hold 'em event. John is such a popular character that the only player who might not welcome this news is Dave Ulliott, until now the only Brit to have won both WSOP and WPT titles. This year the Devilfish is having a far from vintage World Series.

At the other end of the age scale, a film student from Wisconsin called Jeff Madsen has become the youngest-ever bracelet winner, carrying off $661,000 by beating 1578 entrants in the three-day No Limit Hold 'em event, just six weeks after his twenty-first birthday. A few days later he astonished the poker world by doing it again in the short-handed Hold 'em event, as well as scoring two third places, earning himself some $1.5 million in ten days. 'No player has ever skyrocketed to the top of the poker world so quickly,' said the daily report of the WSOP's Nolan Dalla. 'At twenty-one, Stu Ungar was still hustling gin games in New York, Johnny Chan was washing dishes in his parents' restaurant, Phil Hellmuth was a University of Wisconsin student playing in $20 Hold 'em games.' And Madsen, he added ominously, 'is not finished yet'.

'I have a really analytical mind,' said young Madsen coolly. 'I'm good at thinking through every situation as it comes and when I think I know something I just have no fear.' Then off he went to choose between finishing college and accepting sponsorship from all the poker websites suddenly laying siege to him (opting, in the end, for Full Tilt).

The one event I consider entering before the Big One, by way of a warm-up, is the $1000 NLHE – with rebuys. Yet that's what deters me, and eventually makes me decide against; the rebuy element mitigates the skill quotient early on, boosting the prize money but turning the whole thing into even more of a crapshoot – an adventure playground for those with more money than sense. Last year, for instance, Daniel Negreanu famously rebought twenty-eight times and still failed to finish in the money. That clinches it for me.

My judgment is vindicated when this year Negreanu rebuys no fewer than forty-eight times and *still* finishes on the wrong side of the rail. 'Ah,' he shrugs on his blog, after shedding nearly $50,000, 'what the heck.'

Top of the all-time money table with wins totalling $7.5 million, Negreanu is such a superstar these days that this year his WSOP blog comes to you on his website by video. He's too busy to sit down and actually write old-fashioned things such as words like everyone else.

And I do mean everyone else. You've got to be careful what you say to whom around here. It's sure to wind up in cyberspace. My entire dinner conversation of a few nights ago is posted on the blog of a well-meaning friend whose blushes I will spare by letting him twist in the wind nameless. But next time, I've told him, I'll be more circumspect over my oysters and prime rib.

Especially about my private life. It's the first time I've been here without a moll, or the Moll, not in a marriage or even a relationship. And it does make a difference, as Barry Greenstein has the candour to spell out in his memoirs, *Ace on the River*: 'If you have sex before you go to sleep, you will probably be more rested and less distracted when you play. Therefore, a sex partner who travels with you can be a big asset.

'In theory, if your partner isn't with you when you go on an extended poker trip out of town, a relatively steady substitute will give you a competitive advantage.'

What? Well, he does have the decency to add: 'Some spouses of athletes and politicians may accept this as part of the territory, but poker players don't have that kind of status.'

Sage old Barry also informs us that 'sexual frustration occurs more frequently in males than in females, but women players also use sex for relaxation. In addition, women on the road are more likely to seek friendship since they tend to share their feelings more freely than men.'

That so? I'd better head downstairs and find me one, then . . .

12

The Gold Rush

'**K**now yourself' was the mantra of the Ancient Greek oracle at Delphi. It should also be the first principle of all poker players, too many of whom are more concerned to nose around their opponents' minds than their own. The next, in a tournament like this, is to get lucky.

Whoever wins the championship event of the World Series of Poker these days is no longer by definition the best poker player alive. He or she – and before long it surely will be a she – is a very strong player with the skill and stamina to have survived a week and more of fourteen-hour playing days blessed with many strokes of good fortune, when their worse starting hand has beaten a better one more often than the most wide-eyed of statistics can even begin to indulge.

The World Series of Poker's main event is simply the richest, most high-profile tournament in the increasingly long, action-packed poker year. It is *sui generis* – a one-off in which anything can happen, and always does. Over a week and more of play the cream will surely rise to the top and *someone* has to emerge victorious. But the odds are that the winner's name will be a new one to the poker world, maybe even an amateur. Outside of the cash games, to many professionals a keener, less luck-bedevilled measure of expertise, the best poker players are those who can manage this consistently: to win tournaments or get in the money all year round, as reflected in the league tables posted on the web or printed in the back of the poker magazines. And not just at No Limit Texas Hold 'em, the game made so popular by television and the World Series, but across all the many different types of poker, from Omaha and stud to razz and high-low.

Yet the title of world champion, not to mention the gaudy bracelet that goes with it, remains the one life-altering prize that every poker player wants to win. Ten million dollars can come in handy too, especially if a website immediately juices it up by way of sponsorship, the icing on a hash-brownie of fame and fortune. The World Series title, it is frequently said, 'turns a player into a legend'.

So what are my chances? I've been pondering that all the way across the Atlantic, as indeed for the last twelve months, since I fetched up 1137th out of 5619 last year. Will I be able to reach the top 20 per cent again this year, maybe higher this time around, perhaps even get in the top 10 per cent – and the money? Title-holder Joe Hachem puts it this way: 'Let's say there are eight thousand starters this year. Mathematically, 70 per cent of the field can't have a chance of winning. That gives us 30 per cent, about 2400 players, who are in with a shout.

'Then only 50 per cent of those have a good chance, which is 1200, so my chances of winning it again are at best about one in 1200.' A heady mix of confidence and modesty from genial Joe, but it is justified; Hachem has proved his win last year was no fluke, cashing in numerous events over the subsequent twelve months. The bookies at BetUSA have, I see, made him 200-1 to win the 2006 main event, with Anthony ('Big Deal') Holden at 3000-1 against. I am amazed to see my name even on the list.

With more than eight thousand starters, however, 3000-1 seems quite flattering.

My guess is that Hachem would put me down as one of the 70 per cent who 'can't have a chance of winning'. Well, we'll see about that. When it comes to writer-players like me, however, poker watcher Michael Konik calls the march of the poet and novelist James McManus to the final table of the 2000 main event 'a once-in-the-history-of-Western-civilisation achievement'. We'll see about that, too. But McManus' feat was indeed impressive; I myself am on the record as calling it 'the equivalent of NASA sending a poet to the moon'.

In the summer of 2000 *Harper's* magazine sent Chicago-based McManus to Las Vegas to cover the WSOP during the simultaneous trial of Ted Binion's lover and her boyfriend for his brutal, desperately cynical murder (they were convicted but the verdict was reversed on appeal). Picture a 1950s movie in which Chicago journalist James Stewart, wearing a trilby with 'PRESS' sticking from the hatband, walks past a casino en route to the courthouse. Intrigued, he peers in uncertainly, to see a sign saying: 'WORLD'S BIGGEST POKER TOURNAMENT! HURRY, HURRY! THIS WAY!' The more the audience yells, 'No, Jimmy, no, don't go in . . . no, no, Jimmy, go to the courthouse and do your job!', the more obvious it is that stumblebum Jimmy is going to go in and take his modest home-game experience into the Big One – and probably, depending who's writing, depending who's directing, go on to win the damn thing – while also managing, of course, to cover the trial with his usual effortless panache.

Hey, it was something like that – except that McManus is no stumblebum; he knows how to play poker as surely as he knows how to weave the most muscular, vibrant prose. Staying at Binion's while covering the trial, he sat down in a satellite and parlayed his upfront *Harper's* expenses into a $10,000 entry for the world title event. Then he played a blinder, all the way to the final table, winning $247,760 for coming fifth to Chris Ferguson against such daunting opposition as T.J. Cloutier, Dan Harrington and Annie Duke.

McManus' account of it all can be read in a book pulsating with poker (and real) life, *Positively Fifth Street*, the finest poker narrative since Alvarez's *The Biggest Game in Town*. Other writers before McManus had played in the World Series for literary as much as financial reasons – Alvarez, David Spanier, myself – but none had got anywhere near the money, let alone the final table. At last this had been achieved by someone also blessed with the ability to describe the experience with all the one-off vividness it deserves – hence my thought about NASA finally 'sending a poet to the moon'. McManus' poker-playing prowess is no less impressive; he has since proved his 2000 feat no accident with several cash finishes on the pro tour. His poker earnings since then are now approaching $750,000, including four cashes already at this year's WSOP, earning him a total of $88,000.

For all his semi-pro status, McManus still teaches a course in poker literature at the School of the Art Institute of Chicago, with Alvarez and Holden on the syllabus. For a while he wrote the first regular column on poker ever published by the august *New York Times*, but was obliged to give it up after accepting player sponsorship from PokerStars. Now he is writing a history of poker, with special reference to American military and diplomatic crises.

McManus and I have a mutual friend in Peter Alson, who has himself just published a stylish poker narrative in *Take Me to the River*. Its central theme – finally committing to marriage and fatherhood at the (to him, 'astonishing') age of fifty, then putting wife and daughter first for once over his addiction to poker – is reflected in his surprise, if last-minute decision not to play in this year's main event.

'Oh, yeah,' confesses Alson, 'I tried to get in. I played a bunch of $160 double shoot-outs online. I played in a Last Chance event at the Venetian. I played in a 440-person $1060 "mega" at the Rio. And when none of those attempts worked out or resulted in getting me a seat, I put out the word that I was available to be backed. But then when someone actually did offer to put me in I'd already booked my flight out of town. I'd told my wife I'd be home Monday and I'd started getting excited about seeing her and my four-month-old daughter, who were both back on Cape Cod at the seaside condo we'd rented for the summer. Faced with the prospect of playing poker for another week or two and missing out on that time with them, I experienced something I'd never felt before: a desire stronger than the urge to play poker. I went and told my prospective backer: "Thanks but no thanks".'

Peter and I laugh that we're living life in opposite directions. After two fifteen-year marriages, with three grown sons, I have now (finally, after a few false starts, entailing prolonged and considerable agonies) begun to enjoy the freedom – and yes, maybe, the selfishness – attendant upon being single, for the first time in my life, in my own fifties. Having never lived alone, not even as a student, I took a while to get used to it; but it comes down, for the most part, to a question of being comfortable with your own company. Who could manage without a few flings, to be sure? But what about the whole new experience of having, much of the time, no one to be considerate to when you get home at night? Doing entirely as you choose all day? Heading off to Vegas open-endedly without upsetting anyone back home? Making such decisions without reference to a soul? I could go on. But then, well, yes, there are times you do miss, let's say, quotidian companionship.

Before Alson leaves town this conversation continues over dinner with McManus the night before he is due to take part in this year's main event, Day 1-A. And a strange thing happens. Among the many literary names to cross our lips, from Shakespeare to Alvarez, is that of Martin Amis, whose little essay on my own supposed poker prowess McManus has read in John Stravinsky's anthology, *Read 'em and Weep*. As we leave the restaurant, Sensi in the Bellagio (where none of us is actually staying), I am astonished to see one of my oldest friends, the British-born but American-resident writer Christopher Hitchens, sitting at the bar to which half an hour earlier I had repaired for a cigarette. Hitchens lives in Washington, DC. The last place I'd expect to bump into him is Vegas. Of all the journos in all the gin-joints in all the world . . .

Nursing his usual Johnny Walker Black, an elegant plume of smoke arising from his Rothman, Hitchens seems much less surprised to see me. 'Hey, Buster,' he says, at his most languid, 'I knew you'd be here somewhere. You've just missed Little Keith.'

'Buster', for reasons with which I won't detain you, is what Hitchens and I have called each other since the early 1970s. 'Little Keith' is his pet name for his buddy Martin Amis, as if he were a character from one of his own early novels. Until five minutes ago, apparently, Amis had been sitting there with 'the Hitch', ten yards away, oblivious to the fact that his name was in the air at our table.

We arrange to get McManus and Amis together the following evening, the night before Martin himself plays (on behalf of the *Sunday Times*) on his own Day One, 1-B. But, Houston, we have a problem here. McManus is a long shot to make it to the meal; his own first day's play is expected to go on until around 3 a.m.

Halfway through Day 1-A, a couple of hours before I am due to meet up with Amis and Hitchens, I receive a breathless email from McManus:

'Three young guys at the opposite end of my table spent the day trying DESPERATELY to get broke. Playing wild and coming from WAY behind with miracle cards. One misplayed aces on a flushing, straightening board about as bad as aces can be misplayed. He also cracked A-A with A-10. Dozens of other similar plays in the first three hours . . . Then one of them makes it four times the big blind in early position, I call with 9-9, button calls too. Flop comes J-9-7. Early raiser bets $2000, I move in for $7,200, button folds, the bettor is THRILLED to call with Q-Q . . . and rivers a straight.

'Of course this sort of stuff happens thousands of times every minute in this town, to say nothing of the internet. But that is my point: the luck factor is so ridiculously high that I'm really left with no other conclusion that NLHE isn't really a skill game, all things considered. I may as well be putting money into slot machines.'

Then the pain really shows. 'I'm serious, fuckin' serious. I have to re-evaluate the focus of my one and only fucking life. The best poker hand seems to stand up maybe half the time, though at my table today the worst hand rivered itself back from the dead WELL over half the time. I'm typing this about thirty minutes after that straight card landed on the table. The key test will be tomorrow, when I have to begin researching the history of poker again at UNLV [University of Nevada, Las Vegas]. Do I wanna try to be a pretty good writer or a fair to middling poker player who gets spectacularly lucky sometimes, spectacularly unlucky other times?

'Tony, I'll see you at the Fleur de Lys tonight at eight. This dinner is JUST what I need.'

Half an hour earlier Des Wilson had called me to say that his aces have been cracked (on the turn) by kings. Both writers, American and British, had gone out in the second session. Ditto Victoria Coren, who had suffered 'the worst day's poker I've ever had'. When it started with a cab driver who didn't know where the Rio was, Vicky already figured it wasn't going to be her day. 'And it really wasn't. I had to pass aces (two black aces), on a preposterous flop of Q-J-8-8-Q – bang bang bang they came down, until there were no two cards left in the deck that I could beat. When I had kings the ace came down immediately. When I had A-Q, the flop came 4-5-6. I was getting the sense that it wasn't happening today.

'Finally, I got knocked out by a guy who played a hand as if Day Two clashed with his wife's birthday. I'm down to $3700 and I'm on the big blind with A-K. A serial raiser makes it $600 and the button (who has $7000) calls. I move in. They all pass round to the button. He calls the extra $3100 – half his stack – with A-J!!! What in God's name am I supposed to be holding, for this call? The real tragedy is that the 8-9-10 on the flop are all diamonds and I have the ace of diamonds. Much good it did me . . . the queen of spades on the river sealed my doom.

'With numbers the way they are, you need a solid run of luck to have a chance. If you get NO run of luck . . . well, you just have to figure it's handy to be back at the cash tables having wasted only one day of your life rather than four.'*

Mike Craig at least made it past the dinner interval. But *all* of my writer friends had taken the dive on Day One – as indeed the next day would Amis, whose subsequent account weighed up the relative merits of 'loose-strong' and 'tight-weak' play before professing concern at 'how continuously and implacably and world-beatingly *brave* you have to be if you want to exist for ten minutes in No Limit, where every hand might be your last. Brave, and cool, too. Brave-cool.'

All this literary carnage is making me feel quite the opposite of brave-cool. Throw in Peter Alson and maybe this is not to be the year of the Writer. No, surely, a Day One exit – after this whole year honing and polishing my game – cannot be the fate awaiting me?

Forget about writers. After three days of playing down from two thousand-plus to eight hundred, more than a third of the field has been eliminated before I even sit down to play. Among

*Within a couple of months Coren would more than atone for her 'worst day's poker' with her best, winning the £500,000 first prize in the London leg of the third European Poker Tour.

the big poker names to have gone out on their own Day Ones are Doyle Brunson, Howard Lederer, Phil Hellmuth, Phil Ivey, Mike Matusow and Dan Harrington. I have outlasted all these giants without so much as riffling a chip.

After a memorable evening with Amis, McManus and Hitchens, then another with Mr and Mrs Ben Holden, who hit town from LA for the weekend, I wake up early on Sunday feeling completely wrecked. This is not the best preparation for my own tilt at the world title tomorrow. Apart from a farewell lunch with my son and daughter-in-law and a quick look-in at the Rio, I spend most of the day in bed – alone, alas, Mr Greenstein – trying to catch up on lost sleep while playing through some sample hands in my head, the poker player's equivalent of counting sheep. Not until evening do I venture out again, for a couple more glasses of red wine (to put me back to sleep) with Amis before he leaves town. I think of Howard Lederer's advice about big tournaments: go to bed late, wake up between ten and eleven, arrive at the table fresh, so you can last out a fifteen-hour playing day.

So I go to bed at one, fall straight to sleep and awake (as usual since I got here) at five bloody a.m. After ten days here this is more than mere jet lag; it is partly angst at the want of a moll, partly acute apprehension after the long year building up to this moment. There follow a fitful two more hours, tossing and turning, the usual nightmares highlighted by going out on aces on the very first hand, before I begin to prepare myself for the Big Day ahead.

There are good luck messages from my sons, the Moll, the ex-moll, Grub Smith and Nic Szeremeta, who wisely says: 'Good luck in the main event . . . you have to beat only two players – yourself and the guy you get heads-up with at the end.' From his summer retreat in Italy, Alvarez chips in with: 'Good luck, knock 'em dead, avoid bad beats and come back $10 million richer . . . I never thought I'd live to say it, but I don't envy you. As someone said of World War One: "The noise, the people!" Eight thousand entrants is *insane*.'

Next comes the pressing question of which T-shirt/football shirt/dress shirt/jacket to wear of the dozen and more given me by PokerStars, some with my name stitched into them. Anonymity seems a high priority, as does combating the unpredictable temperature in the cavernous Amazon Room, which can be ferociously cold on the edges, stiflingly hot in the centre. I have taken the precaution of checking out the whereabouts of my table in advance, and determined that it is on the edge of the centre. So I opt for a long-sleeved shirt, which will need a slice of masking tape over the dot-com (banned on US television), and pack several alternatives in my kitbag, as if about to climb Everest. Plus a notebook, two pens and a bunch of bananas. Then I head over to the Rio in the shuttle bus for the free breakfast – probably the only square meal I will get all day.

I have arrived, as is my wont, too early. For an hour and more, after a nourishing corned-beef hash, there is nothing for it but to rove the interminable corridors of the Rio, chain-smoking condemned-man cigarettes as I bump into such friends as Des Wilson, Jim McManus, Jenny and Richard Sparks. I eventually arrive in the room and at my seat ten minutes early. The event starts twenty minutes late.

Day 1-A got James 'Maverick' Garner, Day 1-B Doyle Brunson on the thirtieth anniversary of his first world title win, Day 1-C poker-playing Penn (Jillette) of Penn and Teller, resident entertainers at the Rio. We get a vocal group no one at Table 35 has heard of – called, I think, Mosaic – who sing some plainsongish, barber-shop dirge before tournament director Robert Daily at last intones the mantra for which all poker players have been waiting all year: 'Okay, dealers, shuffle up and deal.'

People are still arriving in droves. At my table Seats Ten and One (beside me in Two) are still empty. I see the formidable Vegas pro Kassem 'Freddy' Deeb heading towards us. Is he going to sit down beside me? Please, poker gods, *no* . . .

Deeb goes right by. Seat One remains open as I look around at a table of unfamiliar faces. Next to me in Seat Three is another Tony, a Bodog guy, friendly and clearly expert; on my other side a still empty seat. There is no other PokerStars player at the table, which comes as a relief. A menacing-looking Stetson in Eight, a Unabomber-style hoody in Ten, otherwise all baseball caps – all but one on the right way round.

This is a key part of my strategy: to concentrate on this table and try to dominate it, then the next – one table at a time, rather than thinking you're taking on the entire room. The other thing about Day One, I keep telling myself, is survival to Day Two, like you managed last year. Keep that in mind. But *not*, this time, short-stacked survival. If you're going to play in this thing, you're going to try to win it. Busting out after five days' play, just short of the money, is much worse than going out in style on the first hand. There's no point in just hanging in there. So the slogan for today is: bangs not whimpers.

I draw the big blind on the first hand, which I fold with rags after a raise, winning myself no table-image at all. In the second, on the small blind, I am dealt my Hand of the Year, the wretched A-K. I raise $200, and the other Tony calls from the big blind. The flop brings no ace or king – so this early in the proceedings I feebly check. Big Tony bets $200. I shoot him a sideways glance; he gives me his most winning smile. I'm sure he is playing position, but I fold. So far, so pathetic.

After three minutes of play, the PA announces, 'Congratulations, you have all made it past the first player to be eliminated.' His $10k lasted *three minutes*? This makes me want to guard mine like Fort Knox. A round goes by with nothing but rags, then under the gun I get A-8 – not one of

the starting hands recommended for this first round of the
tournament's first day. With the pot already raised, I fold it.
Coward, says half of me; sage, says the other. Which is the
real me? At this early stage it's hard to tell, while trying to
exude self-assurance.

After half an hour I still haven't seen or really played, let
alone won, one hand. I feel like I'm not handling this too well.
My stack of ten thou is down by $375 but I get the feeling
they've already got me marked as the table tight-ass. Time to do
something about *that*.

On my big blind I raise $250 with the worst of all available
Hold 'em hands, 7-2. Everyone folds. It may still be hyper-cau-
tion time but this little bluff is absurdly good for my morale. I
feel like I've gained some respect here. I'm no patsy to be kicked
around at will. Don't you guys go thinking you can steal *my*
blinds. You may all be solid players – as far as I can yet tell – but
I'm no donkey, either. Okay?

Maybe not. The languid Frenchman in Seat Five now takes
down a huge pot (at this stage), all of $10k, when his jack pairs
on the river against a busted flush draw. Boy, some of these
people are playing even looser than I'd expected. McManus'
email replays in my head. I may have to revise my tight-loose-
tight-occasionally aggressive, above all brave-cool strategy here.
It's too passive to survive at this table. I still haven't won a substantial hand and I'm down to $9525.

After an hour or so a big, burly, bearded – but friendly – guy
called Robert finally fetches up next to me in Seat One. He
had, so he said, overslept – and immediately starts running all
over the table. As I sit stationary and silent, watching the way
the others are looking at me, Robert joshes away while doubling
his stack in half an hour. But I refuse to loosen up in such reck-
less style. This is the first session of the ten-day world title event.
Just one or two double-ups later on will get you through the day
in decent shape, ready to fight another. Wait for the right hand

and pray it comes in the right position. In the meantime don't let yourself get bullied.

At 1.25 p.m., more than an hour since we started, I just limp in (sorry, Annie) with A-9 off-suit. Well, there's a lot of limping going on around here and I'm only too happy to see a cheap flop. I know I should capitalise by raising but I can't as yet muster the nerve with less than monster hands while I feel like I'm still evaluating the company.

Which turns out to be a mistake on this hand. Dealt by our dream new dealer – whose name is, yes, Anthony – the flop brings A-Q-9. I bet the statutory $150, three times the big blind. Only Hoody in Seat Ten calls. The turn brings a four. Surely that can't help him? No, it can't. I read him for an ace with a decent, but unpaired kicker, maybe. Or a paired queen. Face cards, for sure. I bet a thousand; again Hoody calls. Uh-oh.

The river brings a king. I check; he bets another thousand. Only a thousand, same as last time. Is it a trap? A bet so small at this late stage, after a river card that may well have improved him? I go 'into the tank' (or think) for a while and decide he's trying to steal, so wonder about a reraise. But it's early days for that sort of showbiz – and my hand is vulnerable to all sorts of things, notably pocket queens or kings. Yet he didn't raise before the flop . . . yes, for sure, his bet is suspicious. In the end I just call. He shows K-Q, two pair on the river, and winces when he sees my A-9. I haul in a decent pot by current standards, taking me up to more than $12k.

Still, I don't feel I played the hand well. I could have won more if I'd had the heart to raise him at the end. In the end I decide not to give myself too hard a time about that. I'm content with my first two hours, if freezing in the ferocious air con. At the first break I smoke my statutory cigarette in the fetid heat rising from the tarmac outside in the alfresco Food Court – 'like a hair dryer', as McManus puts it, 'held an inch and a half from your nostrils' – then nip into the men's room to put on a

T-shirt under my long-sleeved black PokerStars dress-shirt. The longer you sit in that damned room, the colder it gets.

Back out in the hundred-degree shade, the bad beat stories have begun. More than a hundred players have already been eliminated. Another hour or two and I'll have made the top half of the field.

Well, it's a start.

I return to find the room applauding former world heavyweight champion Lennox Lewis as he arrives at Table 6 as an alternate. They're still bringing people in even after the first level. So we still don't know the total number of starters, but it's going to be nearer nine thousand than eight.

The blinds are now $50–$100 and it's my big blind again. With 7-3, after a raise, I have to let it go. Then Stetson takes a big hand off the Frenchman, A-K against 10-10, when the flop brings an ace. Paris slumps in his seat and orders a massage. He's the loosest yet least communicative player at the table.

Ahah! At 2.30 p.m. I am dealt two red aces. I raise three big blinds, $300, and get how many callers? None. So I show my rockets to the table with a smile to confirm my reputation as an apparent rock. 'At least they didn't get beat,' laughs the other Tony. 'I didn't notice no complaint from you!' He's right. Aces are getting cracked all over the room almost every hand. On the first Day One, apparently, quads were beaten by a straight flush. With this many players in this kind of tournament, bad beats are the norm.

Ninety minutes later, at 4 p.m., I'm getting dispirited again. I've seen very few playable hands during this second session, which still has twenty-five minutes to go. And I haven't mustered the nerve to risk any unplayable ones. If the Frenchman doesn't try to steal my blind, Hoody does. Don't these people *know* I've got here by beating three world champions? Should I tell them? Perhaps not. I decide to sock it to Paris by raising him with J-8.

He calls, natch, as he would with anything. Flop of rags: check-check. The turn brings a jack. I bet $1k, he folds. I'm back up to $12k.

The second break I spend in the dealers' secret smoking corner with the PokerStars blogger 'Mad' Harper and the charming Tom Parker Bowles, financed by the *Mail on Sunday*. Tom played yesterday and made it to Day Two. Down to $2k at one point, he somehow got himself back up to $20k. Now there's an example I should keep in mind.

During session three, with the blinds up to $100–$200, there is sudden devastation at our table. At 5 p.m. Seat Nine (back-to-front baseball cap) goes out. Five minutes later exit Hoody whose A-A is rivered by Q-J when the board comes Q-x-x-x-J. Five more minutes and it's sayonara to the other Tony, whose trip fives are rivered by a back-door flush. A guy in a BMW cap arrives in Seat Nine, a PartyPoker player in Ten, and a silent youth in a biker T-shirt on my left in Three.

Now, during the third level, it's announced that the legendary Amarillo 'Slim' Preston has arrived at Table 13. Last year Slim didn't show, discomfited by domestic turmoil in his mid-seventies. The poker world seems to have taken him back to its heart. But *still* they're introducing alternates! When – if ever – will they stop?

At our table the devastation continues. At 5.30 p.m. the Frenchman is destroyed by house over house; his Q-Q beaten by A-J when the board comes A-Q-x-A-J. At 6.20 p.m. Robert goes, his A-Q beaten by trip fives with a board of Q-5-x-x-x. Next hand I get pocket eights, the first playable cards I've seen during all this carnage. In late position I raise and get one caller. The flop comes 8-9-10. He checks; I bet $2000; after an agonisingly long think, during which I regret not bringing my own hoody and wraparound shades, he folds. I'm back up to $11,500.

At 6.45 p.m., after six hours of play, we've made it to the

ninety-minute dinner break. And I'm in reasonable shape.
Better-organised players than me have booked tables in restaurants; but to make such arrangements for myself, I had long
since decided, would be terminal chutzpah. Thanks to my
bananas, I'm not that hungry, anyway. I head off to the
PokerStars lounge where I have a sandwich and for all of ten
minutes a snooze. Tamar and her colleague Marta Salvado
make encouraging noises but I'm just one of hundreds of players in their care. Frankly, I'm happy just to sit and concentrate,
try to keep myself in the zone.

During the next level the blinds remain $100–$200, plus $25
antes every hand. While adjusting to this – which makes the
blinds much more worth stealing – I see one hand go by, the
only one all day. I put down K-J in middle position after a raise,
only to see the flop come K-K-x-J-x. A horrible sight. But I
know I've got to let it go.

By 9 p.m. there are 1600 players left out of some 2300. And
they've finally stopped introducing alternates. The number of
starters in the 2006 main event is now officially finalised at
8773. The first prize will be not ten but twelve million dollars.
The top dozen players will become millionaires (if they aren't
already). Even 860th place is worth $20,000.

Set these tasty new targets, I look down to see a shiny black
ace. Oh please, revered poker gods, please give me a decent
kicker. I squeeze out . . . another shiny black ace. Two adorable
black aces, pocket rockets: the most beautiful damn sight I've
seen in quite a while. Okay, fasten your seat belts.

I'm on the button too, but the pot is checked, dammit, round
to me. I bet $700. The small blind, the Biker, calls. The big
blind folds, as does everyone else. Damn; I'd like to have got it
all-in before the flop with this hand. Just one raise would have
seen me come over the top with everything in front of me. It's
the only way to play aces in a big, anything-can-happen (and
will) tournament like this.

The flop brings A♦-3♥-7♦. Trip aces! I could live without those diamonds but I have to go for it. Not all-in yet, though. Biker's got about $8k to my $12k. Let's try to get all his chips in the subtle way. So I bet $1500 and . . . YES, he raises me $3000. I know I'm going to reraise him all-in. I've got him covered; I've got the best hand; it's a no-brainer. And with no one else in the pot there's not a lot of point in appearing to agonise over the decision . . . except maybe to persuade him that I'm worried about my hand, and to give the other players something irrelevant to think about after I've won this monster pot.

Brimming with confidence, I enjoy running through the options. What can he have? Trip threes or sevens? Let's hope so. A-7 with the case ace? Ditto, but even Biker wouldn't play that loose. He's relatively short-stacked by the standards of the table. He must be on a diamond draw, probably two face cards. With nine diamonds left and two cards out of forty-five potential unknowns to come that makes him a 4-1 dog, even if the board doesn't pair. If aces are getting cracked all the time around here, they must also be standing up once in a while.

The critic briefly wonders about folding the aces because of the flush draw; the poker player decides this is his moment to approach Day Two with a decent stack. I set Biker in and he calls, rolling over K♦-Q♦. The turn gives my heart a jolt by bringing a red card, the 6♥. 'PAIR THE BOARD,' I cry, suddenly worried, showing too much emotion, as the river brings another glimpse of red: yes, the two of . . . diamonds.

F—! I stifle an f-bomb. For once, as it turns out, the critic was right. But folding boss trips would surely have been *pathetic*? I feel the punch in the stomach that comes with the card that knocks you out of this thing. Yet I'm not out. Way down but not out. I've still got the best part of $4k left. Even so it's a massive blow. There is not a look, not a word, from my left. Biker just hauls in more than $8k of my chips as if they were his due – then proceeds on the very next hand to lose most of it to his left.

Was it for this that I handed over two-thirds of my stack?

Hang in there, Holden, I say to myself, and I manage just that for most of another hour, defending my own blinds, stealing some others, going all-in twice with no callers. I'm beginning to recover from that bad beat, gradually feeling a little more optimistic. Think Parker Bowles. Sure, I'm under pressure, and those cracked aces still hurt, but I'm certainly not on tilt. I put down 8-8 in late position after an under-the-gun raise, which Seat Four shows as Q-Q. So I'm even making good decisions. There may yet be a way back out of this hole.

Then I'm dealt 9-9, a talismanic hand at this table, which has all day been doubling, sometimes tripling up anyone who's played it. Under the gun, but I see no alternative. The way I've been playing lately it may even be an advantage. All-in I go again to the tune of $4.5k. Fold, fold, fold, fold, fold, fold, CALL from a newly arrived Nord on my right, in the big blind, who rolls over K-K. The flop brings me a brief spasm of hope with 7-8-10 – but the turn and river bring the usual rags.

End of story. I'm not even dead money any more. I'm just dead.

The pain seeps in slowly before gradually getting worse. I shake hands with the Nord – despite the fact that he thumped the table in triumph when his hand stood up – then with the only other guy left from the original starters, who bids me farewell with an apparently sincere, 'Bad luck, Tony, you played good.'

I stumble outside to the Food Court, praying not to meet anyone I know. There I stand slumped in contemplation over one of their little cocktail tables with only a cigarette for company. Was it all for this? Ten hours of poker, after a year of practice, and still I exit on Day One without much, if any distinction. Just like the first time around, fifteen years ago, I have finished lower at the end of my year as a seasoned semi-pro than I did at its start as an optimistic amateur.

The bad beat stories all around me – many these days yelled into mobile phones – remind me that aces are getting cracked on all sides. Yes, it was those aces that really did for me. But was I over-hasty with those nines? People have been coming back all day with less than $4k. Should I have folded them and waited for something better?

No, given the way my cards were running I'm glad I played them boldly. I'd promised myself not to get stuck down there again like last year, playing short-stack survival.

I could claim to have come in the top half of the field – around four thousand out of nine thousand – but what did that mean? *Niente.* My main consolation was that this year it hadn't cost me a penny.

Maybe I would have played better if it had? But my ten grand had been won in that PokerStars freeroll, so I felt it a due courtesy to visit their hospitality suite bearing the tragic news of my exit. For once the elusive Tamar was in residence, and her face fell at the sight of me. 'What are you doing here?' she asked with a look of concern, then gave me a consolation hug.

Unable to face anyone else, I crawled home to the Monte Carlo to lick my wounds – and, *au* McManus, consider my revised place in the global scheme of things. After I'd emailed the bad news to the UK support team I lay back to consider the rest of my life . . . and awoke three hours later from a deep and dreamless sleep. It was 4 a.m. The sense of disappointment, of outrage, of injustice flooded straight back into my psyche. There was no way I could go back to sleep for a while, so I got dressed and wandered downstairs to join the graveyard shift – leaving my bankroll in the room's wall safe, to make sure I did nothing rash. No point in compounding my woes.

The casino floor was still abuzz, as if it were mid-afternoon. For a while I just wandered around feeling a rare contempt for these crazy people who really seem to believe they can beat the odds in these joints. Then I began to think the same thing about myself. What was the point of playing in this tournament when the numbers boosted the luck factor beyond the realms of reason? Did you really believe you were in with a chance? This thing gets to be more of a crapshoot every year.

Then I noticed that these nocturnal gamblers were, win or lose, having fun. And I realised that playing in the World Series of Poker is also, of course, fun – as long as your life, let alone your living, doesn't depend on it. I had won my usual $5000 satellite the day I arrived and done okay in a few cash games since; so I was still ahead on the trip financially, which is more than most people can say around here. And I might not have made it here at all if I hadn't won that tournament in London. How many players got a freeroll into the main event?

Gradually, by a major effort of positive thinking, I managed to psyche myself back towards some sort of comfort zone. I'd calmed down enough, anyway, to head back upstairs and sleep till noon. By then the emails had started arriving, beginning with the Moll's savvy, fatalistic take on things: 'It just goes to show that luck is a huge part of the game – something all those whizz-kids with their mathematical calculations can forget. In a way, I suppose, that's what keeps poker a game rather than a sport – where talent is rarely usurped by luck. The awful river, the bad beats. The feeling the other guy must have had when his flush came up – that the universe was, finally, aligned just for him. I do think that's what poker is all about – the moment when you absolutely believe the gods are on your side.'

Among other consolatory messages, I was especially touched by one from son Joe in Berlin: 'Bad luck, poppa . . . You'll be back some day – and we three will all be there with you to shorten the odds.' It was a reminder that at moments like this the best plan is to tick off your blessings in life in the hope that they'll outweigh your passing woes. So: you have three loving sons, one of whom is blissfully married, another ditto engaged. Two ex-wives who are (on the whole) fond of you. Lots of warm, generous friends of both sexes, on both sides of the Atlantic. No moll right now, but that can be remedied. And a Job, if a part-time Job, which you're lucky to find, on the whole, so congenial.

But you're broke. And you've got the best part of two more weeks to hang around here and brood about all this while trying not to lose what's left of your bankroll – and waiting to see who does win that twelve mill.

The days ticked by slowly. As all the name players were eliminated from the main event one by one, people began to talk of it as a sick joke. With this many starters and no qualifying heats, the winner would be a no-name fluke. Next year the winner of the all-round HORSE event should be considered the true world champion. Or there should be a professional league to determine the year's best player, excluding all these online amateurs. The majestic new card room of the Venetian was built with that in mind as the natural home of the Professional Poker Players League devised by Chip Reese (plans for which would be announced in the autumn of 2006).

A few said Harrah's had managed an event of unprecedented scale surprisingly well. Many more were so full of venom as to talk of the internet sites getting together to stage a mega-tournament to rival the WSOP – a felt tournament held on some offshore island, but with the latest no-dealer tables. Uh-oh, include me out.

As the climax approached there were so many chips on one table that for the first time ever they had to introduce $100,000 chips – chocolate-coloured with green inserts and so nicknamed 'cookies'. The event went so fast – faster than its organisers expected – that the last nine players got an unexpected day off before the final table. All nine could spend it savouring their new status as millionaires.

On the morning of the final table I awoke to a message from

that same friend in London who had last year proved the first to alert me to the London bombings. This time it was an email hoping I did not have too 'horrendous' a journey home at the weekend. What was she on about now? Not another strike? No, it turned out to be terrorists again – forestalled this time, apparently by British intelligence, after supposedly planning the simultaneous demolition of several mid-Atlantic flights with liquid bombs. They may have been thwarted; but they did indeed ensure that many people, myself included, would wind up having horrendous transatlantic journeys home that weekend.

At 3.45 a.m. on the tenth day of competition, after a final table of 236 hands over nearly fourteen hours, a thirty-six-year-old TV agent turned producer from Malibu, California, with the apt name of Jamie Gold, clinched the title of 2006 world poker champion when his Q-9 proved too much for the pocket tens of the only other man still standing, Paul Wasicka of Westminster, Colorado. Wasicka trousered $6,102,499 for second place, more than Greg Raymer had for winning two years before. Another queen for Gold was the first card to fall on a flop of Q-8-5. The turn brought an ace, the river a four.

The head-to-head lasted just eight hands over twenty minutes. Gold had begun it with $79 million to Wasicka's $11 million. The most appropriately named world champion since Moneymaker, Gold had led the field for the last four days of competition and embarked on the final table with almost a third of the chips in play. He had displayed due expertise in the role of chip leader, building his stack by stealing many a pot with opening bets which were peanuts to him, life or death to his opponents, and rarely getting involved in dangerous confrontations. Still, the cards had also been running his way.

At the final table alone Gold personally eliminated all but one of his opponents. As the day began the chip standings were:

Seat One – Richard Lee – $11,820,000
Seat Two – Erik Friberg – $9,605,000
Seat Three – Paul Wasicka – $7,970,000
Seat Four – Dan Nassif – $2,600,000
Seat Five – Allen Cunningham – $17,770,000
Seat Six – Michael Binger – $3,140,000
Seat Seven – Doug Kim – $6,770,000
Seat Eight – Jamie Gold – $26,650,000
Seat Nine – Rhett Butler – $4,815,000

Of Gold's opponents only Cunningham was a known quantity, winner of three World Series bracelets across three poker disciplines and the player whose experience was expected to tell.

But it took just five hands for Gold to flop a set of deuces and eliminate short-stacked rookie Dan Nassif, who had gone all-in with dear old Anna K. Nassif's first-ever tournament score, $1,566,858 for ninth place, saw Gold advance to more than $30 million, or a third of the chips in play.

On the fifty-seventh hand, at 5.30 p.m., Gold's pocket queens saw off the pocket jacks of Sweden's Erik Friberg – unusually, these days, the only non-American at the final table – who won $1,979,189 for eighth place.

At 6.30 p.m., on the eighty-fourth hand, it was Wasicka's pocket queens that knocked out the pocket nines of Doug Kim, an online qualifier who had recently graduated from Duke University, where he had learnt his poker, and who would now start in the autumn as a Manhattan financial consultant $2,391,520 to the good for seventh place. PokerStars had begun the day with three players at the final table; now they had all gone, the first three to bite the dust.

As for the six players left, it was Gold (now up to $38 million) who would one by one personally perform their executions. On hand 122 at 8.53 p.m., moments before the dinner break, Gold again held pocket queens to eliminate the pocket jacks of his nearest challenger, Richard Lee of San Antonio, Texas. Lee could now add the sixth-place purse of $2,803,851 to his only previous tournament win, $5600 for twelfth place the previous year in the No Limit Hold 'em event of Larry Flynt's Grand Slam of Poker IV.

This huge pot put Gold up to $51 million, well over half the chips in play. Five hours later at 2 a.m., on hand 170, Gold called the all-in of Rhett Butler – yes, since you ask, his real name; thanks to the enduring popularity of *Gone With the Wind*, there are apparently six thousand Rhett Butlers in the United States. Butler was holding a pair of fours, Gold K-J. Again the first card up was the one he needed, as the flop came J-6-5, turn two, river ten. His first tournament cash earned rookie Butler $3,216,182 for fifth place and put Gold up to $54.5m.

Twenty minutes later on hand 208 Gold finally dispatched the one man local experts were still giving a chance of catching him, the popular twenty-seven-year-old professional Allen Cunningham. A UCLA drop-out described by *Card Player* as 'one of the lesser-known great players in the poker world', Cunningham moved all-in from the big blind for $6.5 million with pocket tens. Gold called with K-J and the board came A-K-8-7-3. Cunningham won $3,628,513 for fourth place, to add to the $4 million he had already accumulated over his eleven-year career. And Gold's chip stack climbed to $57m.

Another forty minutes and hand 229 saw Gold limp from the button and Wasicka from the small blind, only to be raised to $1.5m by Michael Binger of Atherton, California, from the big blind. Both called and the flop came 10-6-5. Wasicka checked, Binger bet $3.5m and Gold moved all-in. Wasicka folded and Binger called, showing A-10. Gold turned over 4-3 for an open-ended straight draw and the turn immediately obliged with a seven. The river was an irrelevant queen and Binger was eliminated.

A Ph.D. in particle physics from Stanford University, who had supported himself for the subsequent six years playing poker, Binger had said before the off that he hoped to win enough money to continue his physics research 'without having to run the rat race of getting a job and impressing all the right people'. His $4,123,310 for third place should do the trick – as did Gold's $79m going into the heads-up. Eight more hands and it was all over.

Gold had been given a freeroll into the event by Bodog boss Calvin Ayre – yep, the same man who had just cancelled that Vegas gaming conference. 'Jamie came to us through our Hollywood connections,' explained Ayre. 'We knew he was a good player with some impressive tourney results so we thought he'd be a strong competitor.'

Originally from Paramus, New Jersey, Gold numbered among his Hollywood clients as an agent such A-list names as *The Sopranos*' James Gandolfini, Felicity Huffman, Lucy Liu (*Ally McBeal, Charlie's Angels*) and the singer-actress Brandy (Norwood). Just six months before the WSOP he had given up agenting to become head of production at Buzznation, 'a branded entertainment, media and production company' based in Los Angeles. He had given himself these two weeks off producing a reality TV series called *America's Hottest Mom*, to which he would now have to return with his prize of $12 million, boosted by a contract to promote Bodog during his year as world champion and global ambassador for the game.

Gold's mother is a lifelong poker player, his grandfather a gin rummy champion. Having grown up in a family of card players, he had been playing some forty hours a week in Los Angeles card rooms and earned almost $100,000 in tournament winnings in little more than a year. His game had recently been 'refined' by none other than Johnny Chan, two-time world champ and winner of a record ten gold bracelets, after they met while working together on a poker TV 'concept'. Chan was beside the final table, alongside Johnny's mother, cheering him on.

But his father, Dr Robert Gold, was not. He was suffering from a condition called amyotrophic lateral sclerosis, better-known as Lou Gehrig's Disease, which rendered him immobile. Dedicating his victory to his dad and saying the prize money would go to 'making him as comfortable as possible', Gold explained: 'He's not well. He can't move in his own body. He can't swallow any more. He has a breathing machine. This is all for him.' (Alas, Dr Gold was to die four months later.)

Of his spectacular World Series debut Gold also said, none too modestly: 'I haven't found it very hard but I have found it to be heartbreaking that most people are playing "donkey" or what I would call jack-ass poker. They just make really bad calls and get lucky. Out of two hundred people that play really poorly, twenty of them are going to rise to the top. All of a sudden you have all these guys that aren't great poker players.

'I aspire to be a great poker player and I take it seriously. I feel like every play I'm making is the smartest play and the right play, yet I've never (before the final table) won a pot with more than $150,000 in chips. I've lost $300,000 pots constantly. Five times I went to the river as the favourite and lost all five. I feel like I've earned my chips while other people are just getting lucky left and right.'

Before the tournament Gold had also said: 'I've been fortu-nate enough to make a lot of money through work. I don't need the money. I'm here for the competition.' Somehow this seemed to bode less well for his year as poker's global ambassador.

As did his apparent disappearance a week later when sued for half his winnings. There ensued an unseemly public dispute between Gold and a British-born 'associate' named Bruce Crispin Leyser, who soon filed a claim for 'injunctive relief and damages' at Las Vegas' Clark County District Court. Gold's deal with Bodog, according to Leyser, required him to secure celebrities who would wear Bodog attire during the WSOP main event. At Gold's request, Leyser had found the 'celebrities' for him: the B-list actor Matthew Lillard, who played Shaggy in the *Scooby Doo* movies, and Dax Shepard, a comedian on the MTV show *Punk'd*. Gold, by way of thanks, promised him half of anything he might win.

On the morning of 10 August, according to Leyser's submission, three hours before play began at the final table, Gold had left a message on his voicemail confirming their unwritten deal. But a week, a month, two months later, he still hadn't paid up. The $6 million were frozen by court order in the vaults of Harrah's, and at the time of writing it looked like only prolonged litigation could sort it all out until Gold was reported in February 2007 to have reached an out-of-court settlement with Leyser.

People of my generation recalled the day when Billy Baxter told Jack Binion that he'd staked the 1997 world champion Stu Ungar and was entitled to half his winnings. So, in poker a man's word is supposed to be his bond. Binion immediately instructed the cashier to give Baxter $500,000. It is hard to believe that an unedifying court case is what Bodog's Ayre had in mind when his spokeswoman, Susan Mainzer, declined to comment on the Gold–Leyser dispute, referring all enquirers to a previous statement saying simply that, 'Jamie truly epitomises the Bodog spirit'.

As the final table was dismantled and the rest of the world slept, BetonSports announced that it was suspending all trading in the USA – giving up, in other words, 85 per cent of its business. Still languishing in his Fort Worth cell, pending a bail hearing, its chief executive David Carruthers had been dismissed from his job. The company said its US operations, based in Costa Rica and Antigua, were 'no longer viable'. It would shut them down 'as soon as practicable', pay liabilities to staff and balances due to US customers 'in an orderly manner', and take steps to ensure that the company would no longer 'knowingly accept any wagering transactions from US-based customers'.

Meanwhile an elite consortium of senior professionals was bringing an anti-trust suit against Steve Lipscomb's World Poker Tour. Chris Ferguson, Howard Lederer, Annie Duke, Greg Raymer, Joe Hachem, Andy Bloch and Phil Gordon were no longer prepared to sign away their names and images without remuneration. 'We cannot let these wrongful actions continue,' said Ferguson. 'We will go on with this lawsuit for as long as it takes to change the WPT's ways.' Greg Raymer said he was 'proud to be part of it. Our success in this lawsuit will benefit all poker players'. Howard Lederer added: 'Poker players have to take a stand and say enough is enough. Without the players there's no show. Until the players and TV producers realise this, the players will never get a fair deal.'

Lipscomb declared himself 'proud' of the WPT's contribution to the growth of the poker industry and found it 'disappointing that a handful of players, of the many thousands who play in WPT events, have decided to make these claims even as the sport continues to grow'. Anti-trust cases 'take a long time', as Lederer conceded, hoping that the WPT would 'come to the table and settle our case'.

All this would be rendered academic, if not irrelevant, within two months when the Senate stunned the multi-billion-dollar world of the new poker by sneaking through Goodlatte-Leach's anti-gaming bill in the early hours of Saturday 30 September 2006, on the last vote before Congress rose for the mid-term elections. In a nakedly opportunist move, apparently designed to appease the religious right and other fundamentalist voters, Senate majority leader (and 2008 presidential hopeful) Bill Frist attached the 'Unlawful Internet Gambling Enforcement Act' to the completely unrelated 'Safe Ports Act', a 'war on terrorism' measure which passed on a mere voice vote.

The effect was to close down a huge slice of the online

gaming business overnight. Washington's weekend ambush wiped £4 billion off the value of online gaming shares. The main victims were those innocents all over the world whose investments and pension funds were crippled by legislation that looked likely to prove as effective in achieving its objectives as had Prohibition in the 1920s. The main beneficiaries beyond the land-based casinos and organised crime, as gambling was inevitably driven underground, would be all the lawyers laboriously trying to work out the legislation's true impact.

Contrary to widespread belief at the time, the act did not make online poker illegal. What it did render illegal was the transfer of funds between online gaming sites and financial institutions from banks to credit card companies. In essence it aimed to stop banks allowing customers to send funds to offshore sites and to criminalise those accepting such funds for the purpose of gambling. Even after it was signed into law by President Bush on Friday, 13 October 2006 – yes, Friday the thirteenth, or 'Black Friday' as it became known in the new poker world – there would be a 270-day 'grace' period until mid-July 2007 for US regulators to spell out the act's precise terms, and banks and other interested parties to work out how to implement them.

The immediate impact was that PartyGaming and ParadisePoker felt obliged to suspend their operations in the lucrative US market. Sporting Bet abandoned its merger talks with World Gaming, who went bust on Black Friday. In the City of London, the industry's financial base since the 2005 flotations, the crisis was compared with the collapse of the dotcom boom. 'It's like a nuclear bomb being dropped on our industry,' said one executive as he surveyed the carnage that had the previous day been his prosperous business. 'Funds and investors will be licking their wounds,' said another, 'after what, I believe, has been a mirror image of the technology crash seen five years ago.' As PartyGaming fell out of the FTSE 100 index, trading at a fraction of its flotation price, founder Russell DeLeon announced that he would now be redeploying his personal, multi-million-pound fortune into becoming a movie mogul.

In July 2006 the British government had failed to protect three British businessmen known as 'the NatWest Three' from deportation to the United States on charges of fraud supposedly committed on British soil. So another internet gambling executive, while describing the US ban as 'corporate terrorism', argued that 'the reason why everyone has stopped today is fear – fear that in the total absence of support from the UK government, who have been breathtakingly silent on this issue, directors run the very real risk of being extradited on trumped-up money laundering charges'. Said another: 'They are not saying, "Here are detailed laws which we are giving you as something you can live with and work with". They are saying, "We don't like internet gambling full stop. Even if you are lawfully and legitimately licensed, say in Alderney or Gibraltar or Malta, we will nevertheless regard you as committing a crime in the US every time a US citizen bets, and we reserve the right to throw you in the slammer".'

The day before Bush signed the legislation two of the largest online companies, Sporting Bet and Leisure and Gaming, sold off their American interests for a mere dollar each. Within a few days, though, NETeller, one of the major players in the money transfer business, and based outside the US, announced that it proposed to carry on conducting business as usual. Within a week it had changed its tune. Handling some $7 billion each year, however, on behalf of more than three million customers in 160 countries, NETeller gave confidence to the larger poker-only sites such as PokerStars and Full Tilt, which also announced business as usual. While all this was going on, the first twelve days of October 2006 – or the twelve days between the Senate ambush and the signing of the bill – saw the biggest online business ever. Unsure how they were going to be affected, American online players went on tilt, getting 'last-day-itis' with the balances in their accounts, worried that their online poker days were numbered.

In fact opaque questions of enforcement and jurisdiction seemed to offer a multitude of ways around the new law. Offshore companies, for instance, could open offshore (or foreign) accounts for their customers – beyond the reach of US legislators. Online poker had already been declared illegal in all of eight American states (including Nevada) under state rather than federal legislation, but there were as yet no signs of any eagerness to enforce the ban; no one had been arrested or charged for playing online poker in the privacy of their own homes. So the main effect of the Senate vote was to anger, while temporarily inconveniencing, the almost thirty million Americans who play poker online. Why should they be prevented from doing something in private that remained legal in public?

For those players who carried on regardless, however, there would almost certainly be less 'value' in the online game. The presence of fewer players seemed likely to make online poker games more competitive and tougher to beat, especially as expert players were more likely to persist than newcomers, while beginners would be deterred from signing on. In the words of my son's online friend Oliver Chubb, 'We could see pretty much all of the recreational and amateur players from the US market drop out of games and only the solid winning players continue. Obviously, increasing the concentration of skilled, winning players in my games will decrease my hourly rate.' Websites making lower profits would also seem less willing to hand money back to players in the shape of 'rake-back' and bonuses. 'Olly' confessed that he was even having to consider coming back to England and getting a 'proper' job.

In Britain (as, of course, around the rest of Europe and the

world), poker life could proceed as normal. The British government, with its plans to open super-casinos within the next few
years, was even inviting the offshore companies to come and
base themselves in London if they would accept government
regulation – and, needless to say, taxation, which could amount
to billions. Why hadn't the US government chosen to go down
this much more sensible and indeed lucrative road? There
would be a period of intense political lobbying ahead, not least
by the newly formed and well-financed Poker Players Alliance
(PPA), which was seeking to up its membership from 125,000 to
more than a million by the end of 2006, to petition and argue
the case for poker to be exempted from legislation against online
sports betting.

As far as the World Series of Poker was concerned, Harrah's
announced that henceforth it would no longer be accepting
bulk entries from the dot-com (or even the dot-net) websites, or
indeed 'third parties' of any kind. The websites countered that
they would continue to hold satellites and simply deposit the
$10,000 entry fee in the winners' accounts so that they could
register themselves. But, asked many a new poker wiseacre, how
many were likely, given the choice, to use it to enter so large and
unpredictable an event? Winners would surely find some other,
more sensible way of risking (or just spending) a windfall of ten
grand.

The 'over-under' on the number of competitors in the 2007
WSOP world title event slumped from 9300 to 4400, as compared with 2006's 8773. And most bets were on the 'under'.
The dot-net logos on the tables and on players' clothing seemed
to have become an endangered species, as did the 2007 Gaming
Lifestyle Expo; and ESPN, *Card Player* magazine and others
looked likely to rue the day they had signed long-term deals
with the WSOP.

Before the legislation the consensus had been that the poker
boom would never peak. The graph might well have flattened

but the future of online poker appeared secure thanks to all those new students arriving at university every year, all over the world, armed with the laptop which is these days a college requirement. 'Hey,' says the guy down the corridor, 'I can show you some fun you can have with that!' And another online poker statistic is born.

Take the United States out of that equation and the global statistics shrink dramatically. Outside of America, meanwhile, television poker seemed likely to stagger on, with the game's rampant popularity spreading across new markets in western Europe, down to South Africa and east towards the Philippines and Singapore. In the Nixonian words of one senior broad-caster: 'Next stop, China!'

But the continuing growth of the World Series of Poker cer-tainly looked to have been seriously damaged, if not crippled. Again, pre-legislation, there was talk of coping with continuing expansion by holding regional heats around the world. Yet a substantial percentage of the 2006 field had been online American qualifiers. With a much lower number converting satellite wins into actual entries, the field for the main event was expected to sink back down to a mere three thousand – or less.

Which might at least give me a better chance of winning the damn thing next year.

All this happened after my second year on the pro poker tour ended at the World Series, which might just turn out to be the biggest year in the history of poker. I left with the resigned feel-ing that I was content to hand on the baton to the next generation, just as I'm happy to pass the world on to my chil-dren. The remarkable, unexpected transformation in poker over a few years of my middle age may have changed the game in ways not all to my taste. More may mean merrier but it also means less collegiate, less companionable. That, however, is beyond my control, really none of my business – and the boom may now, anyway, have turned to bust. So I shall watch the big picture with interest, excitement and occasional horror, while knowing I've got my home and club games to keep me warm.

As for the tournament circuit: I have come to the conclusion that to win one of these things, or improve your chances of winning one of these things, you have to shorten the odds by playing one pretty much every week. In fact you have to do very little else in your life but eat, sleep, drink and play poker, all day every day, most days of the year. And as much as I love poker, I don't have a problem confessing that there are other things in life that I love just as much – and wish to pursue with equal vigour in the diminishing time left to me on this earth.

So I will continue to drop by this brave new world of poker strictly as a hopeful amateur, a player for whom the word 'recreational' might have been coined. I will also continue to enjoy music, read (and write) books, root for my football team, love and enjoy my family and friends, and seek out the next moll, maybe even the next Moll.

But for now it's back to the Job. I'd lay long odds that I'm the only one of the 44,500 players in the 2006 World Series of Poker to be heading straight from Las Vegas to the operas and concerts of the Edinburgh Festival.

As always, Shakespeare said it first: 'There is a world elsewhere.'

EPILOGUE

Before that dread US legislation, Harrah's prediction of 12,000 starters in the 'main event' of the 2007 World Series of Poker seemed entirely credible. By the end of 2006, after Bush signed it into law on 'Black Friday', the 'over-under' bet sank as low as 3500–4000. As it turned out, the final reckoning was 6358 – far from shabby, but a third down on the previous year. Thanks to Bill Frist's so-called 'Safe Ports Act', the world-title field had fallen for the first time in the event's thirty-eight-year history.

Your correspondent again got past the dinner break on Day One before being dealt A♦-J♦ in the cut-off seat, and raising $5000. A dour, bearded Yank with twice as many chips called, and the flop brought J♣-10♦-8♦. Now I've got top pair with top kicker, and four to the nut flush. With $12,000 left in front of me, and much the same in the pot, I pretend to think for a while before pushing all-in. Beardy thinks rather longer before calling; and we roll them over. He has 9-8 off-suit, both black. The turn brings the J♠, giving me trip Jacks with top kicker. Surely this pot is now mine, doubling me up to a very respectable $35,000? The Bearded One has only six outs – for Q♦ or 7♦, which would give him a straight, would also fill my flush. With eight cards seen, and so forty-four unknown, I made that 38-6, so better than 6-1, in my favour.

The dealer banged the table, burnt a card, and showed . . . a black seven, giving Beardy a beyond-flukey straight. He raked in my chips as if they were his natural due – without even looking at devastated me, let alone offering any gallant apology or embarrassed sympathy – as I suavely rose above the Matusow routine of telling him in many colours what a lousy call he'd made on the turn, if not the flop, as indeed before it.

'Wow,' said the guy on my left, 'that was a *really* bad beat.'

'Can I have that in writing?' I replied with a feeble attempt at a smile, and made a dignified exit. Another year, another bad beat story.

Ten days later, after a cosmopolitan final table ranging in age from twenty-two to sixty-three, and containing only four Americans (with the experienced Lee Watkinson as favourite), the $8.25 million first prize went to a forty-year-old psychologist from Laos, now resident in California, called Jerry Yang. Soon he had been snapped up by FullTilt, and four of his fellow finalists by PokerStars.

The World Series itself was deemed to have been the best yet, with the authorities actually listening to the players and taking their views into account. An early row over custom-made, large-print playing cards was speedily resolved. An impassioned speech from former Senator Alphonse D'Amato promised to continue the fight on Capitol Hill to have poker exempted from the legislation. Those websites that had cautiously unloaded their US customers, such as PartyPoker, opened their usual hospitality suites; those that had not – such as PokerStars, now 'the world's biggest poker website' – did not. The Lifestyle Expo was as vulgar, if not quite as big, as ever. The $50,000-entry HORSE title went to a worthy winner, Vegas pro Freddy Deeb, and Phil Hellmuth won a record eleventh bracelet (again at Hold 'em). Hellmuth was inducted into the Poker Hall of Fame, along with its first female member, Barbara Enright.

In poker terms, 2007 eventually turned out to be the Year of the Woman. When the first WSOP bracelet event ever held outside Vegas was staged in London in September 2007, the £1 million first prize was won by an eighteen-year-old Norwegian internet whiz called Annette Obrestad (online name 'Annette_15', a reminder of the age at which she started playing). Already an online millionaire, still three years short of being allowed into a casino in the US, Obrestad became – and will surely long remain – the youngest player to win a WSOP bracelet.

The Norwegian knocked out Annie Duke in twelfth place, making Duke the first woman in poker history to exceed $1m in WSOP earnings; within a matter of hours, Obrestad herself had stolen the distinction by doubling that. The average age at the final table in London's Empire casino was twenty-five. But the victor seemed to presage the latest development in the 'new' world of poker: the arrival of women. As Lee Jones put it on this book's website, BiggerDeal.com: 'Unless I'm badly mistaken, her win will give poker a shot in the arm like nothing we've seen since Chris Moneymaker injected pure go-juice into the business in 2003. I have said for years that the next big growth area for poker will be women players . . . If you've been writing the definitive History of Poker, you've got some editing to do. A nineteen-year-old Norwegian lass has just torn up your previous ending. And started a brand new chapter.'

And given this book a new ending. Obrestad replied with 'tyty', in true online style. She was snapped up by a rival website before I could wonder whether I really wanted her playing in BiggerDeal.com's monthly tournaments, sponsored by PokerStars – and touchingly called, in a 'new' poker nod to the 'old', the Tuesday Night Game.

How to Play Texas Hold 'em, with Ranking of Poker Hands

Hold 'em is the simplest of poker games to follow but one of the most complex to play – so full of possibilities as to require consummate skill, especially in 'reading' your opponents, at the highest level.

It was invented so that as many people as possible can play at the same table – sometimes ten, usually nine, then (in tournaments) fewer as players get knocked out until two players are left 'head to head' or 'heads-up'. (This one-on-one version can itself be a two-player variant of Hold 'em; there are even 'heads-up' tournaments these days.)

Each player is dealt two cards, face down. These are your 'hole' cards or 'pocket' cards. Between betting intervals five 'community' cards will then be dealt in the middle of the table – at first three simultaneously (the 'flop'), then one (Fourth Street or 'the turn'), then the last (Fifth Street or 'the river'). Between them these five communal cards are called 'the board'.

The idea of the game is to combine either or both of your hole cards with the communal cards in the middle to create the best possible five-card poker hand. Occasionally it is possible that the board wins – i.e., no player still in the hand can improve on the five community cards, in which case the pot will be split between the surviving players.

With a professional or non-playing dealer, a button will pass clockwise round the table to indicate which player is nominally dealing the hand. The two players to the dealer's left are called 'the blinds'; before the deal they are obliged to put in compulsory bets to start building a pot. Dealer's left is called the 'small blind', the next seat the 'big blind' (usually double the small blind). This works out the same for every player, who has to do both once a round. In the later stages of a tournament, as the level of the blinds increases, putting pressure on the players with fewer chips, every player will also have to put in an 'ante' every hand, which will also go up with the levels of the blinds.

After the deal, before the flop, the betting starts in the seat after the big blind. This player has three options: to 'call' (i.e., match) the big blind, raise it (by at least as much), or to fold (i.e., surrender his cards, taking no further part in the hand). And so it goes around the table with each player either calling, raising, reraising or folding – and the small blind must match the big blind, and both blinds any raise that may have been made, to stay in the hand.

Once this betting round is complete the dealer will 'burn' a card from the deck face down (a tradition to prevent cheating) and reveal the 'turn'. There is then another round of betting, where the first player to speak may now 'check' (or bet nothing), before another 'burn' and the 'river'. One last round of betting follows before the 'showdown', if more than one player remains in the pot.

Bluffing is a common tactic in Hold 'em – i.e. 'representing' a good hand by betting with lesser ones, or 'rags', in the hope of scaring your opponents into folding.

The other key element to the game is 'position'. The first player to speak, i.e., the first to the dealer's left still in the hand, or 'under the gun', is in the worst position, or 'out of' position. The last player to speak is in the best position as you get to know

what all the other players are up to before making your own decision. Usually, of course, this is the 'button', or nominal dealer;
next best is the 'cut-off' seat, immediately before the button.
Again this evens out with each round as position changes for all
players with each hand. But the best Hold 'em players maximise
their use of position, regardless of the quality of their hand.
Players in late position often try to 'steal' the pot with a bluff if
they sense weakness around the table before it is their turn to act.

Finally, the version played throughout this book (as on television) is No Limit Hold 'em at which any player can bet as much
as he wants or has in front of him at any given time. There is
also Limit Hold 'em, where the betting rounds have fixed limits,
and Pot Limit, where the maximum bet is the total of the pot
(including the raiser's call). But No Limit Hold 'em has become,
in the immortal words of one of its leading practitioners, Doyle
'Texas Dolly' Brunson, 'the Cadillac of poker'.

RANKING OF POKER HANDS
(and the odds against receiving them)

ROYAL FLUSH – A-K-Q-J-10 of the same suit. 649,739-1.

STRAIGHT FLUSH – Five consecutive cards of the same suit. 64,973-1.

FOUR OF A KIND – Four cards of the same rank, with four aces beating four kings and so on down the scale. 4164-1.

FULL HOUSE – Three of a kind, with a pair. 693-1.

FLUSH – Five cards of the same suit, all suits being equal, but the highest card in the hand deciding between two or more flushes. 508-1.

STRAIGHT – Five consecutive cards of different suits. Again the
higher the sequence, the better. 508-1.

THREE OF A KIND – Three cards of the same rank, with three aces
beating three kings, etc. 254-1.

TWO PAIRS – Two different pairs, the higher pair deciding a contest.
20-1

ONE PAIR – Two of a kind, the higher the better. 1.25-1

HIGH CARD – The highest single card in a hand with none of the
above. Evens

Select Bibliography

(Editions cited are those in the author's collection)

Manuals

Brunson, Doyle (ed.): *Super/System 2: A Course in Poker Power* (New York: Cardoza Publishing, 2005)

Caro, Mike: *Caro's Book of Poker Tells* (New York: Cardoza, 2001)

Cloutier, T. J.: *How to Win the Championship: Strategies for the Final Table* (New York: Cardoza, 2006)

Harrington, Dan: *Harrington on Hold 'em*, Vol. 1 *Strategic Play*, Vol. 2 *The Endgame*, Vol. 3 *The Workbook* (Las Vegas: Two Plus Two, 2004–05–06)

Holden, Anthony: *All In* (London: Weidenfeld & Nicolson, 2005)

Jones, Lee H.: *Winning Low Limit Hold 'em* (Pittsburgh: Conjelco, 2005)

McEvoy, Tom and Cloutier, T. J.: *Championship Pot Limit and No Limit Hold 'em* (New York: Cardoza, 2004)

——, *Championship Hold 'em: Tournament Hands* (New York: Cardoza, 2005)

Rodman, Blair and Nelson, Lee: *Kill Phil* (Las Vegas: Huntington Press, 2006)

Sklansky, David: *Tournament Poker for Advanced Players* (Las Vegas: Two Plus Two, 2002)

Sklansky, David and Malmuth, Mason: *Hold 'em for Advanced Players* (Las Vegas: Two Plus Two, 1999)

Narratives, anthologies, fiction

Alson, Peter: *Take Me to the River* (New York: Atria, 2006)
Alvarez, Al: *The Biggest Game in Town* (Boston: Houghton Mifflin, 1983)
——, *Poker: Bets, Bluffs and Bad Beats* (San Francisco: Chronicle, 2001)
Bradshaw, John: *Fast Company* (London: High Stakes, 2003)
Craig, Michael: *The Professor, the Banker and the Suicide King* (New York: Warner, 2005)
Dalla, Nolan and Alson, Peter: *The Man Behind the Shades: The Rise and Fall of Stuey 'The Kid' Ungar* (London: Weidenfeld & Nicolson, 2005)
Fromson, Brett D.: *Hitting the Jackpot: The Inside Story of the Richest Indian Tribe in History* (New York: Grove Press, 2003)
Holden, Anthony: *Big Deal: One Year as a Professional Poker Player* (London: Bantam, 1990; Abacus, 2002)
Kaplan, Michael and Reagan, Brad: *Aces and Kings* (New York: Wenner, 2005)
Konik, Michael: *Telling Lies and Getting Paid* (Guilford, Ct: The Lyons Press, 2002)
May, Jesse: *Shut Up and Deal* (Harpenden: No Exit Press, 1999)
McManus, James: *Positively Fifth Street* (New York: Picador, 2003)
Schwartz, David G.: *Roll the Bones: The History of Gambling* (New York: Gotham, 2006)
Sparks, Richard: *Diary of a Mad Poker Player* (Milford, Ct: Russell Enterprises, 2005)
——, *Getting Lucky* (Milford, Ct.: Russell Enterprises, 2006)
Stravinsky, John (ed.): *Read 'Em and Weep* (New York: HarperCollins, 2004)
Wilson, Des: *Swimming with the Devilfish* (London: Macmillan, 2006)
Yardley, Herbert O.: *The Education of a Poker Player* (London: Jonathan Cape, 1979)

Acknowledgements

By the time I had lived the year as a poker pro chronicled in this book's predecessor, *Big Deal*, and was busy writing it in 1989, the editor who had first commissioned the book at Bantam had moved on – as in those days was so often the case. I was summoned to the office to explain myself to her successor, a new (to me) editor called Ursula Mackenzie. As she sat sternly opposite me with several senior colleagues, I could see them all thinking: 'Who in hell had the barmy idea of giving this guy a handsome advance to go out and play poker? Heads must roll.' Their money, they all looked sure, had gone straight down the plughole.

But disaster was averted, the book appeared and Ursula became a fairy godmother to *Big Deal*. She has personally ensured that over nearly twenty years it has never gone out of print. She steered it through several paperback editions at Bantam's parent company, Transworld, and republished it (complete with gonzo Ralph Steadman jacket) when she moved to Time Warner Book Group as its publisher in 2002. Time Warner has since become Little, Brown and that same Ursula

Mackenzie is its CEO. She it was who responded with immediate enthusiasm to the equally barmy idea, fifteen years on, of a sequel.

I am very glad of this chance to thank Ursula publicly for keeping faith in *Big Deal* all these years and for showing the same confidence in this, its successor. I am also grateful to her London colleague Stephen Guise and his New York counterpart Amanda Murray for proving the most diligent and constructive of editors. Iain Hunt has proved a meticulous line editor. It is as much a privilege as a pleasure to thank my sometime *Sunday Times* colleague Gerald Scarfe for agreeing to lend the jacket such style.

My friends and fellow poker junkies Al Alvarez, Cindy Blake, Michael Craig, John David Morley, James McManus, Joe Saumarez Smith and Des Wilson were all kind enough to read the manuscript, making many helpful suggestions. Thanks are also due for their invigorating company on the road, where many more heated discussions took place over far too many drinks and meals. The same goes for Peter Alson, Ashley Alterman, Joe Barnard, Steve Bartley, Matt Born, Neil Channing, Victoria Coren, Eric Drache, John Duthie, 'Mad' Harper, Jo Haslam, Barry Hearn, Brian Hipwood, Roy Houghton, Hugh Howard, Patrick Marber, Hugo Martin, Matthew Norman, Phil Shaw, Grub Smith, Nic Szeremeta, Kirsty Thompson, Marty Wilson, Richard Whitehouse and many more, not all of whom have made it into the text.

When my latest adventure began, the last thing I expected was any kind of sponsorship. But I wind up indebted to Ladbrokes for an invitation to travel as a guest on their 2006 Caribbean poker cruise; Annie Duke, Howard Lederer and their colleague Rick Bierman for 'comping' me on their Baden poker camp; and above all Tamar Yaniv, Lee Jones, Conrad Brunner and their colleagues at PokerStars.com for looking after me in Monte Carlo and Barcelona – as well as hosting the media event in London at which I won my $10,000 entry fee, plus travel expenses, for the 2006 World Series of Poker. PokerStars has since prolonged our arrangement so I can travel and play on the 2006–07 European Poker Tour.

I am grateful to the UK edition of *GQ* magazine and the writers involved – Al Alvarez, Martin Amis, John Graham and David Mamet – for permission to quote the material from its September 1990 issue which begins Chapter Eight. I am also grateful to Alvarez for permission to quote (on pages 53–4) from his introduction to Ulvis Albert's majestic volume of photographs, *Poker Faces 2* (2006).

While buying me an excellent dinner in London, Dave Woods, editor of *Poker Player* magazine, kindly gave me permission to filch the odd quote from his pages, as did my old friend Nic Szeremeta, publisher and editor-in-chief of *Poker Europa*. Matthew Norman generously shared material from his interview with Doyle Brunson during the 2005 World Series and Richard Sparks from his chat with Mike Sexton in *Diary of a Mad Poker Player*. I am also grateful to Nolan Dalla, media director of the World Series of Poker, and his colleague Nicole Khoury for arranging my accreditation and other assistance at the 2005 and 2006 World Series.

My three sons – Sam, Joe and Ben – have proved terrific company on the road, as elsewhere, while keeping my nose to the rockface with their constant enquiries as to my progress. My literary agent, Gill Coleridge, has remained her ever supportive self, as my obsession with poker has again thwarted her best efforts to keep my literary career on the high road. And last but by no means least my thanks go, for obvious reasons, to my accountant, James Watts; and to my bank manager, John Hughes, who has listened patiently, and indulgently, as I tried desperately to explain the wild fluctuations in my various accounts.

Glossary of Poker Terms

ACE-HIGH: a five-card hand containing an ace but no pair; beats a king-high but loses to any pair or above

ACES UP: two pairs, one of which is aces

ACTION: the betting, as in, 'The action's on you'

ADVERTISE: to show your cards after making a bluff, with the deliberate intention of being exposed as an apparently 'loose' player

ALL-IN: to bet all the chips you have left

ANTE: compulsory stake for all players before the deal

ANTE UP: dealer's request for antes to be paid

AVATAR: online poker term for a player's computer-generated image

B&M: online term for a real card room, short for 'bricks and mortar'

BACK TO BACK: two paired hole cards, as in 'aces back to back' or 'aces wired' (also 'pocket rockets')

BACK DOOR: term used when a straight or flush is filled on the turn and river cards.

BAD BEAT: to lose a pot against the odds, the stronger hand being beaten by a lucky one

BELLY HIT: to fill an 'inside straight'

BET INTO: to bet before an apparently stronger hand, or a player who bet strongly on a previous round

BET THE POT: to bet the total value of the pot (including the call)

BETTING INTERVAL: period during which each active player has the right to check, bet or raise; ends when the last bet or raise has been called by all players still in the hand

BICYCLE: the lowest possible straight, A-2-3-4-5

BIG BLIND: the bigger of the two compulsory bets before the deal – usually, in Hold 'em, two seats to the dealer's left

BIG SLICK: A-K (also known these days as 'Anna Kournikova')

BLIND (1): the compulsory pre-deal bet(s) to the dealer's left

BLIND (2): to check or bet before receiving or without looking at hole cards

BLOW BACK: to lose back most or all of one's profits

BLUFF: 'representing', with a bet, better cards than you actually hold

BOARD: the five communal cards revealed in the centre of a Hold 'em table

BOAT: full house

BOBTAIL: *see* 'open-ended straight'

BOSS: the strongest hand at that stage, as in 'boss trips'

BRING IT IN: to make the first bet

BUCK: the rotating button used by a professional dealer to indicate which player is notionally dealing the hand and so should receive the last card

BULLET: an ace

BUMP: to raise (as in 'bump it up')

BURN: to deal off the top card, face down, before dealing out the cards (to prevent cheating); or to set aside a card which has been inadvertently revealed

BUST: a worthless hand, which has failed to improve as the player hoped

BUST OUT, BE BUSTED OUT: to be eliminated from a tournament by losing all your chips

BUST A PLAYER: to deprive a player of all his chips; in tournament play to eliminate a player

BUSTED: broke or tapped

BUSTED FLUSH: four-to-a-flush, which failed to fill up

BUTTON: *see* 'buck'; also the seat before the blinds, i.e., prime position

BUY-IN: the amount of money required to sit down in a particular game or tournament

BY ME: a (dated) alternative to 'check' or 'fold'

CAGE: the casino's or card room's 'bank' where you exchange chips for cash or vice-versa

CALL: to match rather than raise the previous bet

CALLING STATION: a player who invariably calls and is therefore hard to bluff out

CARD PROTECTOR: a disc or lucky charm placed on top of a player's hole cards

CARDS SPEAK: refers to a face-up declaration at the end of a hand, by which even if a player has not realised he holds the winning hand the dealer or other players can point this out on his behalf

CASE CARD: the last remaining card of a denomination or suit when the rest have been seen, as in 'the case ace'

CASH IN: to leave a game and convert one's chips to cash, either with the dealer or at the cage

CATCH: to pull the card or hand you want

CHASE: to stay in against an apparently stronger hand, usually in the hope of filling a straight or flush

CHECK: to offer no bet, reserving the right to call or raise if another player bets

CHECK-RAISE: to check a strong hand with the intention of raising or reraising any bet

CHIPS: plastic discs of varying colours representing different amounts of cash

CINCH HAND: a hand that cannot be beaten; *see also* 'nuts'

COFFEE-HOUSING: to attempt to mislead opponents about your hand by means of devious speech or behaviour

COLD: a bad streak, as in, 'My cards have gone cold'

COLD DECK: a deck of cards fixed in advance by a cheat

COME: to play an as yet worthless hand in the hope of improving it, as in playing 'on the come'

COME OVER THE TOP: to reraise after the pot has been raised

CONNECTORS: consecutive cards such as 9-10 or J-Q which might make a straight

COWBOY: a king

CUT IT UP: to divide or split the pot after a tie

CUT-OFF: the seat before the button

DEAD CARD: a card no longer legally playable

DEAD HAND: a hand no longer legally playable, due to an irregularity

DEAD MONEY: *see* 'fish', 'patsy', 'pigeon', etc.

DEALER'S CHOICE: a game in which each dealer, in turn, chooses the type of poker to be played for a round

DECLARATION: declaring by the use of coins or chips, in high-low poker, whether one is aiming to win the high or the low end of the pot, or both

DEUCE: a two, the lowest-ranking card in high poker

DOG: poker shorthand for 'underdog'

DONKEY: a weak or bad player; *see also* 'fish', 'patsy', 'pigeon', etc.

DOWN CARDS: hole (or pocket) cards

DRAWING DEAD: calling a bet, or drawing a card, on a hand that cannot win, whatever the 'turn', usually the 'river', may bring

DRAWING OUT: to win a hand on the last card or cards, after staying with an inferior hand, 'on the come' – in Hold 'em, to 'river' or 'suck out' on your opponent

DRIVER'S SEAT (in the): said of a player who is making all the betting and thus appears to hold the strongest hand

DROP: to fold

ELGAR: twenty-pound note

EPT: the European Poker Tour, a series of televised tournaments

FAMILY POT: a pot in which most of the players are still 'in' before the flop

FIFTH STREET: the fifth and last communal card to be exposed in Hold 'em, also known as the 'river'

FILL, FILL UP: to pull the card you are seeking for a straight or above

FISH: an inferior, losing player

FLAT-CALL: to call when a raise might have been expected

FLOORMAN: the card room employee supervising a group of tables, who is the ultimate arbiter of disputes

FLOP: the first three communal cards to be exposed in Hold 'em

FLUSH: five cards of the same suit; ranks above a straight and below a full house

FOLD: to withdraw from, or give up, the hand

FOUR-FLUSH: four cards of the same suit, requiring a fifth to become a flush

FOUR OF A KIND: four cards of the same denomination; ranks above a full house and below a straight flush

FOURTH STREET: the fourth communal card to be exposed in Hold 'em, also known as the 'turn'

FREE RIDE: to stay in a hand without being obliged to bet

FREEROLL: tournament with no entry fee but cash prizes

FREEZE-OUT: a knock-out game, usually a tournament, in which all players start with the same amount and play until one has won the lot

FULL HOUSE: a hand containing trips and a pair. Between two full houses, the higher trips win. Beats straights and flushes, loses to four of a kind

G-NOTE: a thousand-dollar bill

GRAVEYARD: the pre-dawn shift in a Las Vegas casino

GUTSHOT: the card needed to fill an inside straight

HEAD TO HEAD: *see* 'heads-up'

HEADS-UP: a game between just two players, often the climax of a tournament

HIGH ROLLER: one who gambles for large amounts of money

HIGH-LOW: a species of poker in which the highest and the lowest hands share the pot

HIT: to fill, or obtain the card you are seeking

HOLE CARDS: in Hold 'em the two concealed cards dealt to each player at the start of a hand; *see also* 'pocket'

HOT: said of a player on a winning streak

HOUSE: full house or 'boat'

IGNORANT END: the low end of a straight

IMPROVE: to pull a card or cards that better one's hand

IN: a player is in (the hand) if he has called all bets

IN THE DARK: to check or bet 'blind', i.e., without looking at your cards

INSIDE STRAIGHT: four cards requiring (an unlikely) one in the middle to fill a straight, viz. 5-6-7-9; *see also* 'open-ended straight'

INTERVAL: the length of time before the blinds go up in tournament play

JUICE: *see* 'rake'

KIBITZER: a non-playing spectator or 'railbird'

KICK IT: to raise

KICKER: the subsidiary or 'side card' to a more powerful card or cards

KNAVE: a jack

KNOCK: to check; *see also* 'rap'

LAY DOWN: to reveal one's hand in a showdown

LEAK: a tendency to lose poker winnings at other forms of gambling such as dice or sports betting

LEVEL: the level of each (escalating) set of blinds in tournament play, or the time allowed for it (*see* 'interval'); or the stakes in a cash game

LIMIT POKER: a game with fixed betting limits, so £10–£20, £20–£40, etc.

LIMP (IN): to call rather than raise a bet in late position

LITTLE BLIND: *see* 'small blind'

LIVE ONE: an inexperienced, bad or loose player; a sucker who apparently has money to lose

LOCK: a hand that cannot lose; *see also* 'cinch hand' and 'nuts'

LOOK: to call the final bet (before the showdown)

LOOSE: liberal play, usually in defiance of the odds

LOWBALL: a form of poker in which the lowest (or worst) hand wins

MAKE (THE DECK): to shuffle

MARK: a sucker

MARKER: an IOU

MECHANIC: a cheat who manipulates the deck

MEET: to call

MONSTER: a powerful hand, especially used of starting hands

MOVE IN: to go all-in

MUCK: the discard pile, in which all cards are dead. Also used as a verb

NUT FLUSH: the best available flush, i.e., an ace-high flush

NUTS: the best, unbeatable hand at any stage of a game

OFF-SUIT: hole cards of different suits

OMAHA: variant of Hold 'em in which players are dealt four cards, of which they must use two (no more, no less) with the flop. Can be played high-low

ON THE COME: to bet with four cards to a straight or a flush in the hope that it will 'come' on the turn or river; also called a 'semi-bluff'

ON TILT: playing badly, often because of a bad beat, or being 'stuck'

ON YOUR BACKS: to turn your hole cards face up in a hand where there can be no more betting, i.e., after one or more players are all-in

OPEN: to make the first bet

OPEN-ENDED STRAIGHT: four consecutive cards requiring one at either end to make a straight, e.g. 5-6-7-8; also known as a two-way straight or a 'bobtail'

OUTS: the cards still available that could in theory improve your hand

OVER THE TOP: to reraise

OVERCARDS: in Hold 'em cards higher than the flop cards, or those in your opponent's hand, played in hope of catching a higher pair

PAINT: any picture or court card

PAIR: two cards of the same denomination

PASS: to fold; occasionally (wrongly) used for 'check'

PATSY: an inferior, losing player

PICTURE CARD: king, queen or jack, also known as court or face cards

PIGEON: an inferior, losing player

PIP: the suit symbols on a non-court card, indicating its rank

PLAY BACK (AT): to reraise

POCKET (IN THE): synonym for hole, as in 'pocket aces'

POCKET ROCKETS: a pair of aces in the hole

POSITION: your seat in relation to the dealer and thus your place in the betting order, an important tactical consideration

POT: the total of the chips at stake in the centre of the table

POT LIMIT: a game in which the maximum bet is the total of the pot after a player has called

POT ODDS: calculating the percentage of the pot you are required to invest, as against your percentage chances of winning the hand, thus assessing the worth of the investment

PUT DOWN: to fold

QUADS: four of a kind

RABBIT-RUN: looking (when permitted) to see what the 'turn' and/or 'river' would have brought when a hand ends after the flop

RAGS: low, bad, unplayable or irrelevant cards

RAILBIRD: a non-playing spectator or 'kibitzer', often used of a busted player

RAINBOW: a flop of three different suits

RAISE: to call and increase the previous bet by at least as much

RAKE: chips taken from the pot by the dealer on behalf of the house, or from tournament entries by the organisers

RAP: to 'knock' the table to indicate a check

RAZZ: *see* 'lowball'

READ: to try to figure out the cards your opponent is holding

REBUY: to start again for an additional entry fee in tournament play (where permitted)

REPRESENT: to bet in a way that suggests you are holding a particular (usually strong) hand

RERAISE: to raise a raise

RIFFLE: to shuffle chips

RING GAME: American term for cash games (as opposed to tournaments)

RIVER: in Hold 'em the fifth and final communal card to be exposed, also known as 'Fifth Street'

RIVERED: beaten on the river (fifth) card, usually a 'bad beat'

ROCK: an ultra-tight, conservative player

ROLL (A CARD): to turn a card face up

ROUNDER: a poker player who makes his or her living at the game

ROYAL FLUSH: A-K-Q-J-10 of the same suit. The best possible poker hand in all but wild card games

RUN (1): synonym for a straight

RUN (2): a run of good cards; *see also* 'rush' and 'streak'

RUNNER-RUNNER: improving your hand on both the 'turn' and the 'river'

RUNNING BAD: on a losing streak

RUNNING GOOD: on a winning streak

RUSH: a run of good cards; *see also* 'run' and 'streak'. A player on a rush may well play his rush, i.e., play an indifferent hand, because he's feeling lucky and might win against the odds

SANDBAG: (a) to check-raise; (b) to get caught between two players who are raising each other

SATELLITE: a small-stakes tournament whose winner obtains cheap entry into a bigger tournament

SCHOOL: collective noun for the players in a regular game

SEE: to call

SEMI-BLUFF: *see* 'on the come'

SET: three of a kind or 'trips' (in Hold 'em normally used of a pair in the hand and one on the board)

SET YOU IN: to bet as much as your opponent has left in chips

SEVEN-CARD STUD: a poker game in which players make their best five-card hand out of seven they are dealt, four showing and three hidden

SHILL: a card room employee, often an off-duty dealer, who plays with house money to start or fill up a game

SHOWDOWN: showing hole cards after betting has ceased to see which of the remaining players has won the pot

SIDE CARD: an unmatched card which may decide a pot between two hands otherwise of the same strength; *see also* 'kicker'

SIDE POT: a separate pot contested by other players when one or more players are all-in

SIT-AND-GO : a one-table freeze-out tournament

SLOWPLAY: to disguise the real value of a high hand by underbetting it, to tempt players with worse hands into the pot

SMALL BLIND: the smaller of the two compulsory bets; in Hold 'em the player on the dealer's left

SOFTPLAY: to play gently against a friend

SPLIT (POT): a tie or stand-off. Occasionally this can be agreed between two players before the hand is ended

SQUEEZE: to look slowly at the extremities of your hole cards without removing them from the table

SUCK OUT: to 'river' a player, or beat him against the odds on the last card to be dealt

STACK: the pile of chips in front of a player, as in 'short stack'

STAND-OFF: a tie, in which the players divide the pot equally

STARTING HAND: the two hole cards in Hold 'em

STAY: to remain in a hand with a call rather than a raise

STEAL: a bluff in late position, attempting to pinch the pot from a table of apparently weak hands

STEAMING: playing badly or wildly, to go 'on tilt'

STRADDLE: to make a voluntary blind raise (if allowed) before the deal

STRAIGHT: five consecutive cards not of the same suit; beats trips but loses to a flush and above

STRAIGHT FLUSH: five consecutive cards of the same suit. Beats everything but a higher straight flush, viz. a royal flush

STREAK: a run of good (or bad) cards; *see also* 'run' and 'rush'

STRING BET: an illegal bet in which a player puts some chips in the pot then reaches back to his stack for more. He should declare a raise verbally before calling

STUCK: losing

STUD: *see* 'seven-card stud'

SUIT: one of the four suits: hearts, diamonds, clubs or spades

SUITED: cards of the same suit, as in 'A-Q suited'

SWEETEN (THE POT): to raise

TABLE: can be used as a collective noun for all the players in a game, as well as for the green baize itself

TABLE STAKES: a poker game in which a player cannot bet more than the money he has on the table

TAP CITY: to go broke

TAP OUT: to bet all one's chips

TAPPED OUT: broke, busted

TELL: a giveaway mannerism or nervous habit which reveals the strength or otherwise of an opponent's hand

THREE OF A KIND: three cards of the same denomination, with two 'side cards'; beats two pairs but loses to a straight or above. *See also* 'set' or 'trips'

THREE-FLUSH: three cards of the same suit

TIGHT: a conservative player who tends to play only strong hands

TILT: *see* 'on tilt'

TOKE: a tip to the dealer (illegal in Britain)

TRAP: to check or make merely a token bet when holding a strong hand (with the aim of suckering another player into betting, then raising)

TREY: a three

TRIPS: three of a kind or a set. Beats two pairs but loses to a straight or above

TURN: the fourth communal card to be revealed at Hold 'em, also known as 'Fourth Street'

TWO PAIRS: a hand containing two pairs plus a kicker; beats a pair but loses to trips or above

UNDER THE GUN: the player who is first to bet after the two blinds

UNDER-RAISE: to raise less than the previous bet, allowed only if a player is going all-in

UP CARD: an open or exposed card

WHALE: a fish of giant proportion, i.e., a major casino punter, or high roller, who is usually a loser (used less about poker players than other gamblers)

WHEEL: the lowest straight possible, A-2-3-4-5, also known as a 'bicycle'

WHIPSAW: to raise before and after a caller who gets caught in the middle

WILD CARD: a card designated as a joker, of any value

WIRED: said of two paired hole cards, as in 'aces wired' or 'aces back to back'

WPT: the World Poker Tour, a series of televised tournaments

WSOP: the World Series of Poker, held in Las Vegas each summer